TEACHING
and
LEARNING
HISTORY
in
ELEMENTARY
SCHOOLS

TEACHING
and
LEARNING
HISTORY
in
ELEMENTARY
SCHOOLS

Jere Brophy
Bruce VanSledright

Teachers College, Columbia University
New York

Published by Teachers College Press, 1234 Amsterdam Avenue, New York, NY 10027

Library of Congress Cataloging-in-Publication Data

Brophy, Jere E.
    Teaching and learning history in elementary schools / Jere E.
    Brophy and Bruce A. VanSledright.
        p.   cm.
    Includes bibliographical references (p.   ) and index.
    ISBN 0-8077-3608-2 (cloth). — ISBN 0-8077-3607-4 (pbk.)
    1. History—Study and teaching (Elementary)—United States—Case
    studies.   I. VanSledright, Bruce A.   II. Title.
    LB1582.U6B76   1997
    372.89—dc21   96-52833

ISBN 0-8077-3607-4 (paper)
ISBN 0-8077-3608-2 (cloth)

Printed on acid-free paper
Manufactured in the United States of America

04 03 02 01 00 99 98 97   8 7 6 5 4 3 2 1

To Mark Edward Speier

To Gilbert A. VanSledright
in memoriam

Contents

CONTENTS

Preface

Generally history is considered to be the core of the K–12 social studies curriculum. A complete course in U.S. history is usually taught at fifth grade (and again later at eighth grade and eleventh grade). In addition, unit segments or strands dealing with the past are included in the material on families and communities taught in grades K–3, state history is taught in grade 4, and world history is emphasized heavily in courses taught in middle schools and junior high schools.

Recognizing the importance of history as a school subject, other nations (especially Great Britain) have produced considerable research on the learning and teaching of history, as well as textbooks and other books for teachers dealing with history teaching. However, for reasons that are not entirely clear, there has been much less such research and scholarly writing in our country, especially with respect to the learning and teaching of history in the elementary grades. This book is a contribution to the currently small but recently growing U.S. literature on the learning and teaching of history.

We begin with an overview of the past and current status of history in the elementary curriculum. Then we review two relevant bodies of research and scholarship: (1) studies of children's knowledge and thinking about history, considering both general developmental trends and more specific changes induced through educational experiences, and (2) research on the different purposes and goals that may be emphasized in history teaching, the ways that these play out in classroom lessons and activities, and the trade-offs that the different approaches offer with respect to accomplishment of frequently-emphasized history and social studies goals. The literature review presented in the first two chapters brings readers up to date on scholarship in the field and provides a context within which to interpret the research presented in subsequent chapters.

In the remainder of the book, we present and discuss our research on the teaching and learning of U.S. history in fifth grade. The research on teaching focused on detailed case studies of U.S. history units taught by three skilled but contrasting fifth-grade teachers. The work of all three of these teachers was worthy of detailed description and analysis because they all had earned local reputations as good fifth-grade teachers in general and good teachers of U.S. history in particular. However, they contrasted with one another in their goal priorities and approaches to curriculum and instruction.

Mary Lake was primarily a storyteller who sought to stimulate interest in history by communicating much of the content in the form of engagingly related stories, then helping her students to remember and connect the key ideas by embedding them within narrative formats. In doing so, she exposed her students to traditional historical accounts and socialized them into traditional American values. In contrast, Ramona Palmer was more of a scientific historian, using her course to introduce history as an academic discipline. She taught her students about how historians use evidence and engage in historical reasoning in order to construct defensible accounts of the past, emphasized historical cause–effect relationships and the generalizations that might be derived from them, and attempted to build in her students an appreciation for the importance of facts, details, and research in making historical claims. Finally, Sara Atkinson was a reformer who approached history as a tool for developing understanding of and policy positions on current problems and social issues. She was less interested in teaching a detailed chronology of the past than in using selected historical content as a basis for helping her students to become critical readers and principled social activists.

Our case studies illustrate in detail what these three approaches to history teaching looked like in the classroom. Our discussion of them emphasizes the trade-offs involved in adopting them and also in adopting recognized alternatives, most notably the frequently observed but widely criticized parade-of-facts approach that treats content coverage as an end in itself rather than as a means for accomplishing more fundamental instructional goals.

Influenced by recent research and scholarship on the social construction of knowledge, comparison of novice versus expert learners, and learning as conceptual change, our research also involved detailed analyses of students' knowledge and thinking about the history topics they studied. Each case study unit included a KWL exercise that called for students to tell what they knew (or thought they knew) about the topic and what they wanted to learn about it prior to studying it, and then after studying it, to tell what they had learned. In addition, stratified samples of students were interviewed individually before and after the unit, to develop information about the prior knowledge they possessed upon entry and about how this knowledge changed in response to the instruction and learning activities they experienced during the unit.

In analyzing the KWL and student interview data, we emphasized qualitative indicators of the students' knowledge and thinking (including misconceptions) about key topics and issues, not just whether or not they were able to supply correct answers. In addition to the KWL and interview data, the case studies also included student data in the form of contributions to public discourse during lessons and activities (tape recorded and transcribed for analysis), responses to tests administered by the teachers, and samples of work done on assignments.

Finally, our research included a year-long study of developments in one group of students' historical knowledge and thinking as they experienced their first chronological survey of U.S. history. Beginning in the late spring of fourth grade and extending through the end of fifth grade, we used KWL and interview methods to probe these students' knowledge and thinking before and after they experienced curriculum units on history and the work of historians, the Native Americans, European exploration and colonization of the New World, the English colonies in America, the American Revolution, and westward expansion of the new nation. Embedded in this research was longitudinal study of developments in the knowledge and thinking of a stratified sample of 10 students who were interviewed repeatedly. Along with several other unique aspects, our book is the first source of scientific information on history learning to provide this kind of detailed information on students studied longitudinally.

In discussing our findings, we emphasize the value of teaching school subjects by connecting their content with students' current knowledge and thinking about topics, and, in the process, building on valid information but also addressing students' naive ideas or outright misconceptions. In this regard, our student data provide a great deal of information about qualitative features of the initial understandings that elementary students develop about history and the kinds of naive conceptions or misconceptions that teachers are likely to encounter. In discussing the potential implications of the work, we address such issues as the trade-offs involved in emphasizing various purposes and goals in teaching history to elementary students, the trade-offs involved in teaching state history in fourth grade prior to introducing students to chronological U.S. history in fifth grade, and the trade-offs involved in using children's historical fiction selections instead of conventional textbooks as content sources. The findings should be of interest to psychologists who study developmental aspects of learning and cognition as well as to teachers and teacher educators interested in history and social studies.

Acknowledgments

This book was completed in part while Jere Brophy was on sabbatical leave from Michigan State University and in residence as a Fellow at the Center for Advanced Study in the Behavioral Sciences. He wishes to thank both of these institutions for their financial support during that sabbatical year. In addition, he wishes to thank the Spencer Foundation, which provided part of the funds for the support he received through the Center for Advanced Study in the Behavioral Sciences (Spencer Foundation grant B-1074).

Some of the research that led to the writing of this book was done under the auspices of the Center for the Learning and Teaching of Elementary Subjects, located in the College of Education at Michigan State University. That center was funded primarily by the Office of Educational Research and Improvement, U.S. Department of Education (Cooperative Agreement #G0098C0226). We wish to express our appreciation for this support, and also to note that opinions expressed in this publication do not necessarily reflect the position, policy, or endorsement of the Office or Department.

We also wish to thank the colleagues, students, and teachers who have collaborated with our work and enriched our understanding of social studies, especially the three teachers who were the focus of the case studies presented in Chapters 3, 5, and 6.

Finally, we wish to express our appreciation to June Benson, who has made enormous contributions to our work, not only by consistently handling manuscript preparation and other normal secretarial tasks with efficiency and good humor, but in addition by producing remarkably complete and accurate transcriptions of our observational field notes and our interviews with teachers and students. She has made our work both easier and better, and we are most grateful for her help.

CHAPTER 1

The Place and Importance of History in the Elementary Curriculum

Although this book is primarily about three fifth-grade teachers and their students, we begin by considering theory and research on the learning of history and on its place in the curriculum. This overview situates these teachers and students in the context within which we came to understand their teaching and what their students were learning. The field of theory and research on history teaching and learning is still young and full of controversies. Understanding these controversies is a way to locate these particular teachers and their students with respect to key ideas about history and history education. Before exploring those controversies, we briefly examine the past and current state of history in the elementary curriculum.

HISTORY IN THE CURRICULUM, PAST AND PRESENT

U.S. history, in one form or another, has always been emphasized in the elementary school curriculum in the United States. At the beginning of the twentieth century, it was viewed as one of the "basics," a fundamental tool for socializing the large numbers of immigrants then pouring into the country (Jenness, 1990). This period gave rise to what we now call the Progressive Education Movement, from which was born the "social studies." Although there is some dispute (Saxe, 1992) about the exact origins of social studies as a school subject, many attribute its formation and definition to the National Education Association's Committee on Social Studies of 1916. The history instruction common in that age featured recitation of factual chronicles to note-taking students (some argue that this approach is still common today; see Cuban, 1984; Tyack & Tobin, 1994). Influenced by John Dewey and

1

other progressive, reform-minded scholars and social welfare advocates, the 1916 committee sought to transform history instruction into something more interesting, child appropriate, and active, and to embed it within the emerging social studies curriculum. Dewey's *The Child and the Curriculum* (1902/1950) is a good source for understanding what those reformers had in mind.

The evolution of social studies and its influence on history education have been uneven. Those who accepted the social studies approach advocated by the early social welfare reformers and the Committee on Social Studies sought to use history as an integrative discipline. That is, history would remain as the core of the elementary social education component of the curriculum, but it would be fused with geography, economics, and political science, and it would pursue education for civic competence as its primary goal (Saxe, 1992). Beginning in the 1920s, history became increasingly integrated with these other curricular offerings. In the process, it lost some of its unique identity, especially in the lower grades.

In 1963, Paul Hanna wrote an article in which he rationalized what in many ways had become the dominant approach to elementary social studies during his generation—the expanding communities curriculum sequence (Hanna, 1934, 1963). This now quite familiar model was rooted in Hanna's understanding of Jean Piaget's ideas about child development. It suggested that children in the elementary grades should begin by studying the social world they knew (themselves and their families) and gradually expand, grade by grade, into the neighborhood, the community, the state, the nation, and finally the world. Following this general progression, U.S. history became lodged in fifth grade, preceded by a unit on state history taught as a part of state studies in fourth grade. Earlier grades featured short offerings on the Pilgrims at Thanksgiving and on Washington and Lincoln around their birthdays, as well as occasional units on Native Americans and pioneer life and occasional studies of "famous Americans." However, there was no systematic, chronological treatment of history prior to fifth grade. Fifth-grade U.S. history became a survey course, to be repeated in eighth grade and again sometime during the high school years. This remains the predominant curriculum pattern today, despite limited empirical research on its educational efficacy.

The widespread adoption of the expanding communities sequence prompted Naylor and Diem (1987) to call it the "de facto national curriculum" in elementary social studies. Nevertheless, debates continue about the "rightful place" of history relative to the other social studies subjects, how history should be taught, and what students should learn.

GOALS FOR TEACHING HISTORY
TO ELEMENTARY STUDENTS

One of the most hotly contested landscapes involves the purposes or goals that scholars, teachers, and the public think ought to be addressed through instruction in history. Why teach history? What history ought to be taught and how should it be approached? These questions hinge on value commitments. Currently, they are far from being settled and show little promise of being settled in the near future.

For example, a debate of considerable force has arisen over the substance, goals, and perspectives of the National Standards for United States History released in the fall of 1994 by the National Center for History in the Schools (1994). Lynne Cheney, who was the director of the National Endowment for the Humanities when that agency provided funding for the creation of these standards, accused the document's authors of leftist bias and extreme political correctness in their choices of historical sources recommended for curriculum inclusion. The co-directors of the Standards project, Gary Nash and Charlotte Crabtree, dismissed these claims as bean counting and accused Cheney of seeking to rework the definition of political correctness to satisfy her own conservative leanings.

Essentially, the battle here was over what the history curriculum ought to look like. Cheney favored a "consensus," celebratory history that largely glorifies the major accomplishments of individuals who made important political, military, or economic contributions to the nation's development. This position no longer has much credibility within the discipline of history (Seixas, 1993b). The major alternative view reflects the structural forces in society that are beyond any one individual's control and accomplishment. Also, along with coverage of traditionally emphasized "great men," it includes attention to individuals and groups who have influenced U.S. history but have been largely invisible in previous consensus accounts. This approach taken by the Standards' authors reflects the "new" social history perspective that has been popular within the historical profession over the past 2 decades. Its proponents favor balancing coverage of political, military, and economic history and the exploits of famous individuals with increased coverage of evolution in social and cultural trends and the everyday lives of ordinary people.

Ultimately, conservative opposition to the 1994 version of the Standards forced their withdrawal. A rewritten version was released later, representing a compromise between the two contrasting views. This was only one recent skirmish over the history curriculum. In varying degrees of intensity, disputes over facets of historical study have persisted throughout the century. We will focus on aspects of those debates that have special relevance to elementary teachers and students.

Three goal-rationale frameworks have had the most influence on decisions about the elementary history curriculum: the child development, social studies, and disciplinary history perspectives. We consider these perspectives briefly, offering general portraits without probing the complexities that lie beneath the surface. Currently and across time, there has been considerable variation in the ways that these perspectives have been implemented through curriculum and instruction.

Child Development

Child development advocates argue that social studies or history teaching must be developmentally appropriate for young children (Bloch, 1986; Hahn, 1986). They place children, rather than subject matter or something else, at the center of the curriculum. They often are child development specialists or lower-grade elementary school teachers. Most of them would dispute Diane Ravitch (1987), who argued that even very young children (in Grades 1 and 2) are quite capable of studying history seriously. By contrast, they would suggest that young children are not developmentally ready to tackle the intricacies of historical study, often have trouble with "pastness," and are better served by a curriculum that is closer to their personal experience (e.g., home, family, school), such as the expanding communities curriculum.

Social Studies

Social studies advocates concern themselves primarily with citizenship education (Engle & Ochoa, 1988; Parker, 1989). As a result, they wish to design school subjects based on history and the social sciences that emphasize this goal. They press for integration across disciplines to achieve a curriculum that promotes civic learning, commitment to the public good, and active participation in the nation's democratic political process through decision-making and problem-solving experiences. Although they value the knowledge that disciplinary historians produce, they are not especially concerned about maintaining history's disciplinary integrity or teaching it in isolation from citizen education. In their view, promoting civic competence and a disposition toward participatory citizenship is the reason for social education in elementary school, and history is just one of the disciplines that contribute content to this effort.

Disciplinary History

Finally, many disciplinary historians and others who favor an emphasis on subject matter (Cheney, 1987; Gagnon, 1989a,b; Ravitch, 1987; Ravitch & Finn, 1987) would like to replace the social studies strand in the elementary curriculum on the grounds that it destroys the integrity of the disciplines and results in an intellectually fluffy and bankrupt course of study. Taking a primarily cultural literacy approach to history education (Hirsch, 1987), these detractors of social studies would restore the disciplines, especially history, to what they perceive to be the disciplines' rightful place in the curriculum. Most of them are history proponents who advocate that children should begin the serious study of history in grades 1 and 2 with historical myths and stories and biographies of famous Americans. A more rigorous chronological examination of history (combining fact-concept mastery with historical inquiry) would follow in the remaining elementary grades. Geography also would play an important role but it would be subsumed within this essential "history curriculum." Proponents of the history curriculum believe that study rooted in the disciplines not only teaches content more effectively but makes for more thoughtful and cognitively sophisticated students.

The current federal government plan for rejuvenating education, America 2000, uses the history-geography language favored by disciplinary historians; there is no mention of the social studies. However, most elementary school curricula feature the expanding communities approach, which is a "child development-friendly," "social studies" curriculum. The debate goes on.

These debates are important because their arguments become part of public consciousness and therefore spill over into schools in various forms. Once in the schools, different points of view and goal-rationale frameworks influence curriculum policy and architecture, and, in turn, influence how teachers teach history. This raises questions about the educational trade-offs that arise in choosing to pursue, say, citizenship education goals over disciplinary history goals, or vice versa. The three fifth-grade teachers introduced in forthcoming chapters offer us front row seats for observing how these trade-offs can play out in the classroom.

RECENT SCHOLARSHIP ON THE DEBATES OVER HISTORY IN THE CURRICULUM

Debates over goals and rationales for history education are not confined to well-publicized exchanges between Lynne Cheney and the co-directors of the National History Standards Project, or to public policies such as America 2000. They also take place on the pages of scholarly journals and in the forums of educational research conferences. Arguments in the scholarly fields tend to parallel the more public debates, but they also serve to inform those debates.

Kieran Egan (1983) offered a rather caustic critique of the expanding communities curriculum, claiming that instead of educating students, it promotes blind allegiance to simplistically presented Americanist ideals. He added that the historical strand of this curriculum is mostly indoctrination and of dubious educational value. He argued that history and the social science disciplines should assume prominence in the elementary curriculum. In his book *Teaching as Storytelling*, Egan (1986) offered a storytelling model of history teaching, using a "Great Stories of the World" curriculum. He maintained that good storytelling resonates with even very young children because it often is dramatic and connects with their sense of right and wrong, good and evil, heroes/heroines and villains, or other binary opposites. Egan viewed history as one of the richest sources of these human interest stories.

More recently, several U.S. groups have created a history curriculum reform movement. The Bradley Commission, a group of distinguished historians, met periodically from 1987 to 1989 to discuss issues related to the teaching and learning of history in the schools. They produced an edited volume entitled *Historical Literacy: The Case for History in American Education* (Gagnon, 1989b). Its contributors argued for the central importance of history in the curriculum and suggested different ways of teaching it well. Following the lead of Diane Ravitch (1987), who had dismissed the early-grades social studies curriculum as "tot sociology," the Bradley Commission expressed strong support for moving history into the primary grades, through stories and studies of the biographies of famous Americans. Chronological treatment still would begin in fifth grade, but it would be augmented by historical study and preparation in the earlier grades. The Bradley Commission also released guidelines for its vision of a renewed and reformed history curriculum (Gagnon, 1989a).

During this same time frame, educators and state officials produced the History-Social Science Framework for the California State Board of Education (1988). In it, they virtually eliminated the idea of social studies and moved aspects of the study of history into Grades K–3, while retaining the chronological, consensus-history focus of the fifth grade. That same year, the National Center for History in the Schools was formed at UCLA. The Center received the contract for the development of national history standards and since has become the focus of considerable controversy because of the standards it produced.

These California efforts reflected a hope for and commitment to making history a pivotal feature of the elementary curriculum. Charlotte Crabtree (1989), one of the co-directors of the Center for History in the Schools, in advocating the power and virtue of history in the elementary curriculum, directly challenged the social studies expanding communities curriculum model on grounds that it was without any core foundation or research support in work on cognitive psychology. What Crabtree did not say, however, was that her center's curriculum, teaching, and learning recommendations (and many of those of the Bradley Commission as well) also were put forth without any empirical evidence to support them.

In 1989, a group called the National Commission on Social Studies in the Schools released the document *Charting a Course: Social Studies for the 21st Century*. Its authors argued for a more prominent place for history in the K–12 curriculum at all levels. They recommended a considerably revised scope and sequence for the social studies curriculum that would give chronological, survey history a more prominent role. Their efforts mirrored much of the work done in California. As with its predecessors, there was little about the *Charting a Course* document that was anchored in empirical research on the teaching and learning of history (Levstik, 1990).

These direct challenges to the long-standing elementary social studies curriculum by reform groups that sought to replace it with more history did not go unnoticed (see, for example, Whelan, 1992, and the critical exchanges surrounding the *Charting a Course* report in issue 7, volume 54 of *Social Education*, 1990). We look here at one example, an article by Thornton (1990) entitled "Should We Be Teaching More History?", to provide a sense of the debate between those who advocate an academic-disciplines approach to history and those who favor the social studies model that integrates history with other subjects to pursue active citizenship education goals.

Thornton (1990) stated that he welcomed history's place in the school curriculum but was concerned that the proposals described above were misguided in their top-down curriculum reform emphasis. Most of the would-be reformers were not school people or K–12 teachers, but university professors and state education officials. Likening this late-1980s curriculum reform movement to the generally failed top-down New Social Studies Movement of the 1960s and 1970s, Thornton argued that reforming the curriculum alone, without direct attention to teachers' practices and to the impediments to change embedded in school cultures, would do little good. He also noted that the recommendations of the reformers lacked a research basis.

> In sum, the supposed benefits of teaching more history are unproven. If the case for teaching more history is to rest on its efficacy as civic education in areas such as informed decision-making about public issues, then the case cannot be sustained from the research evidence. Little is known about the effects of students' exposure to either more "history" courses 50 or 60 years ago, or to fewer "history" courses in recent decades. (p. 55)

Thornton concluded by restating his main point: Until more is learned about how teachers teach history and how this teaching in turn influences students, simply adding more history to the curriculum will contribute little to enhancing citizenship education in American schools.

In a later review of research on the social studies curriculum, Thornton (1994) returned to this same point and repeated his cautionary assessment. A possible subtext of Thornton's caution is his worry that a renewed role for history in the curriculum would mean a revival of the fact-mastery, politically conservative history teaching that early-twentieth-century reformers sought to eliminate by introducing the social studies perspective into the curriculum.

Child development advocates also have weighed in on the issue of history in the elementary curriculum. One of the more notable and direct statements came from Carol Seefeldt (1993), an early childhood education specialist and researcher. As her point of departure, Seefeldt examined Egan's and Ravitch's arguments for eliminating the expanding communities curriculum in the early grades and replacing it with more history, particularly history of story and myth. Echoing Thornton's cautions but from a different angle, Seefeldt contended that stories and myths may be engaging but they have the potential to teach young children unfounded ideas about the past. To avoid this, she argued for an early childhood history curriculum (if one is to replace the expanding communities model) that is rooted in concepts that "characterize the field," such as time, change, continuity in human life, and the past. These concepts would be introduced through a teaching framework designed to make history meaningful (by connecting it to the students' here-and-now experiences), age appropriate (by focusing on initial exploration of concepts rather than in-depth, detailed understandings), personified (by having students study their own histories), and intellectually stimulating (by featuring content that has disciplinary integrity but also connects to the children's lives).[1]

Peter Seixas (1993b) addressed disagreements about the place of history education in the school curriculum within the context of the wider sweep of changes in late-twentieth-century educational affairs. He noted that not only is there a "crisis" going on in schools over the role of the social studies and history in the curriculum, but a similar "crisis" pervades the discipline of history itself. At least four areas of historical debate have arisen—over the role of objectivity in scholarship, the place of the "new" social history relative to the traditional economic and political history, the broadening purview of acceptable historical inquiry, and the explicit politicization of historical study. Given this bumpy terrain, Seixas cautioned that proponents of more history in the curriculum will find little solace or solid ground if they rely on the discipline of history as a model for school curriculum reform efforts. However, he also suggested that promoting the development of a conversation between social studies educators and the new generation of historians (those responsible in part for the "crisis" in history) might provide the means necessary to achieve lasting social studies curriculum reform. Such a coalition, Seixas argued, could accomplish more than the limited, narrow band of history reform suggested by neoconservative proponents such as Lynne Cheney (1987).

As we have seen, the debates about history in the curriculum remain far from settled. Many of those (e.g., Cheney) who advocate more history in the elementary grades appear to be conservatives who nostalgically seek to return to an older version of consensus history. Others (e.g., Egan and perhaps the Bradley Commission and Ravitch) champion more history because of their disdain for the weaknesses and "fluff" they have identified in the expanding communities curriculum. Citizenship education proponents (e.g., Thornton), along with some child development advocates (e.g., Seefeldt), appear wary of a "more history" reform agenda. Social education advocates prefer that history be integrated within the social studies and taught in service of citizenship education goals rather than isolated within a separate curriculum strand that emphasizes disciplinary goals. Child development proponents do not object to more history per se, but caution that it should be intellectually stimulating, not an irrelevant academic exercise, and that it should be reality- and concept-based rather than centered on stories and myths.

The foregoing analysis has set the stage for examining how contrasting positions on the role of history in the curriculum can entail significant differences in classroom practices. Our portraits of three teachers will reflect some aspects of the positions taken by the various groups of reformers. The teacher portraits illustrate what we refer to as trade-offs—the practice-related results of following one general direction rather than another. The portraits will not answer definitively the questions: More history or not? and What is the best way to teach history? Rather, they will provide opportunities for reflection on the trade-offs embedded in contrasting goals and purposes for teaching history.

In the remainder of this chapter, we focus on recent research studies that also bear on the portraits of the three teachers. Accompanying the history reform movement, there has been an upsurge of interest in research on history learning. Less polemical than reformers' positions on the purposes of history in the curriculum, this research focuses on what it means to learn history. It has extended from the elementary grades to the college years. We will focus on studies that apply primarily to *learning* history at the elementary level, especially fifth grade, where history is taught chronologically for the first time.

RESEARCH ON THE LEARNING OF HISTORY

Several wide-ranging classroom studies of history education have been conducted, initially in Great Britain but recently in the United States as well. Many of these studies have focused on the learning of history, especially on students' developing historical understanding and empathy, textbook usage, knowledge development during units of instruction, and the character of "novice" and "expert" historical knowledge.

Early British Studies

In Great Britain, many early studies on history learning were influenced by Jean Piaget's ideas about developmental stages. These studies focused on (1) historical time (West, 1978, 1981); (2) children's understandings of the past (Biggs & Collis, 1982; Hallam, 1978, 1979; Jurd, 1973); (3) gender and history testing performance (Bryant, 1982); (4) developments (across the middle and high school grades) in students' reasoning related to causation, the nature of historical evidence, and empathy with people from the past (Shemilt, 1980, 1983, 1984); and (5) older students' historical understanding and empathy (Ashby & Lee, 1987; Dickinson & Lee, 1978, 1984).

Martin Booth (1993), a British researcher whose own work in Great Britain parallels the period when much of this research was compiled, has reviewed salient aspects of it in connection with his assessment of the British national history curriculum. We draw on relevant aspects of his account of the influence of this British research on early theories, beliefs, and arguments about history learning.[2]

Controversies Rooted in Piagetian Ideas. Hallam's (1978, 1979) research was based largely in Piagetian stage-development processes. Piaget argued that children move through a series of progressive stages—sensorimotor, preoperational, concrete operational, and formal operational. During the first two stages, infants and young children do not yet possess the levels of understanding and logical reasoning abilities observed in older children and adults. Starting around age 6 or 7, however, children begin to develop concrete operations—cognitive capacities that enable them to solve concrete (hands-on) problems logically, adopt the perspective of another person, and consider intentions (not just actions and their outcomes) in moral reasoning. Starting around age 12, they begin to develop formal operations—cognitive capacities that enable them to engage in more abstract, hypothetical, and purely symbolic (complex verbal) thinking, without being so dependent on direct experiences or concrete examples.

Hallam viewed movement from the concrete to the formal operational stage as crucial to the development of historical thinking. He assumed that schools should cultivate in students the type of historical thinking that is valued in the discipline, and that such reasoning requires formal operational ability. Based on interviews with students concerning their understandings of historical accounts given to them to read, Hallam concluded that disciplined historical reasoning did not develop until students were in their middle teens. This conclusion carried discouraging implications for elementary school curriculum designers and teachers. It seemed to dispute Jerome Bruner's (1960) contention that any subject could be taught in an "intellectually honest way" to students at any level of development.

These and other early findings appeared to support child development advocates who wanted the curriculum to reflect learning opportunities closer to children's immediate experience, something that the history of the past often was not. However, subsequent British studies began to challenge the idea that only older students were capable of historical thinking. Hallam's conclusions were questioned on a number of fronts, but most notably on the grounds that Piaget's studies had been constructed around thinking in the natural sciences, and historical thinking is qualitatively different from scientific thinking.

Booth (1993) argued that historical thinking requires "adductive thought"—a form of analysis that combines both inductive and deductive cognition in a process that lacks the linear structure found in applications of the scientific method used in the natural sciences. Also, historical reasoning is applied with the intention of developing a detailed account of a unique case (history is about unique particulars), whereas scientific thinking is applied with the intention of developing generalizable theories and explanations. Booth applied this theory of historical reasoning in his own research with 14–16-year-olds—younger students than Hallam had predicted could manage historical thinking successfully. Booth (1979) showed that these students could do so if their teacher helped to promote it through open-ended discussion formats.

Shemilt (1980, 1983, 1984) conducted extended work on students' ability to empathize with people from the past. He also showed that students were able to imagine past events in ways that supported historical empathy even when still in the concrete operational stage. Shemilt interpreted these possibilities optimistically, stressing that the ways children are taught, their direct involvement in thinking historically, and the types of sources at their disposal could affect their development of historical thinking in early adolescence.

Dickinson and Lee (1978, 1984) conducted a series of studies that further challenged Piagetian ideas about history learning. Based on their empirical work with early adolescents, these British researchers suggested that the development of historical understanding depends on three overlapping and interactive factors: (1) cultivating a sense of historical actors' range of motives and intentions, (2) developing a context in which to situate the range of their possible motives, and (3) constructing a range of potential events that may have influenced their actions. They also argued that historical imagination and empathy are necessary and crucial features of historical understanding, which (1) develops by degrees; (2) can be stimulated by teachers; and (3) may depend heavily on discussion, questioning, students' prior knowledge of other historical periods, and the ability of teachers to connect the period under study to the students' lives. Dickinson and Lee warned that Piagetian notions about students' ability to reason historically could cause teachers to underestimate the complexity of their students' thought processes and, in particular, to underappreciate the possibilities for teaching history to younger students.

Implications of Early British Studies. Sansom (1987) reviewed the British studies and considered their implications for curriculum and instruction. He noted the increasing evidence that children were capable of meaningful historical understanding much earlier than Hallam had suggested. He also concluded that historical knowledge and reasoning abilities develop gradually without any clear "breakthrough" points, rather than being tied closely to Piagetian stages or other generic developmental phenomena. Based on Shemilt's work, he emphasized gradual developments in four key conceptual clusters.

1. *Causation.* At first, children do not perceive any logic to historical causality—things happen without relationship to one another. The story "unfolds" but doesn't develop. Once they begin to understand that historical events have causes, they tend to take a mechanistic view of causal determination. That is, they seem to think that events were the inevitable results of their preceding causal chains, that they had to happen the way they did. Later, children begin to understand that events have multiple causes that act in combination, that things could have turned out differently, that we can't know all of the causes and give a comprehensive and final picture of the past, and that events are unique because they develop from complex interactions of factors that are unlikely to be duplicated exactly.

2. *Change and continuity.* At first, children view changes as unrelated rather than as progressions that transform a story. Later they begin to view change as a series or causal chain. At this point they believe that everything can be traced back to a first cause and that everything that happened in the past is an antecedent to the present. Finally, they begin to view historical change as the gradual transformation of a situation, realizing that only some aspects of the situation change and that these changes may range from the trivial to the radical.

3. *Motivation and intentions of historical actors.* At first, children do not empathize with people from the past. When exposed to accounts of what seems to be inexplicable behavior, they adopt a patronizing attitude, suggesting that the people acted as they did because they were stupid or not as developed as we are. Subsequently they begin to understand that the people were acting rationally from their own perspectives. Initially they attribute vague or stereotyped motivations to the people ("his character," "their religion"). Later they attribute more specific motives, although still by projecting from a twentieth-century viewpoint. Finally, they begin to appreciate the need to reconstruct the probable perceptions and beliefs of historical actors, reasoning from whatever historical source materials may be available.

4. *Evidence and historical method.* At first, children equate evidence with factual information. They don't notice or don't know how to make sense of contradictory evidence. Later, they gradually come to

understand that evidence must be interpreted, that different sources of evidence may conflict, and that historians need to follow disciplinary rules for evidence collection and use and then develop interpretations that are defensible but not final or definitive.

More Recent Studies

There has been an upsurge in research on history learning in recent years. Having reviewed early British studies, we now examine more recent work, done mostly in the United States. We confine our selection primarily to studies that have explored younger students' knowledge growth, learning from historical texts, and developing historical understandings. We draw from several of these studies later in the book where we analyze what students learned in the classrooms of the three teachers.

Surveys of Historical Knowledge. There have been occasional surveys of students' knowledge about particular social studies topics (e.g., Guzzetta, 1969; Ravitch & Finn, 1987). These have concentrated mostly on isolated facts such as names, places, or definitions, with analysis and reporting of findings being limited to the percentages of students in various categories who were able to answer each item correctly. There is not much to say about these studies other than that the results have not been encouraging. Given their failure to address qualitative aspects of students' thinking, these studies have told us little about what we are particularly interested in here—students' developing historical understandings, their thought processes, and what they learn from curriculum units on historical periods.

Studies of Learning from History Texts. History textbooks have been criticized roundly by a variety of scholars for their inconsiderateness to readers, incoherence, emphasis on details at the expense of overall main ideas, and mundane expository style (e.g., Beck, McKeown, & Gromoll, 1989; Brophy, 1992a; Larkins, Hawkins, & Gilmore, 1987; McCabe, 1993). These criticisms have spawned a number of studies that have examined the use of textbooks in classrooms and related contexts, exploring their limitations and how they might be improved. The criticisms also have prompted study of the burgeoning use of textbook alternatives—history tradebooks and fiction—to identify whether and how they might improve on the expository textbooks.

McKeown and Beck (1990, 1994) studied what fifth graders learn from commonly used textbooks. They interviewed these students before and after a unit on the American Revolution in which the textbook was their major source of information. They also interviewed sixth graders who had taken the same fifth-grade history course the year before, to see how much of what they learned was retained. Both sets of interviews indicated that students had considerable difficulty making sense of the textbooks and retaining what they "learned." Among other problems, the textbook authors tended to assume too much background knowledge on the part of students, used a "language of objectivity" that distanced the students from the text content, and produced passages that lacked textual coherence. To illustrate the problem, Beck and McKeown (1994) invited readers to consider the following "historical" account:

> *The Langurian and Pitok War.* In 1367 Marain and the settlements ended a 7-year war with the Langurian and Pitoks. As a result of this war Languria was driven out of East Bacol. Marain would now rule Laman and other lands that belonged to Languria. This brought peace to the Bacolian settlements. The settlers no longer had to fear attacks from Laman. The Bacolians were happy to be a part of Marain in 1367. Yet a dozen years later, these same people would be fighting the Marish for independence, or freedom from United Marain's rule. This war was called the Freedom War or the Bacolian Revolution. A revolution changes one type of government or way of thinking and replaces it with another. (p. 239)

This passage was constructed simply by changing the names of people and places referred to in the following passage from a fifth-grade U.S. history text:

> *The French and Indian War.* In 1763 Britain and the colonies ended a 7-year war with the French and Indians. As a result of this war France was driven out of North America. Britain would now rule Canada and other lands that had belonged to France. This brought peace to the American colonies. The colonists no longer had to fear attacks from Canada. The Americans were happy to be a part of Britain in 1763. Yet a dozen years later, these same people would be fighting the British for independence, or freedom from Great Britain's rule. This war was called the War for Independence or the American Revolution. A revolution changes one type of government or way of thinking and replaces it with another. (pp. 239–240)

Beck and McKeown pointed out that, given most fifth graders' limited prior knowledge about history, the second passage is no more coherent and meaningful to them than the first passage is to adults. Reading sparse, poorly connected historical accounts without rich background knowledge gives one the feeling of being bombarded with meaningless labels and makes it difficult to emerge with a coherent account that "holds the pieces together."

Addressing this problem, McKeown and Beck (1994) applied "repair" strategies to textbook passages to see if this would help students to develop greater historical understanding. Their repair strategies involved making improvements in two areas: providing more background context to the passages to help overcome students' limited prior knowledge, and rewriting sections to make them more coherent (especially regarding cause-and-effect linkages). Of the two repairs, increased coherence produced stronger gains in student understanding, but broadening the context also helped. McKeown and Beck argued that the chronological survey curriculum was partly to blame for the poor quality of the textbooks. They suggested that students would benefit by encountering a curriculum that addressed fewer historical topics, but covered them in greater depth and with more of the contextualized information that enhances coherence.

Levstik and Pappas (1987) also looked at young learners' responses to the history texts they read in school. Specifically, they investigated the connections between textual narrative and historical understanding in Grades 2, 4, and 6. They explored the effects of narrative on children's concepts of chronology, the significance of the past, the ambiguity of historical knowledge, historical change, and what counts as knowing history. They concluded that (1) the children were capable of constructing their own intelligible historical narratives, (2) even the youngest children were receptive to historical information and found aspects of social history very appealing, (3) historical context and style of presentation were both key elements affecting what students learned, and (4) echoing Dickinson and Lee (1984), educators consistently have underestimated young children's ability to make sense of the past and think intelligently about it.

Levstik (1989) examined the relationship between history narratives or stories (e.g., historical fiction) and history learning in the case of Jennifer, a fifth grader. Levstik suggested that narratives were appealing to Jennifer because they provided a sense of wholeness and moral resolution (see Egan, 1986, on this point), and emphasized the humanness of history. Jennifer's satisfaction with historical narratives caused her to use them as a reference point to judge the quality of the textbook.

The social studies [text]book is old and doesn't have as much information in it like [fictional] books do . . . and they give you a lot of information that no social studies book ever tells you. . . . The social studies book doesn't give you a lot of detail. You don't imagine yourself there because they're not doing it as if it were a person. That would be a very interesting social studies book if they told a few things about the people as if it were from their own eyes. . . . But the textbooks don't like to be interesting, especially. (p. 114)

Levstik concluded that it is important to provide students with more than just textbooks as sources of historical information. She recommended integrating language arts with historical study as a means of bringing the learning of history together with the art of interpretation and the creation of narratives (two processes that are taught more commonly in language arts, yet are closely linked to history).

More recently, Levstik and Pappas (1992; see also Levstik, 1995) broadened the argument for emphasizing narrative texts and instructional methods in teaching history to young students. They suggested that narrative forms not only appeal to children, but are basic to the "culture" of history as a discipline. Historians have long used narrative as a way of structuring historical accounts, in the process transforming a collection of "facts" into a sequence of events—a story—that includes interpretation of the causes that account for these events. Imposition of the narrative format shapes events, assigns greater significance to some events than to others, and embeds them all within a causal interpretation. Even primary grade children can follow narrative structures so long as they can understand the motives and goals of the central figures.

Others also have been interested in the fusion of language arts and children's literature with historical study. Many are teachers, which has caused a significant rise in the classroom use of tradebooks for historical study. The use of these tradebooks as attractive alternatives to uninspiring textbooks prompted Richgels, Tomlinson, and Tunnell (1993) to do a detailed study of the textual similarities and differences between children's history tradebooks (fiction, literature) and expository textbooks. They examined sentence predicate organization, sentence length, sentence structure and complexity, overall organizational features, and coherence in both types of texts. Their analysis demonstrated that the tradebooks frequently contained longer, more complex sentences; used better organizational strategies and predicate constructions; and provided for deeper topic exploration than the textbooks. Despite their richer vocabularies and more complex sentence constructions, the tradebooks were more comprehensible to students than the textbooks. This may account in part for their greater appeal.

McKinney and Jones (1993) studied the use of a children's trade-book as an alternative or supplement to the textbook in teaching U.S. history in three fifth-grade classes. For a unit on the American Revolution, one class received instruction based on a tradebook about the American Revolution (a nonfictional account written for children), a second class received instruction based on the regular textbook, and a third class received instruction based on the textbook but were encouraged to read the tradebook at home. Assessment data indicated that the classes did not differ significantly on knowledge of content contained in both books, but that the two classes that read the children's book learned additional information that was contained only in that book. The authors concluded that children taught with tradebooks may learn more because more content can be included in children's books than in textbook units. Howe (1990) also reported an achievement advantage to fifth graders who read selections from historical tradebooks, but Kovalcik (1979) reported better results for students taught with the textbook, and Cunningham and Gall (1990) found no group difference.

Kinder and Bursuck (1993) taught junior high students a strategy for studying history texts that was based on the narrative structure that includes a problem, an individual or group's attempt to solve the problem, and a resolution that describes the effects of this attempted solution. Research findings indicated that students taught to take notes using this problem-solution-effect analysis showed significantly improved achievement and attitudes in history.

Barton (1993) described an emphasis on children's historical fiction in a case study of a fifth-grade unit on the American Revolution. He observed a heavy reliance on narrative structures, by both the teacher and the students, in representing knowledge about this historical period in speech and writing. The teacher and students used five overlapping structures to place their study of the Revolution into a narrative framework.

1. The unit as a whole was treated as a sequence of causally related events that together formed the "story" of the American Revolution.
2. Each event was treated as a story in itself, with characters, problem, and resolution.
3. These stories emphasized the feelings and actions of individuals.
4. Fictive conversations (e.g., between King George and his advi-

sors) were spontaneously created in order to convey information.
5. Nations were endowed with human characteristics (e.g., motives, goals, plans, and other features common to central figures
in stories).

Clearly, tradebooks have much to offer as sources of curriculum
content in teaching about history. However, as Levstik (1989) noted,
reliance on these resources can lead to distorted understandings if students are not clear about the distinctions between historical accounts
and fictional recreations, or if they are exposed to fictional selections
depicting events that are not historically accurate.

VanSledright and Brophy (1992) encountered some evidence to support Levstik's (1989) concerns. Interviews with 10 fourth graders who
had read fictionalized historical accounts during their study of state
history that year indicated that some of them, particularly the lower
achievers, produced stories and fancifully elaborated accounts as responses to questions about what they had learned. Several students
appeared to equate history with storytelling or narrativizing, so that
they viewed an account as a historical rendition if it was based in the
past, was dramatic, contained action, was personalized, and was constructed around a story grammar framework. These students seemed
unaware that historians work from evidence-use rules when constructing their accounts and that they seek to provide accurate details.

The use of narrative or storytelling, especially in fictionalizing history, operated as a two-edged sword. It promoted reading motivation
and engagement because the students found the fiction interesting, but
it fostered beliefs about history and historical evidence that were at
odds with how historians do their work. This indicates the need for
teachers to teach students about the difference between fictional and
nonfictional texts, and about evidence use in constructing the latter.

In a more recent study, VanSledright (1994; VanSledright & Kelly,
1995) further explored how students make sense of history by reading
from expository textbooks and fictionalized tradebook accounts. Based
on data from interviews with six fifth graders, a think-aloud protocol
in which the six students read a first-person account of the Boston
Massacre taken from a tradebook and a synoptic account taken from a
textbook, and a motivation questionnaire used with an entire fifth-
grade class, he concluded that students

1. enjoyed reading the tradebooks more than the textbooks because of their narrative style, but found the textbooks more use-

ful in gathering a wide array of information for their assigned research projects;

2. viewed history as an objective, fact-laden account of the past, with their task being to get those facts (but did not know how they might judge the viability or accuracy of the historical representations found in the texts);

3. were unsure about what to do when information from one text type conflicted with another, having learned few strategies for reconciling or dealing with the differences (which they often simply ignored); and

4. as in the earlier study, were unaware of the various ways that historical evidence had been treated in constructing the different texts, causing them to believe that both accounts were equally accurate in representing history. When pressed, students chose the textbook as more accurate because its apparent objective, encyclopedic nature fit more readily with their view of history, and because many of their classroom activities involved searching for facts.

Becoming able to make distinctions between texts and aware of the problems that contrasting types can produce in learning about the past may require the development of what Wineburg (1991) called reading for subtext. Although his study dealt with how historians and bright high school students read different types of history texts and documents, it may have implications for how younger learners develop historical understanding and respond to various accounts. Wineburg asked historians and high school students to think aloud as they read documents and texts concerning the battle at Lexington on the eve of the American Revolutionary War. He found that students tended to read for authorial intent and viewed the texts as authoritative. They were interested in establishing the facts of the events and appeared to be confused by the documents' shifting points of view. Wineburg argued that this was a consequence of learning to read for information to satisfy the demands of standardized tests.

Historians, by contrast, were interested in the subtexts of the documents; that is, the underlying points of view and political positions of the authors that helped frame their descriptions of events. The historians used interpretive strategies that allowed them to understand the events more deeply by plumbing their subtleties. Reading for subtext was a crucial ingredient in helping the historians build "event models" that reconstructed what probably happened (and why). Wineburg identified such reading for subtext as a hallmark of expertise in understanding history. He recommended that young learners be taught to read historical accounts for the subtexts they often contain, the indeterminacy of their authority, and the slipperiness of their meaning.

Studies on Historical Understanding, Time Concepts, and Knowledge Acquisition. Hallden (1994) raised an interesting issue encountered in work with Swedish children: the "paradox of understanding history" that arises when novice learners produce naive conceptions. Invoking Bruner's claim that when pupils give wrong answers they are in fact answering other questions, Hallden explored "alternative frames of reference" held by young learners that influence how they understand the "open" structure of history and its array of concepts. Classroom dialogue samples were used to illustrate the paradox: As students are asked "to understand the explanatory power of a fact, [they] have to find an interpretation of the fact in the context of what needs to be explained. Yet, what needs to be explained is what is intended to be stated by the presentation of these facts" (p. 33). In other words, it appears that in order to appreciate the import of new information, learners must already possess a contextualized understanding of it!

Hallden found that novice learners brought their own ideas about the discipline of history to the interpretive process, helping to account for their naive conceptions and their difficulties in understanding historical explanations. They approached history by personifying explanations; that is, by focusing on the actions and intentions of individuals. This focus caused them to miss or fail to appreciate structural explanations that often appear in historical accounts (e.g., the working of an economic system over which no individual person has control). The question this raises for instruction involves discovering how to help students construct a desired interpretation when they do not possess the contextual background (e.g., a structural explanation) necessary for achieving that interpretation. Hallden suggested asking students to process simultaneously a meta-level explanation (the larger, often structural, context) and its lower-level facts and concepts. In the process of working back and forth between the two levels, both the facts and the explanation would gain meaning for students.

In interviews with eighth graders who were about to embark on a lengthy study of British colonization in North America, VanSledright (1995a) found that, even though they had studied this same period in fifth grade, students had difficulty remembering much of what they had learned. In preunit interviews, five of the six students recalled the name Jamestown from fifth grade, but could say little more about it.

This was the case with most of the questions that asked about what they remembered from their fifth-grade study of colonization. The one exception concerned Plymouth Rock and the early Plymouth colony. Students were able to tell a fairly detailed, celebratory story about the colonists' arrival there and the first Thanksgiving. They claimed they remembered this so well because they had heard the story in several elementary grades as part of the Thanksgiving holiday celebration. VanSledright attributed, in part, students' difficulty recalling what they ostensibly had learned in fifth grade to the concern of the curriculum objectives with the pursuit of facts, details, and content coverage at the expense of cultivating a deeper historical understanding of the colonial period. Beck and McKeown (1994) also found that eighth graders offered mostly vague or confused reconstructions of U.S. history that they ostensibly had learned in fifth grade. They attributed the problem to similar causes.

Levstik and Barton (1996) explored how 58 elementary students (approximately eight students in each grade from K–6) constructed understandings of historical time (in contrast to clock time, or contemporary calendar time). The authors were interested in testing earlier research conclusions that indicated that children below the age of 7 or 8 generally were unable to make reliable distinctions about events in the past. These conclusions have been employed to argue that young children are not ready for historical study, but research by Levstik and Pappas (1987) had suggested that this was not necessarily the case.

Levstik and Barton (1996) asked students to place nine pictures drawn from a variety of historical time periods (e.g., colonial era, the late nineteenth century, the 1950s) into chronological order. As expected, the responses varied by age. The youngest children were capable of making distinctions in historical time (e.g., far past versus recent past versus today), but dates had little meaning for them. They used context clues such as clothing and hairstyle to base their choices. It was not until about third grade that dates began to take on significance, and not until fifth and sixth grades that children began to associate dates with background knowledge about event epochs (e.g., the colonial period). Levstik and Barton concluded that the sizable agreement across grade levels in placement of the pictures indicated the presence of a reasonably large body of knowledge about historical chronology at children's disposal, and disputed earlier claims that young children were not ready for historical study. Elementary school teachers, they contended, could help to enhance young learners' ideas of the past and chronology by building on their existing knowledge.

CONCLUSION

More research on history learning is still required to enable anyone to draw firm conclusions about how best to assist students in making sense of the past. However, the studies described above suggest, among other things, that

1. even the youngest elementary students do have a sense of history and bring prior conceptions (even highly overgeneralized ones) to bear on the new learning that takes place;
2. texts provide a fundamental entree into the past, requiring that students learn to appreciate the different purposes for which different types of texts are written and the expectation that historical texts will be constructed based on evidence and rules about how to use that evidence;
3. students have difficulty retaining what they learn if it is not connected to their prior knowledge, lacks coherence, or is not embedded within a context that enables them to situate it; and
4. the fact-laden, objectivist view of history may distort students' perspectives on what history is and potentially prevent them from developing the critical, interpretive, and synthetic thinking abilities required for cultivating historical understanding.

We will return to these ideas later as we explore how the three teachers taught their fifth graders and what the students learned.

NOTES

1. For a slightly different early childhood perspective on history learning, see Low-Beer and Blyth (1983). For a defense of the expanding communities curriculum on the grounds that it "comes closest to bringing understanding to how the real world works and operates" (p. 17), see Bragaw and Hartoonian (1988).

2. For additional assessments and critiques of this early British work, see Laville and Rosenzweig (1982), Levstik (1993b), and Knight (1989b).

CHAPTER 2

Teaching History

The image of good [history] teaching . . . is one that is grounded in subject matter. It is a disciplinary conception of history teaching that presupposes that one major goal for teaching history is the communication of historical knowledge—the central facts, concepts, and ideas of the discipline—and the nature of the methods employed by historians, for example, the role played by interpretation and narrative.

—Wilson, 1991, p. 101

Teachers need knowledge of the ways in which the social sciences are interrelated and should be able to view issues, concepts, and problems in an interdisciplinary way. Teachers also need an interdisciplinary orientation to the social sciences because disciplinary boundaries are often blurred in the real world of schools as units are taught that include insights and perspectives from several different disciplines.

—Banks, 1991, pp. 120–121

There is as much controversy surrounding the teaching of history as there is about the role of history in the curriculum. In this chapter, we begin by examining the various positions advanced in scholarship on history teaching, especially those that seem most relevant to history in the elementary school. Then, to further situate the three teachers and their students within the wider arena of work on this subject, we review research on history teaching. Finally, in preparation for introducing the teachers and students, we discuss the questions that guided our research and the methods we employed in collecting data.

APPROACHES TO TEACHING HISTORY

A careful look into the scholarly literature on history teaching unearths two interesting results. First, there is a large volume of work on analyses of possible orientations to the teaching of history—as the quotations from Suzanne Wilson and James Banks attest—and numerous recommendations and prescriptions for appropriate methods and practices. Second, there is surprisingly little actual research (systematic or otherwise) on history teaching, and much of what one does find is very recent and focused largely around history teaching in secondary schools. The latter point makes sense in that, with the exception of fifth grade, much of the history that is taught in elementary schools has been integrated into the social studies. Secondary schools teach more discipline-based content and appear far less concerned about integrating subjects (although some middle schools have been moving toward integrated models).

The Three Traditions

One influential assessment of teaching in social studies and history came from Barr, Barth, and Shermis (1977). In *Defining the Social Studies,* they posited that social studies can and should be defined by its citizenship education mission. They linked this assertion to the goal frameworks for social studies derived from the historic and progressive Report of the Commission on Social Studies of 1916 (Barr et al., 1977, p. 25). With this citizenship education mission in place, they described what they termed "the three traditions" that historically have competed over the purpose, content, and teaching methods of the social studies, including history. The three traditions are (1) social studies as citizenship transmission, (2) social studies as social science, and (3) social studies as reflective inquiry.

Barr and colleagues (1977) stated that "the essence of Citizenship Transmission, as the name suggests, is that adult teachers possess a particular conception of citizenship that they wish all students to share. They use a mixture of techniques to insure that these beliefs are transmitted to their students" (p. 59). The purpose of this tradition hinges on the process of "inculcating right values as a framework for making decisions" (p. 67). Concepts and values are introduced and mastered through the use of authoritative textbooks, lectures, recitations, discussion, and structured problem solving. Content is appropriated by teacher choice using criteria that entail the authoritativeness of the "right" values, beliefs, and attitudes that are to be communicated. Typically these emerge from an analysis of traditional cultural values such as the work ethic, individualism, the free market system, the wisdom of merit-based social stratification, representative democracy, and so forth. The teaching and learning of history has been understood as a very effective method for accomplishing this citizenship purpose as long as it follows the celebratory, consensus model.

Barr and colleagues noted that all teachers practice some form of citizenship transmission implicitly, if not explicitly.

The second tradition, social science, competes for prominence in social studies teaching by promoting citizenship through "decision making based on mastery of social science concepts, processes, and problems" (Barr et al., 1977, p. 67), rather than on ostensibly "right" cultural values, beliefs, and attitudes. Its content therefore must revolve around the knowledge generated by history and the social science disciplines both individually and, where possible, in an integrated fashion. The method mirrors the pursuit of concepts, structures, and problems emergent in the work of social scientists themselves (i.e., following the scientific method derived from the natural sciences). As a result, the curriculum embraces the individual (and possibly integrated) subject matters of history, geography, and the behavioral sciences as they pertain to citizenship decisions.

Barr and colleagues (1977) traced the third tradition, citizenship as reflective inquiry, to John Dewey's active, participatory, and reflective involvement in a developing democratic vision. It argues that "citizenship is best promoted through a process of inquiry in which knowledge is derived from what citizens need to know to make decisions and solve problems" (p. 67). Content is determined by an "analysis of individual citizens' values yield[ing] needs and interests which . . . form the basis for student self-selection of problems. Problems, therefore constitute the content for reflection" (p. 67). The method of reflective inquiry itself operates by testing the insight of the student against the standard of that insight's viability for creating skillful decision-making practices within democratic communities.

Barr and colleagues developed an instrument called the Social Studies Preference Scale (ssps) to measure the presence or absence of the three traditions in teachers' orientations and thoughts about social studies. The ssps is a 45-item Likert response questionnaire with three 15-item scales, one for each tradition. Barr and colleagues (1977) reported that social studies teachers' responses to the instrument justified their description of the three traditions. Factor analysis suggested that the teachers surveyed tended to cluster around one of the three traditions, although some of them could be called eclectics because they used approaches from all three. Two replication studies followed. Andres (1981) administered the ssps to 193 secondary social studies teachers, and White (1982) administered it to 190 secondary social studies teachers. Both studies yielded similar factor analysis results: The citizenship transmission approach emerged as a coherent (and commonly endorsed) orientation, but the social science and reflective inquiry orientations collapsed into a single factor instead of maintaining their separate integrities.

These replication failures did not entirely discredit the three traditions as descriptive constructs. Rather, their findings suggested that teachers' approaches probably varied more than Barr and colleagues (1977) initially suggested (Goodman & Adler, 1985). Nonetheless, the three traditions have remained in the literature well into the 1990s and have influenced how a number of people understand the teaching of history and social studies. In their calls for more detailed and complex studies of teaching practices in actual classrooms, some (e.g., Armento, 1986) have suggested that the field move beyond the three traditions. Recently, detailed case studies of teachers have begun to appear that suggest that, although the three traditions are useful as descriptions of alternative approaches to history (and social studies) teaching, teachers commonly exhibit aspects of all of them at different points throughout a school year (and perhaps even within a given lesson).[1] This prompted Evans (1989), following Barr and colleagues (1977), to refer to teachers as eclectics. Others have abandoned the use of the three traditions altogether, inventing new metaphors to describe and categorize history-social studies teaching.

Common Teaching Practice

If Cuban (1984) and Goodlad (1984) are accurate in their analyses of the state of teaching in American classrooms, the most common approach to history teaching offers a perfunctory overview of as many facets of U.S. history as can be crammed into a school year. School district curriculum guides for fifth-grade social studies typically advocate coverage that extends from the early Native Americans through at least Watergate, and sometimes as far as the present. Textbook publishers continue to produce thick, encyclopedic history texts that "cover" this vast span of time.

Greene (1994) argued that this type of "school history" is rooted in what he called the "tradition of archivism," which views history as the gradual accumulation of facts drawn from historical documents and held together by a storyline. In this view, the task of historians is to study documents and amass the facts using rigorous scientific research methods; the task of school teachers is to teach these facts to students in order to provide them with an account of how things actually were in the past. According to Cuban and Goodlad (see also Shaver, Davis, & Helburn, 1979), a common response to this configuration of curriculum architecture, textbook augmentation, and the tradition of archivism has been for many teachers to provide their students with a lightning trip through the historical chronology found in the textbooks. Students attempt to acquire enough facts to pass the end-of-chapter multiple choice tests and then promptly forget most of those facts, which held little meaning for them and were poorly (if at all) integrated into knowledge frameworks structured around key ideas.

Teaching History for Understanding

A number of people have decried this parade-of-facts approach to history teaching as inappropriate and suggested alternatives. For example, Brophy (1990b) argued for examining fewer periods of history during the year, but in considerable depth. He identified how this might work by situating it within the framework of a unit on Native Americans. The major ideas to be represented to students would include

1. the nature of the trek across the land bridge in the Bering Strait into North America;
2. variation in tribal development over time;
3. specific differences in tool development and other unique adaptations to geography, climate, and natural resources among tribes;
4. influences on the indigenous peoples by the Europeans who later came to North America (and vice versa); and
5. the present status of North American native tribes.

Brophy also suggested alternative teaching methods and forms of assessment.

Many of Brophy's recommendations are rooted in ideas about teaching history for understanding, higher-order thinking, and life applications. Proponents of this view contend that in-depth approaches give students better opportunities to construct knowledge in ways that form lasting historical schemas that connect to their everyday lives. These conceptions reflect recent shifts in cognitive psychologists' thinking about how students learn (e.g., Resnick & Klopfer, 1989). The prior knowledge of history that students bring with them to the classroom, it is now believed, has a significant impact on the new ideas they form about the history they learn (see also Hallden, 1994). To the extent that history knowledge is disconnected from students' prior knowledge, they will have difficulty constructing meaningful ideas about the past. Those who advocate teaching for understanding posit that perfunctory treatment of a great many topics leads to the learning—and prompt forgetting—of isolated, decontextualized pieces of information (VanSledright, 1995a). This, they suggest, is one reason why students tend to do poorly on gauges of their historical knowledge (Ravitch & Finn, 1987).

Newmann (1988, 1990) advocated what he called "thoughtfulness" in social studies classes. After studying social studies teaching that emphasized understanding and higher-order thinking, Newmann concluded that classrooms high in thoughtfulness feature

1. content coverage that focuses in depth on relatively few topics rather than providing shallow overviews of many;
2. classroom discourse that reflects continuity and coherence of ideas;
3. encouragement of students to think before responding to questions;
4. requests that students clarify and justify their responses and assertions;
5. teacher modeling of thoughtfulness through articulating problem-solving processes and acknowledging the difficulties inherent in such processes; and
6. student generation of novel ideas and understandings concerning the topics studied, rather than routine recall of textbook contents.

Disciplinary Perspectives

Differing from Brophy (1990b) and Newmann (1990) in that she does not appear to rely on the conceptual framework of teaching for understanding, Reed (1989) suggested 10 attributes of good elementary history teaching.

1. cultivating historical empathy;
2. developing an appreciation of cultural diversity and shared humanity;
3. engendering an understanding of the interplay of change and continuity in history;
4. establishing a grasp of the complexity of historical causation;
5. developing a respect for historical details;
6. creating a suspicion of abstract generalizations;
7. constructing an appreciation for the importance of the personal character of individuals as they influence human affairs;

8. developing the ability to recognize the difference between fact and conjecture;
9. developing the ability to recognize the difference between evidence and assertion; and
10. developing the ability to recognize "useful" historical questions.

Reflecting the position of the Bradley Commission, Reed's attributes draw from disciplinary understandings of the nature of historical knowledge and, in turn, how they should influence good history teaching. Several of her ideas about good elementary history teaching overlap with the findings and recommendations of Dickinson and Lee (1978, 1984) and with suggestions commonly made over the years by authors who have addressed issues involved in making history interesting and meaningful to children, helping them to develop historical empathy and imagination, and engaging them in working with historical sources and artifacts.[2]

Others also have focused on aligning the teaching of history more closely with its disciplinary roots. The National Board for Professional Teaching Standards (1994) produced 11 criteria for Board certification in the teaching of history and social studies. The criteria were designed to facilitate the ongoing professional development of and a move to higher standards among the nation's history-social studies teachers. These criteria address teachers'

1. knowledge of learners;
2. knowledge of subject matter;
3. advanced disciplinary knowledge;
4. promotion of social understanding in learners;
5. development of civic competence;
6. awareness and use of effective instructional resources;
7. creation of dynamic learning environments;
8. employment of a variety of assessments;
9. regular reflection on practice;
10. cultivation of family partnerships for learning; and
11. collaboration with others in their schools and academic fields.

The Board was concerned especially with teachers' academic disciplinary knowledge and their promotion of that disciplinary knowledge with students. Criteria (1) and (2) alone were devoted to this disciplinary focus, and within them, U.S. history plays a predominant role. Among other things, Board-certified teachers who specialize in history know that history is an interpretive enterprise, that there are better and worse analyses of every event or time period, and that the way we understand such analyses changes over time. These teachers develop in their students a sense of historical perspective, helping them to enter the patterns of the past and see through the eyes of the people who were there. . . . [T]hey work with students to review evidence about the event or idea in question in order to understand how the descriptions and interpretations were created. Teachers use history to help students analyze the ways that societies change over time. On a regular basis teachers make choices among the compelling stories to be told and the perspectives to which they expose their students. (p. 14)

Most standards or criteria in the draft were treated in two or three pages, but "knowledge of subject matter" received nine pages. The Board laid out a view of exemplary teaching in the disciplines of U.S. history, world history, economics, geography, and political science. An integrated, interdisciplinary focus received a scant two paragraphs.

Hertzberg (1985) suggested that teachers attend to three aspects of immersion into the historical: (1) the importance of developing historical imagination in learners, (2) the cultivation of cause–effect understandings of historical events, and (3) the construction of broad historical syntheses (central to the teaching task despite only limited help from the history profession). Promoting historical inquiry as the pivotal classroom method, she added three recommendations: that teachers assist students in (1) learning how to interpret the past, (2) developing skills for using documentary evidence and historical source material, and (3) seeing connections across the curriculum (e.g., linkages between the humanities and the social sciences).

Howard and Mendenhall (1982) made similar recommendations. In addition, they focused heavily on the preparation of history teachers, noting that they should

1. obtain a rigorous liberal arts education;
2. be taught by professional historians and take coursework in related fields such as literature, anthropology, and the social sciences;
3. take courses on historical methods and historiography;
4. learn to write well;
5. receive training in how to teach history well; and
6. realize that they must think of themselves as learners (as well as teachers) of history.

Along with other authors (Gagnon, 1989a; Ravitch, 1987), Howard and Mendenhall expressed concern about what they perceived as slippage in the place of history in the curriculum. They argued that better preparation of history teachers would enhance the presence of history in the curriculum because it would lead to teaching that would "make history come alive" for students. Howard and Mendenhall's recommendations appear pitched primarily to the secondary level, where teachers are educated as disciplinary specialists. However, their recommendations may have some import for the preparation of elementary teachers, particularly those who teach the fifth-grade American history course.

Also pitched toward the secondary level, but containing some interesting recommendations, is Green and Watson's (1993) review of the status of American history in the schools. In a rather caustic analysis, Green and Watson observed:

> The teaching of American history continues to be characterized by superficial surveys, simplistic literal mindedness, and little emphasis on historical process or critical inquiry. To students, history appears meaningless and dead. Yet, American history, as reflected in developments in the discipline, is alive and dynamic. (p. 69)

They then surveyed what they perceived to be the robust nature of disciplinary historical inquiry over the past several decades, noting the growth of social history—or history "from the bottom up"—and the emergence of histories about groups and individuals previously left out of historical accounts (women, minorities, labor groups, etc.). They argued that school history could be improved significantly by tying teaching more closely to the dynamic developments found in the discipline of history and by fostering social historical inquiry.

> *It is critical for history teachers to understand that their subject is a scholarly activity.* Scholars ask questions. Their answers are necessarily tentative and subject to revision. To teach history merely as a body of information to be set to memory is an injustice to the discipline itself, as well as to the students. (p. 85, emphasis in the original)

These authors concluded that, in order to improve the teaching of history, more needs to be done with the professional development of history teachers. For example, rather than offering a smattering of history courses followed by a cluster of education courses, all of which appear only loosely connected, teacher educators and historians could work together to provide prospective teachers with a more coherent, discipline-based program. Such a program purportedly would enhance the quality of history teaching.[3]

In ways similar to Howard and Mendenhall (1982) and Green and Watson (1993), Wilson (1991) argued for the importance of deep subject matter knowledge in the teaching of history. She suggested that teachers must understand the interpretive factors that characterize the discipline of history and how historians frame these interpretations as they go about representing the past. Teachers would need to teach these aspects to students, rather than asking them merely to reproduce what they find in textbooks. Such understandings, according to Wilson, are minimum necessary ingredients for fruitful learning of history. Without them, students will continue to encounter bland lecture-recitation-seatwork experiences in American history classrooms (see also Wilson & Sykes, 1989).

Barton (1993) suggested that characterizations of historical reasoning have focused too narrowly on reading for subtext and other aspects of the evaluation of source materials. He argued that at least as much attention should be paid, especially in teaching elementary students, to the kinds of thinking involved in piecing elements of evidence together and imposing a narrative structure. Long before they are able to assemble and evaluate an array of historical source materials, children are able to understand basic ideas such as that writing history involves constructing storylines and that different stakeholders will be predisposed to write contrasting accounts of the same events.

Interdisciplinary Perspectives

As his quotation near the beginning of this chapter made plain, Banks (1991) disputed the value of teaching history as a discipline by focusing on how it is practiced. Taking a social studies (rather than a disciplinary history) perspective, Banks recommended that history be taught as a framework for understanding current public policy and social justice issues, with a view to involving students as active citizens in promoting a better future. He would use historical records as means for addressing present citizenship education questions and policy issues, rather than as ends in themselves. Similar views have been put forth by other social studies scholars who prefer to see history taught within an interdisciplinary framework, organized around policy issues and participatory citizenship goals.[4]

Engle and Ochoa (1988) offered detailed recommendations for teaching history (and social studies more generally) from a goal framework that employs an active, participatory citizenship agenda. They favored an interdisciplinary approach, noting that the social sciences and history were resistant to integration because they were organized around different questions and understandings of the social world. However, the traditional school subjects—of which history would be one, along with geography—can be used effectively to accomplish the purpose of teaching participatory decision making and reflective inquiry; teachers can engage students in the reflective study of social problems, engage them in decision making about course-related content, promote citizen internships (e.g., community service experiences), and create democratic classroom environments.

In reflective classrooms, the teacher's role is to stimulate thinking, encourage dialogue, and guide students in evaluating the worth of ideas. The role of teachers becomes a facilitative one where teachers raise questions, foster doubt, present competing views, challenge the ideas of students, and promote rigorous democratic dialogue. At the same time, teachers must be informed of the issues under discussion. To enhance the reflection process to be cultivated in students, Engle and Ochoa recommended a number of strategies: identifying problems for discussion; using probing, open-ended questions; identifying value assumptions; identifying alternative understandings and exploring their consequences; and pursuing justifiable solution decisions. The disciplines would be drawn upon for substantive knowledge to inform the decision-making process. In a number of ways, these ideas parallel those of Newmann (1990).

Storytelling Perspectives

Levstik (1986) took a somewhat different slant toward both the disciplinary history perspective and the interdisciplinary study and active citizenship perspective. Focusing on younger students' learning of history, Levstik advocated a "reader response" approach. Likening history to literature and other humanities (as opposed to the social sciences), Levstik argued that using narrative accounts and stories (e.g., historical fiction) can enhance the quality of history teaching, if teachers help young students respond to these accounts in critical and reflective ways. Teaching the art of interpretation would be one such method. Levstik contended that her research suggests that young students learn more by focusing on history as a story rather than as a fact archive to be mastered and memorized, and that they find narrative, storytelling accounts much more compelling than encyclopedic textbook treatments.

Levstik's recommendations for teaching history to elementary students are similar in some ways to Egan's (1986). Egan suggested that young students benefit from history represented as a dynamic story replete with conflict and resolution, heroes and villains, good and evil, and other binary oppositions pitted against each other. Contending that stories that make use of these binary oppositions resonate most effectively with students' desire to see the world in these terms, Egan argued that the entire elementary curriculum could be organized around stories and taught using the storytelling approach. However, Levstik (1995) disputed this notion, arguing that students need exposure to textbooks and other analytic historical sources in addition to narrative sources, because they need to learn that historical accounts are tentative interpretations and that historical analysis is a way to put one's own time and place into larger perspective.

This array of arguments concerning the ways in which history might be taught includes some of the same patterns (and authors) discussed in Chapter 1. With the exception of those who propose teaching history for understanding and Levstik's (1986) and Egan's (1986) storytelling (narrative) approaches, teaching recommendations follow generally along two lines: (1) using a disciplinary history framework as the backdrop for teaching practice, and (2) adopting an interdisciplinary, issues- and policy-guided social studies approach that would promote active citizenship before introduction to the disciplines. Levstik's and Egan's approaches might be characterized as developmentally oriented. Those who advocate teaching history for understanding appear drawn more to applications of cognitive science and recent advances in learning theory, with less immediate concern for developmental, disciplinary, or interdisciplinary commitments.

The approaches recommended by various authors reflect their positions and assumptions with respect to the goals to be accomplished in teaching history. For example, those with disciplinary affinities hope that students will emerge from their study having cultivated disciplinary habits of intellect and historical perspectives on the world and their past. Advocates of interdisciplinary social studies and decision making hope to prepare students to use historical knowledge to address contemporary policy issues and societal concerns and to become actively engaged as citizens of a participatory democracy. Proponents of teaching for understanding and those concerned about developmentally appropriate teaching hinge their recommendations on learning theory, engagement, and application, and are less influenced by debates over disciplinary or interdisciplinary connections.

These various recommendations suggest that there may be a variety of good ways to teach fifth-grade history, involving trade-offs among goals and purposes. Few useful or compelling goals are likely to be accomplished, however, when teachers emphasize breadth of coverage at the expense of developing key ideas, perfunctorily moving students from point A to point Z as quickly as the textbooks pages will turn. Unfortunately, it appears that all too much of this goes on in classrooms across the nation (Cuban, 1984; Goodlad, 1984; Shaver, Davis, & Helburn, 1979). Choosing a discipline-based set of goals, or a developmental perspective and the goals it entails, or any of the other approaches we have reviewed, may lead to much more robust and meaningful learning for students than operating from the default approach, wherein goals reflect nothing more than routine content coverage. In our portraits of the three fifth-grade history teachers and in our assessments of what students learned in their classes, we explore this premise in more detail.

RESEARCH ON TEACHING HISTORY

There is surprisingly little empirical information available to support or refute the plethora of recommendations for effective ways to teach history. Brophy (1990b), in his summary of research in elementary history and social studies, noted that

> Not much research has been done in social studies classes, and most of the available findings are focused on relatively narrow issues. . . . The paucity of research is especially noticeable at the elementary level. There . . . has not been systematic descriptive, let alone comparative, research on the implementation and effects of elementary social studies instruction considered holistically (i.e., with attention to purposes, goals, content selection and organization, instructional methods, activities and assignments, and evaluation methods). Information of this kind is badly needed if practice is to become . . . informed by something other than relatively abstract scholarly debates. Detailed description of what occurs during typical units of exemplary programs taught by outstanding teachers is particularly needed to provide models of excellence for practitioners. (pp. 396–397)

Others who have examined the social studies research literature also have noted the absence of descriptive, contextualized research. For example, Marker and Mehlinger (1992) argued:

> Social studies could profit from in-depth case studies focused on specific classrooms. It is important to observe systematically over an extended

period of time how [a] course is mediated by a teacher. Such studies are needed in order to gain more exact understanding of how social studies varies across grade levels, across schools serving different social classes and student abilities, across urban and rural schools, and by subject areas. (p. 847)

Downey and Levstik's (1991) chapter in the *Handbook of Research on Social Studies Teaching and Learning* (Shaver, 1991) stated that

The research base for the teaching and learning of history is thin and uneven. There is a dearth of research studies on history teaching in large part because little of the research on teaching and learning within the social studies has been discipline-centered. Consequently, most of the systematic research that has been done in history education is of relatively recent origin. A number of areas of critical importance to the field still remain largely unexplored. (p. 400)

Downey and Levstik (1988) earlier had indicated those unexplored areas of importance. Talking about history education in general, and U.S. history in particular, they argued:

We know little about how interaction among students, teachers, and others whose influence is felt in the classroom affects how history is taught and learned. We . . . need more research [for example] on how teachers introduce concepts of historical time, and whether current practice contributes to rather than eases the difficulties children have in these areas. . . . [W]e need to develop and test empirically curricula based on new understandings of human cognition that have emerged in recent years. (p. 341)

Regarding research specifically on the teaching of history, Downey and Levstik (1991) further observed that, beginning in the 1950s and extending through the 1980s, most studies were limited to surveys of the pedagogical methods teachers used in their history classrooms. They cited the National Science Foundation-sponsored survey of school science, mathematics, and social studies education (see Shaver et al., 1979) as the most extensive. It found that class discussions, lectures, and tests and quizzes were the most commonly reported history teaching methods at the high school grades. Several other studies found similar trends (Goodlad, 1984; Gross, 1952; Wood, 1966).

As Downey and Levstik noted, surveys of reported teaching methods tell us very little about how teachers use these methods, with what duration in a given class period, in what particular sequence, and with what results—hence the calls for more detailed studies. Such studies have begun to emerge in the past decade, including the accounts of the three teachers we present in the following chapters. We are beginning to see detailed accounts of classroom practice, probing of history teachers' views about their teaching, and comparative studies. We review several of the extant studies here, focusing again on those that provide richly descriptive portraits, demonstrate relevance to elementary school history teaching, and/or assist in situating the three teachers represented in our studies.

McNeil (1986) spent a year regularly visiting four midwestern high schools and collecting data on their history-social studies teaching practices. She found considerable variety in the methods and procedures teachers used. Each teacher appeared to carve out a bargain with students over how much work they would be required to do in exchange for in-class cooperation with school and teacher mandates. Some of the bargains effectively dumbed down curricular requirements, so that students were required to do very little work. Other history classrooms featured more rigorous demands, such as more reading and writing and higher expectations for involvement in classroom discussion of historical issues. The nature of the bargain (and consequently how teachers taught) seemed most influenced by the expectations of school administrators. McNeil found irony in this, noting that rigorous curricular and academic demands made on students were inversely related to administrators' requirements for student compliance with technical behavioral regulations (e.g., orderly passage in hallways, prompt arrival to class, prudent attire).

Kobrin (1992) worked with four high school history teachers who asked students to use historical evidence, artifacts, and primary documents to generate their own student-produced textbook. His purpose was to show (1) how history is a result of socially constructed meanings, (2) that those who construct accounts control how we come to understand things historical, and (3) that students themselves can be enabled to construct a history of their own making. Kobrin concluded that students were more engaged with history and developed more thoroughly historical understandings because they were made responsible for and had control over the outcome. This contrasts with traditional practices that ask students to learn only "other people's facts" (see Holt, 1990).

Case Studies

Levstik (1993a) presented a case study of a first-grade teacher who included a strong history component within an integrated approach to instruction. This teacher did not attempt to teach history chronologi-cally, but she did provide her students with age-appropriate informa-tion and learning experiences designed to teach them worthwhile knowledge about life in the past and historically significant people and events. Her students applied their developing reading, writing, and ar-tistic skills to their learning of history, and they participated in a vari-ety of hands-on activities designed to make their history learning per-sonalized and concrete.

Even though she was teaching first graders in an inner-city school, this teacher was able to engage her students in meaningful historical inquiry activities that included addressing the moral dimensions of the content. She made considerable use of children's literature sources and emphasized heroic figures for their inspirational value. However, her tradebook selections involved history-based children's fiction and non-fictional sources, not fables, myths, or purely fictional selections. Thus, she genuinely taught history, rather than merely using stories as socialization devices.

Barton (1993) presented a case study of a fifth-grade teacher who focused on developing historical perspective and empathy in her stu-dents. When presenting information about historical events, she pointed out ways in which stakeholders' opinions and perceptions dif-fered, and she often placed more emphasis on the feelings of the parti-cipants than on the flow of the events. In addition, she frequently fol-lowed up these presentations with assignments that involved role play or other opportunities for students to assume the perspectives of his-torical actors. Interviews with her students indicated that they had developed understanding that different participants may take con-trasting perspectives on commonly experienced historical events, and that the same is true of people in the present who incorporate accounts of historical events into arguments about historical interpretation or social policy issues.

Thornton (1993) presented a case study of a high school history teacher who used a variety of methods to help his students appreciate and use history for the perspective it provides on the evolution of the human condition. In particular, he strove to help his students under-stand how and why the United States has developed as it has, how the students' own family histories fit into this big picture, and the poten-tial implications of this for critical thinking and decision making about current social and civic issues. His approach illustrates what it means to teach history as citizen education rather than just as an in-troduction to an academic discipline.

Wineburg and Wilson (1988, 1991) reported case studies of two high school history teachers who taught units on the American Revolution and Constitutional period. One of the teachers—Jensen—was cast as the "invisible teacher" or the "choreographer," whereas the other teacher—Price—was described as the "visible teacher" or "performer." Jensen preferred to construct activities for students that allowed her to recede into the background of the classroom process. For example, she staged a debate on salient issues influencing colonists' decisions to resist British law prior to the Revolutionary War. She prepared students for this debate by asking them to read from a booklet of primary and secondary sources that dealt with themes such as "authority" and the "nature of man." Jensen provided the choreography while students engaged in the dance. By contrast, Price preferred to work from a notebook of details and accounts of the period that he had built up over time. After introducing students to these accounts directly, he asked them to examine primary texts drawn from his notebook to search out author bias. This became a focus for classroom discussion and promoted ways to understand the revolutionary period by interpreting authors' intentions and motives. Wineburg and Wilson observed that, although these approaches were quite different, both were constructive and powerful methods for representing history to students. The teachers' different stances on the issue of how to interpret the past helped to demarcate the ways in which they represented the period to students.

Later, Wilson and Wineburg (1993) explored in detail how two additional high school history teachers responded to three performance assessments—evaluation of student writing samples, planning a lesson using primary historical documents, and textbook analyses and evaluations. Wilson and Wineburg were interested in what these performance assessments might tell them about how history teachers understand the discipline they teach. Once again, the teachers were quite different. As the performance assessments revealed, the older, more veteran teacher held a view of history that he learned primarily as an undergraduate history major, one in which careful research, accumulation of facts, and accuracy were important. The second teacher, younger and more of a novice, held a "newer" view of the past, one that focused on history as a socially constructed account and on the importance of the historians' frames of reference as they write history. The two teachers approached the assessment tasks (and by extension, teaching) quite differently, in accordance with their contrasting views of the discipline.

Wilson and Wineburg (1993) withheld judgment on the relative effectiveness of each teacher's approach, suggesting that decisions about how to teach history cannot be made without taking into account how the purpose of the teaching is defined. They also observed that school structure, through what it promotes or constrains in teaching, plays an important role in how history is taught. Thus, teachers may not be able to teach in whatever fashion they choose. Our research on the three fifth-grade teachers also indicated that curricular and time constraints, classroom management dilemmas, administrative support, and school culture factors had an impact on the ways in which the teachers approached their teaching tasks.[5]

Evans's Typology of History Teachers

Evans (1989, 1994) developed a typology of history teachers connected to Elbaz's (1983) concept of images of practical knowledge. Evans identified five types of secondary history teachers: (1) the storyteller, an analytic idealist (11% of the teachers investigated), (2) the scientific historian, an analytic positivist (18%), (3) the relativist/reformer, an analytic relativist (45%), (4) the cosmic philosopher, a speculative, meta-historian (3%), and (5) the eclectic (23%) who demonstrated no central tendency. He argued that the storyteller teaches by telling stories in a knowledge transmission mode; the scientific historian fosters disciplinary inquiry as found in historiography and the social science research tradition; the relativist/reformer relies on mixed methods to promote inquiry into historical events and engage students in reflective thinking about past and present social problems; the cosmic philosopher challenges historical accounts from a cosmological perspective, and the eclectic pursues a variety of methods related to practical teaching choices.

These types were identified among and probably apply more readily to secondary teachers, but they offer possibilities for understanding elementary history teachers as well. We have found them useful as descriptive shorthand for distinguishing among the three teachers in our study. Mary Lake (all identifying names of teachers, students, and schools are pseudonyms), the first fifth-grade teacher portrayed, was primarily a "storyteller." Ramona Palmer, portrayed next, taught mostly from a "scientific historian" perspective. The last teacher, Sara Atkinson, was best characterized as a "reformer."

Two qualifying observations are in order regarding the use of Evans's types to describe these teachers. First, the distinctions between types are slippery. To some degree, they depend on one another for their distinctions. For example, storytellers, scientific historians, and reformers all may transmit knowledge of the past (as Barr, et al., 1977, noted), but they accomplish it in different ways—storytellers and reformers mostly through direct explanations and other didactic means, scientific historians mostly through indirect means such as inquiry into the past using disciplinary methods. Eclectics may use both direct and indirect approaches, as well as stories and moralistic tales to accomplish their goals. In applying Evans's descriptors to the three teachers, we think of them as general metaphors for the teachers' most common form of practice. Like other metaphors (e.g., "performers" or "choreographers"), these help us to differentiate between the teachers and their views of history. Metaphors serve as placeholders that allow us to amalgamate a cluster of ideas and practices around a single term, but they also oversimplify. In one sense, all three teachers could be thought of as eclectics.

A second qualification is that, although Evans (1989, 1994) lumped relativists and reformers into one type, in some instances they may take different approaches. Those who view history from a relativist position try to understand agents of the past on their own terms. Strong relativists frequently refuse to pass judgment on the morality of these agents' choices. As a result, they are reluctant to display the types of commitments to correcting "past mistakes" and righting "historical injustices" that frame the work of reformers. Reformers adopt a present-oriented approach that leaves them more willing to form the "right vs. wrong" commitments needed to confront what they perceive to be historical misjudgments that have contemporaneous implications. Given our understanding of Atkinson's case, we believe that she was more of a reformer than a relativist, so we refer to her as such.

RESEARCH GOALS AND DATA-GATHERING METHODS

Our research on elementary history teaching and learning proceeded in a series of phases. Data for the case of Mary Lake were gathered during the 1990–1991 school year. Data for the two subsequent fifth-grade cases, Ramona Palmer's and Sara Atkinson's, were collected during the 1991–1992 school year. The teachers were selected on the basis of recommendations from district and school administrators, social studies curriculum coordinators, and these teachers' peers. Data gathering for the case studies also involved studying six students from each class during the history unit that was being observed and recorded. In addition, during the 1991–1992 school year, we followed 10 fifth graders across the entire year, interviewing them before and after each of their U.S. history units. These students were drawn from Mary Lake's classroom.

Case study methods were employed to generate data on each teacher. Classes were observed daily for the duration of the history unit studied (Lake taught about the English colonies; Palmer and Atkinson taught about the American Revolution and Constitution). We compiled detailed fieldnotes and the classroom discourse was audiotaped and transcribed. Portions of these transcripts were used to construct lengthy descriptions of teaching practices and teacher–student and student–student interaction (Brophy, 1990a, 1992b; VanSledright, 1992a, 1992b). The teachers were interviewed in depth to elicit their views about teaching history, their goals for the units, their teaching approaches and assessment practices, their beliefs about students, and their overall philosophies of education. These interviews also were audiotaped and transcribed. Finally, teaching documents and student work samples were collected and analyzed. We provide more specific information about the teachers, the schools in which they taught, and their students in each of the case study chapters.

Our goals for this series of studies were fairly straightforward. We wanted to understand how reportedly effective fifth-grade teachers approached the task of teaching history to their students: what their approaches entailed; how they were similar and different; how they represented content to students, developed understanding, and assessed learning; and how their knowledge of history, goal frameworks, philosophies, and interpretations of the curriculum influenced their history teaching. This effort was informed by Thornton's (1991) concept of teachers as curricular-instructional gatekeepers. Thornton maintained that teachers are responsible for interpreting, making sense of, and representing the curriculum to students. Therefore, in large measure, they control students' access to knowledge and how their understandings develop. Students, the public, and school administrators also play a role, but it is largely up to teachers to tend the curriculum gate in the context of their classroom interactions with students. We were interested in how each teacher accomplished this gate tending, with what consequences for students.

In studying the students, we addressed the need for research information concerning how elementary grade students—fifth grade in this case—make sense of the history they learn. Consequently, we asked mostly open-ended questions and analyzed students' responses with attention to the qualitative nuances of the understandings (and misconceptions) they communicated, not just to determine whether they supplied accurate answers. Additionally, the interview protocols were constructed to reflect how and what the teachers taught and how school district curriculum objectives were represented in the teachers' practices. The purpose for this was to preserve the ecological validity of the teacher case studies relative to student learning, and also to allow us to draw comparisons across the teacher cases where it was appropriate (e.g., the American Revolution unit taught in all three classes).

To the extent that our methods were ecologically valid, the resulting data on student learning allowed to us to make some inferences about the relative merits of each of the teachers' practice. However, we prefer to characterize the case comparisons as trade-offs. Each teacher's approach entails doing some things very well while necessarily holding other important matters in abeyance. Therefore, we make no definitive claims about which methods or approaches are best, or which teacher should be emulated. Each teacher approached her teaching task from a different goal framework. As with most important educational questions, how one defines "best" will depend on the goals one wishes to accomplish. Goal questions are heavily laden with value and ethical dimensions, which empirical research studies cannot address directly. However, we do believe that these cases will inform reflection about history teaching goals and their potential consequences for practice.

NOTES

1. For example, see Brophy (1990a, 1993), Cornett (1990), Levstik (1993a), VanSledright (1992b, 1992c), Thornton (1993), Wilson & Wineburg (1993), and Wineburg and Wilson (1988, 1991).

2. See Chase (1961), Coltham (1971), Dawson (1989), Little (1989), Myers (1990), Sylvester (1989), and Willig (1990).

3. On related points, see also Seixas (1994) and Wineburg and Wilson (1991).

4. For example, see Engle and Ochoa (1988), Parker (1989), Parker and Jarolimek (1984), and Shaver (1987).

5. We take up some of these issues in the following chapters, but for more detailed discussions, see Brophy (1992b) and VanSledright and Grant (1994).

CHAPTER 3

Storytelling: The Case of Mary Lake

I was telling my kids the story of how they found a flint arrowhead in Arizona in the early 1900s. We were pretending that we were cowboys. I was riding along and they were following me. Previously I had put down, in the back of the room, some sand and a flint arrowhead buried in it. I reached down and picked it up and right there I had them. They'll never forget my picking up that flint arrowhead to illustrate how it was found. Then we continued the story. "What did he do with it? What would you do with it if you found something that was unusual? You'd take it to a scientist. That's what he did. . . . " I just try to be a professional story-teller with them.

—Mary Lake

Mary Lake, a 14-year veteran teacher, taught in a predominantly white, working-class suburb in the northern Midwest. She taught several sections of language arts and several of social studies in a semidepartmentalized arrangement. This allowed her to concentrate on these two subjects, as well as to integrate them. Lake allowed time for depth of development of key ideas by covering U.S. history only up to the Civil War and by restricting coverage to content that was directly relevant to the main ideas that she emphasized. For example, she omitted Magellan from her unit on explorers because her main themes focused on the development of the United States as a country, and Magellan's voyages were less relevant here than the voyages of those who explored the New World. She taught units on (1) history and the work of historians, (2) Native Americans, (3) the explorers, (4) the colonies, (5) the Revolution and establishment of a new nation, (6) westward expansion and the frontier, and (7) the Civil War.

Lake taught in a well-equipped and flexibly furnished self-contained classroom. A chalkboard extended across the front wall. Above it was a timeline describing and illustrating salient events in U.S. history. Front and center was a roll-down projector screen, as well as some roll-down maps. To the left was Lake's desk, and to the right was a utility table used as work space for projects. Windows took up most of one side wall, with bookcases and storage space beneath them. The other side wall contained the door to the hall, storage space, and closets. In one back corner was a personal computer that students used for various purposes. In the other corner was a reading center that included a display of books related to the current social studies unit. The back of the room was Lake's social studies teaching station.

Lake operated a largely teacher-directed classroom, which generally is consistent with the storyteller's more traditional philosophy (Evans, 1989, 1994). Her room took on three different "looks" during her social studies teaching. When she told stories, she sat in a chair at the back and her students sat on the floor. Behind her chair was a display space for key words and other materials from the social studies unit, and nearby was a chart stand. When she used the overhead or gave directions for assignments, she stood at the front and the students sat in rows facing her. When the students worked in pairs or small groups, they sat in four-desk clusters and Lake circulated among them.

PHILOSOPHY OF TEACHING

Asked about her general philosophy and approach to teaching, Lake began with affective goals: "Every child needs to feel that he or she has a place, can learn, and can be successful in school . . . every learning style that children have should be addressed daily so that all children have an opportunity to feel successful about themselves and about what they are learning." Asked how she has grown as a teacher and how she differs from other teachers, Lake stressed three themes. First, she has moved beyond the reading-recitation-seatwork method to develop a more varied approach that primarily involves storytelling but also makes use of artifacts, cooperative learning, and detailed writing assignments. Second, she integrates across subjects, especially by using social studies themes as the basis for language arts writing assignments or for projects in art or music. Third, she emphasizes understanding of key ideas and major themes rather than memory for a great many facts. She has shifted from the textbook to her own storytelling as the main source of content for students (so she can emphasize key ideas), and she has shifted from tests to writing assignments and activities that call for synthesis and communication as her main basis for assessing learning.

GOAL FRAMEWORKS AND TEACHING METHODS

Lake's main knowledge goal was "that every fifth grader can tell me the story of United States history." Skills goals focused on general study, research, and writing skills, although she also addressed the skills involved in acting as a historian and reading historical accounts critically. Value, attitudinal, and dispositional goals focused on socializing students to school as a society in which they were expected to participate in "safe and thoughtful" ways.

Lake projected enthusiasm for the content of history and presented it using concrete examples and props.

> I think that it is very important that the kids see that I love what I'm doing and think, "Gosh. She really likes this stuff and she's willing to share with us." I bring in things for the kids to hold, such as a butter churn, so they can see how butter was really churned. They're amazed because so many of them have seen it in pictures, but to experience the real thing helps to bring history alive to them.

She continued:

> I do a lot of storytelling—retelling of what they would normally read, bringing it alive to them. I subscribe to the history magazine *Cobblestone,* and I read it for anecdotal information that will make my coverage of topics more interesting for the kids. Social studies texts tend to take the approach of, "These are the facts, that's what you need to know." Well, there are more interesting things for 10-year-olds than the basic facts. So if I can grab them on the interesting aspects, they will remember the whole sequence of the story and be able to tell it back to me, focusing on those interesting tidbits but bringing the other information along with them.

Lake's stories—communicating the wisdom of "our" heritage— were central to her approach. When telling stories, she used repetition, visual aids, and story mapping techniques to help the students remember the main themes. She emphasized key ideas and repeated them in reviews and follow-up activities. She posted key words (organized within "people," "places," and "events" columns) as they were introduced and kept them posted throughout the rest of the unit. She also developed story maps and other content outlines or diagrams on the chart stand and posted these when she finished teaching from them.

Lake had a flair for theatrics that made her a gifted storyteller. She maintained student engagement through enthusiastic dramatic readings and theatrical role enactments, effective use of timing and pauses, questions that invited speculation about what happened next, and other dramatic techniques. Occasionally she would don a costume to enact a character. When she wanted the students to see an illustration, she would hold the book out close to them or pass it around. She also circulated props (arrowheads, pieces of wool, colonial household implements), often using them with dramatic flair (see the quote at the beginning of the chapter).

When teaching at the front of the class, Lake moved around rather than remaining stationary. She frequently used the overhead or the chart stand. When students were working on assignments, she circulated to monitor progress and give assistance. Before or after her storytelling sessions, Lake often led students through fast-paced reviews by asking about the main points or pointing to her posted key words and calling on students to explain about the designated person, place, or event. She sequenced these response opportunities so that the students retold the story as the review progressed. Both at these times and during storytelling itself, she invited student comments and questions.

Many of her activities and assignments called for students to work in pairs or small groups, and a great deal of content-based discourse occurred at these times. However, Lake did not structure much discussion in whole-class settings. She reported that she would have used more discussion if the students had more experience-based knowledge, but because so much of the content was new to them, she concentrated on building initial understandings. Lake viewed activities and assignments primarily as means of reinforcing and elaborating on the main themes that she developed through her storytelling, rather than as contexts for engaging students in attempts to generate new learning through inquiry and discovery. She tried to keep activities and assignments varied and interesting. To help students see how content strands fit into the developing timeline of U.S. history, she had them keep completed assignments together in a folder.

> We have a map and other things that they have made to look at the total unit, so that they can refer back to these things. The assignments in themselves blend together. Students can look at their assignment folders and see the progression of the topics that we've covered. . . . We do this in our review. And if I'm going to

give an end-of-unit test, we would go through those things and I would indicate the things they need to look at and be familiar with.

Lake found most of the worksheets and activities supplied with social studies series to be boring to students, low level, and disconnected. She had culled a few good ones for use with her students, but most of her activities and assignments were ones that she had developed herself or encountered in workshops or magazines for teachers. Most of her activities involved either working with maps that incorporated salient aspects of unit content or writing about that content in some way. One common assignment called for recording key ideas about a topic within organizing categories given on the assignment sheet. She reported that such assignments provided students with a purpose for their reading and helped them to remember key information. Also, breaking the information into subsets provided helpful structure to students who otherwise might find the assignment overwhelming.

Certain activities were planned with an eye toward helping students to develop initial understanding of life conditions in the past. In addition to showing illustrations and routinely trying to paint rich verbal pictures, Lake occasionally led students through visualization exercises or simulation activities designed to help them see and feel aspects of the past that they might have known about as abstractions but did not yet appreciate in more concrete ways (e.g., slavery, the conditions of everyday living prior to electricity and modern inventions).

Lake offered optional extra credit activities, mostly worksheets that reinforced unit content. She also offered enrichment opportunities via the computer, although these were related more to geography than to history. Her students participated in Kids Network, a program that engaged them in geographically based research and allowed them to compare their findings with those of students in other schools around the world. The students also used the computer to play educational games, including those in the "Where in the World Is Carmen San Diego?" series, that reinforce knowledge of geography facts.

Lake tended to give detailed instructions before she released students to work independently on assignments. Because she saw great variation both in their abilities to acquire new information through reading and in the degree to which their parents were prepared to help them, Lake avoided requiring students to do schoolwork at home unless she was confident that they could do it successfully on their own.

CONTENT SELECTION AND ASSESSMENT

Lake reduced breadth in order to provide for more depth in her content coverage. Working within district guidelines, she made content choices according to (1) the degree to which she viewed a topic as basic to the story of the development of the United States as a country; (2) students' interest in and readiness to understand and appreciate the topic; and (3) availability of good teaching materials and activities. Much of her colonies unit was based on tradebooks that conveyed the conditions of everyday life in the colonies. Lake believed that fictional but factually based and well-illustrated narratives in tradebooks were more effective for this purpose than the more generalized, but less memorable, treatments in textbooks.

At least once during each unit (not always at the end), Lake administered a test, usually after leading students through a review. Although these tests provided her with useful information, she used them mostly to familiarize students with test taking (something they would have to do a lot more of the next year in middle school). To evaluate the effectiveness of her teaching and provide a basis for grading, she relied more on her activities and assignments. She routinely inspected, graded, and communicated with students about their assignments. Simpler assignments were graded as plus or minus, and more complex ones received letter or percentage grades. Significant writing assignments received one grade for content and another for writing mechanics. Students could redo assignments to raise their grades, within limits.

Lake also got information about her social studies teaching from two interesting end-of-year assignments. The first required her fifth graders to write letters to fourth graders telling them what fifth grade was going to be like. She led her students through a review in which they "brainstormed" about the things they did in fifth grade, going back to the first day of school. Then the students decided what they wanted to mention in their letters, which provided information about the activities they found most salient and enjoyable. The second end-of-year assignment called for fifth graders to write letters to the sixth-grade teachers they would have the next year in middle school. These letters described what they had learned in fifth grade and what they hoped to learn in sixth grade. The letters provided the sixth-grade teachers with information about the interests and writing skills of their incoming students, and the fifth-grade teachers with information about their students' perceptions of what they learned during the year.

TEACHING ABOUT THE COLONIES

In this section, we describe how Mary Lake taught her students about British colonization (see also Brophy, 1990a, 1992a; VanSledright & Brophy, 1995). We provide a detailed, day-by-day account complete with several extended excerpts from classroom dialogue as a means of illustrating how her goal frameworks, teaching philosophy, and storytelling practices played out in a typical history unit. We present the unit in its entirety, reserving discussion of her teaching for the conclusion of the case. We follow the same procedure for the two remaining cases.

Lake began the first lesson in the colonies unit by having students fill out the first two sections of a KWL sheet (Ogle, 1986). These sections asked the questions, What do I *Know?* and What do I *Want* to know? The third section, to be filled out at the end of the unit, asked, What have I *Learned?* She then introduced the concept of colonies, pointing frequently to the illustrated timeline on the front wall.

> If you look at our timeline up here we can see that the Americas, or the land we're talking about, had Indians and they lived here 30,000 years ago. We began learning about those people that were here. Then we began looking at the explorers. . . . So on our timeline we have covered the Indians. We have covered the explorers. We finished the explorers so we should be right about 1600 on our timeline and that's exactly where we're going to begin today. We're going to begin looking at the New World that has been discovered. We know that there are flags from all the other countries all over the land from where the explorers were. Now, what are we going to do with that land? That's what our next unit is all about. What happened to the land that the explorers discovered, and we're going to begin right about 1600.

At this point, the class moved to the back of the room. Before telling about the first settlements in the New World, Lake showed pop-up ship illustrations from the book *Sailing Ships* (by Ron VanderMeer and Alan McGowan, published in 1984 by Viking Press, New York), noting that ships had become bigger and more complicated by the time of Columbus compared with the earlier time of the Vikings. Then she segued into the story of Roanoke Island. This part of the lesson is quoted in detail because it illustrates quite well Lake's storytelling style and manner of interacting with students.

Lake: Columbus's ship had more sails. It looked a lot sturdier and was a lot bigger. After Columbus and the explorers used these kind of ships in the 1600s, people started hearing about all the new land. People started thinking, "I'm going to move there." So they built bigger and better ships. They wanted a lot of people to be able to fit on these ships and they wanted a lot of supplies to fit on these ships so they built better and bigger ships. The ships that were now sailing to the new land looked like this. A lot bigger, more sails. These are the ships that brought the people to the new land. We're going to talk about the first colony. Colonies are the towns and villages like states that people moved to in the new land. Today we're going to meet three colonies. These colonies came from the country of England and the people left England in a ship just like this. They left England for the new land. They came over here to live. They put England's flag in the land or the village that they lived in. Because it really wasn't England, they called it a colony. It's a colony of England. England is the big country but somewhere in the new land, there was a small village that belonged to England called a colony. So a colony is a piece of land where people lived, much like a city. Sometimes they would put a fence up—a boundary up around these villages. They would call it a colony. They called it a colony because it belonged to England. They weren't in their own country. They still had England's flag. The King and Queen of England had a lot of information about all that land that was out there and the king and queen had a really favorite person. His name was Sir Walter Raleigh. They thought he was just a great person. He was an adventure seeker, he liked to find new things, and the queen called him in one day and said, "Hey, why don't you take a group of people to the new land and start living over there and you stay there and you be their leader in that colony and you will work for me." So Sir Walter Raleigh thought that was just a great idea and he loaded up this ship with people and he crossed the ocean and he went to what is now, in your mind, you locate where you know North Carolina is in our United States, that's where he went. He went to North Carolina. When he landed on this island, he named it Roanoke Island. In Kidsnet, some of you wrote to a school in Roanoke, Virginia, didn't you. How many wrote to that school? Well, Roanoke, Virginia was named after this same island that in 1585 Sir Walter Raleigh went to. When they landed at that island they met some very unfriendly people. Who do you suppose those unfriendly people were? Tell me.
Students: The Indians.

Lake: The Indians. The Indians didn't like these people coming to their island. They had a big fight and the settlers that came over on the ship said, "I don't want to live here." They all climbed into this ship and they turned right back and went home to England. Well, Sir Walter Raleigh was convinced that the best thing to do was to try another trip. So he waited a year. He thought maybe people would forget about all those unfriendly Indians. A year later, Sir Walter Raleigh knew a guy named John White. He said to John, "Why don't you gather some people up, take your wife, take your family, and take several families on a ship and go settle at the island I found." Well, John White said, "Well, why not!" Women had not gone to the new land yet. Children had not gone to the new land yet. Here was an opportunity for whole families to go and start a new life. So John White loaded up this ship with some supplies and families and he turned around and went back to Roanoke Island. When he got there, it wasn't too bad. There were some Indians. They did fight so they built a fort. They thought that would be the best thing to do is build a fort to protect you. Well, it was a new land. They didn't have a lot of things. There weren't supermarkets. They couldn't go buy hammer and nails. There wasn't a 7-Eleven to run and get milk from. Do you think they had it really easy?

Students: No.

Lake: It was pretty hard?

Students: Yeah.

Lake: John White had an idea. He said, "I'm going to leave you guys here and I'm going to take some guys back with me, we'll get on our ship, we're going to sail back to England and we're going to fill this ship up, not with people but with supplies. I'm going to bring back food, I'm going to bring back wood, I'm going to bring back anything we would need to make it easier for us here." Do you think the people thought that was a good idea?

Students: Yeah.

Lake: Yeah. So John crawled back in his ship, turned around and went back to England. Well! England was in a war and he did not get to come back to that island for 3 years. There was a war and people of England couldn't leave so once he returned he had to stay there and help fight the war. So his family stayed on Roanoke Island for 3 years while he was gone. He finally was able to return. He filled his ship with supplies, turned around, went back to Roanoke Island. He got off his ship, walked onto the island, looked all round, and did not see a single person. He saw the remains of the fort he had helped build. He didn't see anybody and on the ground and under some of the dirt there were like tin cups that the colonists that were there had used—there were head gear, you know when knights would wear head gears over their helmets, there were some helmets lying around, there was no sign of life anywhere. Nowhere! He walked around the island and didn't see anybody. He started walking back to his ship and he saw on a tree a word that had been carved in that tree. He walked over to it and it was the word Croatoan [spells word] carved in a tree. He knew that was the name of another island. What do you suppose he thought? Tom?

Tom: That it was a message to go there.

Lake: To go to that island. Maybe it was a message of some sort. So he went to the other island and didn't find anyone. He went back to Roanoke Island. Nobody. His entire family and his friends had totally disappeared. What do you suppose happened?

Student: They died.

Lake: They might have died? How do you think they might have died?

Student: Starvation.

Lake: They might have died from starvation. Tom?

Student: Well, if he can't find their home anywhere, maybe they tried to build a ship and tried to sail away and they sunk or drowned.

Lake: One possibility is they built a ship and they sailed off, something happened, and they drowned.

Student: They could have built a ship and went off and [inaudible].

Student: Or like they didn't have any shelter so they could have got like sick.

Lake: Illness, disease. Steve?

Student: They may have said, "Let's not wait here anymore cause this guy ain't going to come back." They may have run off and gone more inland.

Lake: Found a new place to live. Judy?

Student: Maybe those Indians could have attacked and got them.

Lake: Indians might have attacked and killed them or took them away, took their bodies away, took everything that they had.

Student: Another ship could have came along.

Lake: OK.

Student: Maybe they could have tried to go to Croatoan.

Lake: Maybe they did go to that island and then something happened there and they couldn't stay there. There's no answer. It's an unsolved mystery. It's the mystery of the lost colony. Roanoke Island was a colony, people lived there. In fact, the first baby ever born in the new land was born on Roanoke Island and it was John White's granddaughter. He brought over his daughter and her family, and before he returned to England, the first baby born in the new land happened to be on Roanoke Island. We don't know what happened, but Roanoke Island was the very first colony from England in the new land. It didn't last very long, it's not there now. The historians have no idea what happened. They have ideas. They have the same ideas as you. But no one knows because there's no proof of one being valid or right over the other.

Lake continued with her story of the early Virginia colonies, then assigned a brief worksheet that required students to copy five key terms in a "word bank" box and then write answers to three questions (If you were one of the first settlers, why would you have wanted to come to the New World? What natural resources would you consider important for your survival? What were the names of two important settlements, and in what years were they started?).

In lesson two, Lake checked the worksheets, reviewed the Roanoke Island story (now focusing on what a colony is rather than on its "mystery of the lost colony" aspects), then told her version of the founding of Jamestown. Following the Jamestown story, the students worked in pairs on an assignment that required them to explain five key aspects of the Jamestown settlement.

Lake: So 22 years later, after Roanoke, the settlers came to Jamestown. I've already added our Jamestown words. John Smith, Pocahontas, and Jamestown. England and colony still are important to Jamestown, aren't they [referring to two other words]?

Students: Um hum.

Lake: Because where did the settlers from Jamestown come?

Students: England.

Lake: And was Jamestown a colony?

Students: Yes.

Lake: What flag are they flying in Jamestown?

Students: English.

Lake: The flag of England. That's important. So our words for today that I want you to be able to know are John Smith, Pocahontas, England, colony, and Jamestown, Virginia.

Lake: [Sits down, begins Jamestown story.] Jamestown. Twenty-two years after Roanoke Island, more settlers came on what?

Student: Ships.

Lake: Ships. To the new land. Twenty-two years after Roanoke Island. There were a lot of people still coming to the new land for a lot of different reasons. Jamestown was going to happen because a company in England, a store, hired some people to go look for gold, and the company got three ships, filled it with men, and sent them to the New World to make money for the company. "Go. I will pay for your ships, I will pay for everything you need. You go, and you find gold for my company, and you bring the gold back. I'll give you some gold and I'll keep some gold." So these three ships went sailing across the ocean to look for gold. They landed in what is now known as Jamestown, Virginia. To help us out, I've got a poem up here [on the chartstand]. "Southern Ships and Settlers." It was written by Rosemary Vincent Benet. This is not the entire poem, it's just a few verses from the poem, but it talks about the trip to Jamestown. I'm going to read the poem to you, but I want you to be able to tell me what the three ships' names were, what they were looking for in the new land, and what were some of the problems the settlers faced when they got here.

> Oh where are you going, Goodspeed and Discovery
> with meek Susan Constant to make up the three?
> We're going to settle the wilds of Virginia.
> For gold and adventure, we're crossing the sea.
> And what will you find there? Starvation and fever.
> We'll eat of the adder and quarrel and rail.
> All but 60 shall die of the first 700.
> But a nation begins with the voyage we sail.

Lake: What were the names of the three ships?

Student: Goodspeed, Discovery, and Susan Constant [students are reading as Lake points].

Lake: OK, look at the first ship [shows pop-up ship from book]. Those are the three ships. The first ship up there is Goodspeed [spells]. In this poem and in a lot of documents, that's how it's spelled, but the English people, they have an accent unlike how you and I talk and when they say that word that we would say Goodspeed, they say Godspeed. What does that first sound sound like to us? What word? What English word?

Students: God.

Lake: God. So in history books and in other things that you're going to see and even sometimes I refer to it as Godspeed, change it to mean, "May God take care of the ship on the voyage." So you're going to see both spellings. Both are correct depending on which one you're reading. So the Godspeed, Discovery, and Susan Constant were the names of the ships that brought the settlers to Jamestown. What were they coming here for? What did they want to find? Tell me.

Students: Gold.

Lake: They were coming over here for gold. Did they find gold when they got here?

Students: No.

Lake: What did they find?

Student: Starving and fever.

Lake: They found starvation and fever. Did they find gold?

Students: No.

Lake: What did they find when they got here?

Students: Starvation and fever.

Lake: They didn't find a lot of good luck, did they?

Students: No.

Lake: Adder and quarrel and rail. Those three words are important. "We'll eat of the adder." Does anybody know what an adder is?

Student: No.

Lake: Tom?

Tom: A snake.

Lake: A snake. They didn't have a lot of food when they got here, did they? They could find snakes and so if they found a snake, that's what they ate because they didn't have a supermarket to go to. "Quarrel." Why did you suppose they would fight? Mark, why do you think they would fight?

Student: Because . . . [no response].

Lake: Steven, why do you suppose they would fight?

Steven: Since they had so little food, they might fight over the food.

Lake: Yeah. If there was one little piece to eat and there were 700 men to feed, do you think they would fight?

Steven: Yes.

Lake: Do you think they expected to find gold? When they got off that ship, do you think they were ready to find gold?

Student: Um hum.

Lake: Was there any gold?

Student: No.

Lake: No. So they probably were unhappy over that. So they started fighting with each other. "Rail." In England, the word rail means to work hard. Why would they have to work hard when they got here? Judy?

Student: Because they had to work because they had to find gold . . . they were looking and hoping they would find it and they didn't have any food.

Lake: They had to work really, really, really, really hard and you know what? Some of the men on that ship never had to work hard because they were just rich kids from England and they got over here

and said, "What do you mean chop down a tree and build a house?"
They didn't want to work. It was really hard for them.

Student: They had to use other natural resources.

Lake: Right, they had to use the natural resources.

Student: [Inaudible].

Lake: That's right. All but 60 shall die of the first 700. How many
people died?

Student: Six hundred forty.

Lake: Right, 640 men died. Do you think it was easy living here that
first year? No. But 60 survived. What did those 60 men do for you
and I? Did they give up and go back to England?

Students: No.

Lake: Let's read the last line together. What does it say, class?

Students: The nation begins with the voyage we sail.

Lake: What nation are we talking about?

Students: Our nation.

Lake: What do we call our nation?

Students: America.

Lake: Or the?

Students: United States.

Lake: If those 60 guys went back to England, do you think the United
States would have been here right now?

Students: No.

Lake: They stayed, didn't they? And because they stayed and they con-
tinued to grow in Jamestown, more people started to come over.
We began to become a nation with Jamestown. Unlike Roanoke
Island, Jamestown survived. With how many men?

Students: Sixty.

Lake: Only 60. When the men left England, they had three ships: The
Goodspeed, the Discovery, and the Susan Constant. The name of
the company in England was the Virginia Company. Why do you
suppose we have a state called Virginia today? How do you suppose
it got its name, Mary?

Student: The Virginia Company.

Lake: Yeah. The Virginia Company set sail and the owner of the Virginia Company had a small wooden box and in that small wooden
box he had seven pieces of paper. And he had numbers, number
one, number two, all the way to seven. On those pieces of paper,
he put the names of the people he wanted to be the leader or the
ruler when they found the colony. The box was put on the ship,
the Susan Constant, and a man we're going to talk about later,
name was Israel Worth. He was one of the passengers and he kept

a diary of what went on on the ship, the Susan Constant, and also when he landed in Jamestown and started helping to build James-town because he was one of the 60 men that survived, we have a diary that helps us as historians understand what Jamestown was like. But Israel Worth in his diary talks about opening that box when they first got to the new land. And on that piece, on the first piece of paper was the name John Smith. John Smith was going to be the ruler chosen by the Virginia Company, of the colony in the new land and if something happened to him, the other people, the person on number two, the second piece of paper, would become the leader. But the other people, the other six men were going to be his helpers. So John Smith was the leader of Jamestown.

Lake continued in this vein to tell the rest of the Jamestown story, then returned the students to their desks where they worked in pairs on an assignment that required them to explain five key aspects of the Jamestown settlement (why the people came, how they got there, their rules and laws, their Indian friends, and their hardships and problems). To prepare them for the assignment, she showed a story map, led them through a review of key facts, and gave directions.

This class typified Lake's history teaching. She led the students through a review of the Roanoke story using key words posted the previous day, then introduced a new set of key words in the process of telling the Jamestown story. She placed the material within a time and space context, referred to related prior learning, told the new story with gusto, based it on children's literature sources (and in this case a poem as well) included props and illustrations, and finished with an assignment that called for the students to write significantly (in this case, in collaboration with a partner).

Lesson three was similar to lesson two. Lake checked work on the previous assignment, then reviewed Roanoke and Jamestown, then told the story of Plymouth, and then started the students on an assignment calling for them to answer questions about Plymouth and to compare Plymouth with Jamestown. Lesson four was spent reviewing, catching up on uncompleted work, and filling out a sheet on five key aspects of the Plymouth colony (the same five aspects that the students had written about for Jamestown in lesson two).

For lesson five, Lake used the language arts period to give instructions for a major writing assignment—the Jamestown journals. Students were to pretend to be survivors of the first year in Jamestown and compose journal entries that they might have made on May 14, 1607 (arrival on three ships), August 5, 1607 (futile search for gold, developing relationships with local natives, building a fort, hunting and fishing), January 4, 1608 (the travails of winter), and June 28, 1608 (survivors heartened by arrival of new settlers). The journals were to be fictional but historically accurate. To help students plan, Lake distributed a list of key words that might be included. Students were to plan carefully before starting, edit several times, and then copy the final versions into simulated journals.

Lake: When we studied Native American Indians, we made a book and that book was my way of finding out if you knew the information on the various Indian groups. And when we did explorers, you wrote a letter or a report on which explorer you would have wanted to be with and why and what your expedition would have been like. That gives me information on how much you know about those explorers. Our writing assignment for this unit on Jamestown, Roanoke Island, and Plymouth is going to be a diary based on the first year in Jamestown. When you write the diary, I am then going to be able to find out how much information each of you have on exactly what happened in Jamestown during that first year. We've done a lot of talking about that first year. From the people coming over to those who survived, the problem between John Smith and Pocahontas. You have a lot of information. By writing the diary as if you were there, I will know how much information you have. Your work on this assignment will be a part of your grade for the next report card. It will be taking the place of a specific test on Jamestown. Before we begin I want you to look up here [points to poster hung in air on clothesline]. "Historical fiction." We shared with you, yesterday and today, some books that kids got at the library. Those books are historical fiction. Let's read to find out what historical fiction is. [reading this] "Historical fiction is a special kind of fiction in which events and characters from the past seem to come to life. A story that is historical fiction is based on real events or people from history. But in historical fiction, the author creates details and dialogue to make the story more interesting to the reader." The people who write books, the authors of the books that we shared in class, they were not there. They did not see what life was really like during this time period. They researched, they read other books, they read diaries, and then they wrote a story. Everything in that story may not be 100 percent accurate, but we can do our best job of trying to make it historically correct. For instance, we wouldn't write about the settlers of Jamestown coming over on the Mayflower, would we? What would be wrong with that information? Ken?

Student: It's not historically correct.

Lake: It's not historically correct. Very good, Ken. We want the correct information and then we add words to that to make it more interesting. I have here a book, *Jamestown: New World Adventure* [by James Knight, published in 1982 by Troll Associates of Mahwah, New Jersey, as part of the "Adventures in Colonial America" series]. [Holds up the book throughout this introduction.] This book is written in diary form. The book you're going to be writing is in diary form. Let's talk a minute about diaries. How are diaries set up? Can you think for a minute how diaries are set up? Mary?

Student: They're set up like on one page it would say February 1 and February 2 on every page.

Lake: At the top of the page there is a date. Mary is correct. And then on that page beneath the date, the person writing the diary would share information about what happened on that day. In this diary, it happens to be the diary of Israel Worth. Israel Worth was a real settler in Jamestown. How do you suppose we know there was an Israel Worth? Alice?

Student: A diary.

Lake: He left a diary or he left a journal. They did not call them diaries—they called them journals back in the 1600s. So Israel Worth left a journal. This author, James Knight, took part of his journal and put it in diary form to share with you through a book. Books are so important for that very reason. We can learn from them. This book, this diary, this journal of Israel Worth begins May 14, 1607. You can see the date written right at the top of the page. It was the day, or around the day, that they arrived and saw the land that they were going to name Jamestown. Israel Worth, in this book, he did not write in it daily, he did not write in it May 14, May 15, May 16. If he did that for a solid year that book would be this thick. So what is in this book are diary entries. Some are weekly, some are monthly. Some he skipped 3 months and then he would write what had been happening. Cathy?

Student: Was it like he put all the important information in?

Lake: Right, the important information about what was happening in Jamestown. It was a way for the people in England to find out what was happening in Jamestown because, remember, they left relatives and friends in England. This was his way, keeping a journal on what was happening. Listen as I read to you about May 14, 1607. "This journal will record the adventures of Israel Worth in the new colony of Jamestown. At the time of this first entry I am 28 years old and in good health. I am one of four master carpenters on this expedition." What do we call the writing, as I read this, I'm using the term "I," what do we call that, does anybody remember? Robert?

Student: Biography.

Lake: Cathy?

Cathy: Autobiography.

Lake: It's like an autobiography because it did happen to him, but he's not describing his life, so it wouldn't be an autobiography. "First person." We're writing in the first person. He was there, he's the first person to tell us this story, so we use the term "I." You also are going to write in first person. Your diary is going to have "I" because we're going to take a step back in time, and you're going to be living in Jamestown as you're writing your journal. "As I write, I am aboard the ship Susan Constant with the captain, Christopher Newport, in command. Two other ships are also anchored in the bay. They are the Goodspeed and the Discovery. I will write as often as I am able for I know that we will be laboring hard for this new colony of the Virginia Company as we look for gold and time will be scarce." Was the information I've read so far historically correct?

Student: Yes.

In lesson six, Lake led the students through a review of the English, French, and Spanish explorations and land claims, then started them on an assignment calling for them to color and label maps (green for English land claims, brown for French, and yellow for Spanish). During the last 15 minutes, groups of four students played a "Jeopardy" game that required them to listen to clues (e.g., "It was carved on a tree at Roanoke.") and then supply the answer, using the question form used on the TV show ("What is Croatoan?"). This lesson was devoted to consolidation of prior learning, without introducing any important new information, because Lake wanted the students to concentrate on completing the Jamestown journals. She continued this consolidation phase in lesson seven, when she collected the journal assignments and administered a test. Plans for lesson eight were changed because a local veterinarian came to lead the fifth graders through dissections of pig lungs. While half of them worked with the veterinarian; the other half came to Lake's room for social studies. Consequently, instead of beginning new material, Lake reviewed the unit to date and then engaged students in a worksheet about the English colonies.

To begin lesson nine, Lake read the class *Sarah Morton's Day* (by

Kate Waters, published in New York by Scholastic in 1989), depicting a day in the life of a 9-year-old who lived in the Plymouth colony in 1627. She then assigned students to write about Sarah Morton, using not only information from the book but other information about the Plymouth colony. To help them plan, Lake listed key information about Sarah Morton on the chart stand:

Born in Holland, 1618
Came to America, 1623
Came on ship, the *Anne*
Father died during first winter
Sarah had to do chores: Roll up bedding, tend the fire, muck the garden, polish the brass, milk the goats, feed the chickens, do lessons, pound the spices, memorize Bible verses
Manners: Children should be seen and not heard; stand at the table
Best friend is Elizabeth Warren
Describe her home

This class had missed social studies for several days due to various special events, so Lake began lesson 10 with a review. Then the students worked in groups of four on a map activity. Each group received an outline of the 13 colonies drawn on large poster paper. They were to color the three main regions (New England, the middle colonies, and the southern colonies), print the names of each colony, and add a title at the top and a map key and their names at the bottom. As groups finished their assignment, she had them "share" (take turns reading) their historical profiles of Sarah Morton.

In lesson 11, Lake had a few students read their Sarah Morton profiles while she complimented their work and reviewed key ideas about biographical writing. Then she had the students open their social studies texts to a section comparing and contrasting the New England, middle, and southern colonies. She distributed a worksheet on which they would record salient facts about the three sets of colonies, then got them started on it by leading them through instructions and starting to record information about the New England colonies. Students worked quietly on it during lesson 12.

Lake began lesson 13 on life in the colonies by focusing on the contrast between life on an eastern seaboard plantation and life on the inland frontier. She had the students visualize while she talked about cutting a clearing and building a cabin in the wilderness.

Lake: I want to paint a picture for you and you need to help me. You need to shut your eyes, and I want you to think about a forest. A forest without paths, trees after trees after trees after trees. When you look through your forest, you just see more trees. . . . In order to survive, these people chopped down some trees. I want you to visualize a man chopping down, taking his saw or an ax, chopping down some trees to form a clearing. The trees are lying on the ground. Some of you might even be able to hear the trees falling to the ground as you paint your picture. . . . Then this person by himself is going to take those trees and he's going to build himself a small log cabin. Don't you see a picture of a man by himself dragging logs and laying them across each other until he built a log cabin. Picture the log cabin in your mind. Trees surrounding the log cabin. The only clearing is from where he chopped down the trees. You might picture a wife and two or three children. That's their home. . . . Open your eyes. That's what the people faced who lived out here. There was no place for them to live along here [the coast]. You had to be very wealthy to afford the land here. So you left with your wife and your children and maybe your grandmother and you walked until you found an area that you could clear some trees and build yourself a log cabin. That land that you just pictured in your mind is called the frontier. Alice?

Student: It's almost like the [inaudible] where the guy is cutting them all down.

Lake: OK. The frontier was all the land that has been unsettled, and the pioneers are the people who went out here to build their houses. They just went a little ways. They didn't go all the way out west yet. This area was known as the what? [Lake shows "Frontier" word card.]

Student: The frontier.

Lake: What type of houses did they have in the frontier?

Student: Log cabins.

Lake: Were there lots and lots of people who helped build these log cabins?

Student: No.

Lake: No. In here [the coast] . . . Mary shared with us that they wanted to make lots of money. They were greedy. Do you think the people who lived out here on the frontier were concerned about all the stuff they had in life? No. They didn't have a lot of stuff at all, did they?

Student: No.

Lake: People who lived along here lived in huge mansions. We're not talking about castles. We're talking about huge houses. Twenty to 30 rooms in one house. Three living rooms. Two dining rooms, four kitchens because the people who lived on these plantations had a lot of money. . . .

Following the story, students began on an assignment that showed a schematic outline of a plantation and called for them to color different components (blacksmith shop, owner's mansion, etc.) according to a "map key." The assignment called only for coloring, not significant writing. Lake might have done something more substantial in other circumstances, but several social studies periods had been devoted to special events and assemblies, and at this point she was cutting back on her original plans and hurrying to finish the colonies unit before the holiday break.

This final class was devoted to filling out the "What have I Learned?" section of the KWL sheet and review. During the KWL exercise, many students looked at the key word cards displayed at the back of the room or at the Sarah Morton outline on the chart stand. Some students just copied from these sources, but others composed more individualized responses. Lake then concluded the unit by gathering the students on the floor for a final review.

I think that everyone in here has learned a lot of information. I think that every one of you could tell me something about the colonies. You could tell me something about Jamestown. You could tell me something about Roanoke Island, and you could tell me something about Plymouth, and you could tell me something about the New England colonies, the middle colonies, and the southern colonies. I think that we could shut our eyes, and if I asked you to picture a map of the colonies, you could do that. If a month ago I would have said, "Close your eyes and find the map of the colonies," you wouldn't have known what to picture. How many can shut their eyes and think about and draw a map of the colonies in their minds and see that map? [two-thirds] How many can see the exact colors that you and your group put on your maps? That shows you have learned a lot. I'm very proud of all of you because I know I could ask varying questions. If I wanted to give an oral test right now, and I went around and asked each one of you a question, I'm sure you would give me an excellent response. So I want you to know that I'm really proud of the information you've learned. This was new information. It wasn't information you learned in first grade or second grade. I

want to share with you before I give Shirley back hers—she chose
to draw a picture of a plantation and the log cabin because that
was something she remembered that she thought was important
in this unit—the difference between the frontier and the plantation. That was neat because that was one of the ways you could
express what you've learned. I know by looking at this, Shirley
knows about plantation life and she knows about life on the frontier, what it was like to live in a log cabin. I would like some of
you to share some of the information you learned with us.

After several students shared what they had learned, Lake asked
them what were the favorite things they learned or did during the unit.
The biggest favorites were the maps that they worked on in groups of
four and the story times in the back of the room. Surprisingly, the
Sarah Morton book and assignment did not draw much enthusiasm.

Time pressures prevented Lake from implementing all her plans
for the unit. She never used certain materials and activities built
around profiles of colonial women (although in the next unit she
planned to include material on women who played significant roles in
the Revolution). She also omitted certain "hands-on" activities that
she had used in the past, such as preparing colonial foods or making
and wearing colonial costumes. Nor did she include any role play or
dramatic activities, although she planned to do so in later units.

EFFECTS OF THE UNIT ON STUDENT MOTIVATION
AND LEARNING

No formal measures of student motivation were administered, but informal observation suggested that the students found the class enjoyable and the material engaging. They paid consistent, often rapt, attention to Lake when she was telling stories; they frequently initiated
comments and questions; and they typically engaged in assignments
with apparent seriousness of purpose. They also read additional tradebooks on colonial times, completed the extra credit assignments, and
discussed the content during out-of-class times and at home with family members. In summary, there were numerous positive indicators,
and no negative indicators, of desirable motivational outcomes.

Lake's effects on student learning are harder to assess. She administered no standardized tests that would make it possible to compare her
students' scores with established norms. She taught social studies to
all fifth graders at the school, so we couldn't compare her homeroom

students to peers taught by other teachers. However, she used the KWL sheets, administered a test, quizzed the students orally several times, and engaged them in a variety of writing assignments. In addition, we interviewed six of her students at length before and after the unit.

Student performance on these various indicators suggested that Lake was quite successful in accomplishing her stated knowledge goals. Her students learned a great deal, especially the main ideas and associated basic facts that she emphasized repeatedly. Most students began the unit knowing little about who came to live in the colonies except for the Thanksgiving story, and little about life in the colonies except that it did not include modern conveniences.

Following the unit, they displayed considerable knowledge about different people who came to the colonies and why they came, about the early colonies at Roanoke, Jamestown, and Plymouth, about life on the frontier, and so on. Most of what was reported was accurate as far as it went and reflected what Lake had taught. However, there were occasional conflations and misconceptions, reflecting students' difficulties in assimilating so much new information to a limited knowledge base. There also was frequent evidence of vagueness or naivete regarding the time and space dimensions of the events they learned about, the reasons for or implications of these events, and the larger context in which they took place (i.e., the nature of everyday life and of global political developments during the sixteenth to eighteenth centuries). The clues to the nature of fifth graders' historical understandings that emerged during the interviews done for this case study piqued our interest in exploring this area more systematically, which we did the following year. This work is described in Chapter 4.

ASSESSING LAKE'S CASE

Much of what Lake taught in the unit depended on stories. Not only did Lake tell "her" stories, but she relied on other forms of storytelling—historical fiction, journals, and diary accounts—to augment her own approach. The stories tended to convey the impression that history is a singular account of our past, constructed from the cloth of interesting and myriad details, conflicts and resolutions, and heroes and villains. Students appeared to enjoy these stories and sat attentively at the back of the room when they were told, or engaged quickly in constructing their own fictional journals under Lake's direction.

As Evans (1989, 1994) points out, storytellers focus on fascinating historical details and events, emphasize the importance of developing

a collective identity through the study of history, tend to be traditionally conservative politically, and find that the storytelling approach
works well in motivating students' interest in the study of history.
Also, as Egan (1986) might note, they attempt to build a sense of the
past by inspiring students' imagination through those unique and
sometimes strange historical events (e.g., the mysterious disappearance of the first Virginia colony). In their ideal form, such stories transport students into the context of a long past era and breathe life into
their study of the period. It is easy to see why Lake found the storytelling approach effective and useful with her fifth graders.

Lake had a clear vision of what she was trying to accomplish that
featured well-articulated goals and supporting rationale; she had developed an approach that appeared to be well suited to her goals; and data
from classroom observation and from student interviews, tests, and
work samples suggest that she was generally successful in accomplishing what she set out to accomplish. Although with notable individual
differences in degree of sophistication, completeness, and connected-
ness, her students appeared to be learning the key ideas and related
facts that Lake stressed in introducing them to the development of
the United States as a nation. Furthermore, the students displayed the
affective characteristics that she strove for (interest in the content
communicated through storytelling, engagement in the activities, ap-
proaching tasks with a sense of competence rather than anxiety, coop-
erating well with peers).

Lake's teaching also would be judged as effective according to a
variety of other criteria. First, she exemplified virtually all of the personal qualities and general teaching strategies that process-outcome
research has identified as correlates of student achievement gain (Brophy & Good, 1986). She was extraordinarily good at establishing her
classroom as a learning environment in which students spend most of
their time engaged in ongoing academic activities. Activities got
started briskly, transitions were brief and orderly, and very little time
was lost getting organized or dealing with disruptive behavior. She presented information with enthusiasm and structured it around main
ideas that were emphasized during presentations and followed up
using key word cards, story maps, study guides, and related techniques
for engaging students in meaningful learning of connected content
rather than rote memorizing of isolated facts. She used an active teaching approach in which much classroom time was spent in whole-class
lessons and teacher–student discourse rather than in silent work on
assignments; she made sure that students knew what to do and how
to do it before releasing them to work independently; she circulated to

monitor and assist students as they worked; and she frequently allowed them to work cooperatively in pairs or groups.

Lake's teaching also exemplified many features of teaching school subjects for understanding and knowledge use (Brophy, 1990b; Newmann, 1990). She limited her breadth of coverage in order to develop limited content sufficiently to foster conceptual understanding; she organized this limited content around a few key ideas; she emphasized the relationships and connections between these ideas; she provided students with frequent opportunities to actively process information and construct meaning; and she developed skills through activities that capitalized on naturally occurring opportunities for students to communicate or apply the history content that they were learning, rather than by requiring the students to work on isolated skills exercises. Her students did not get many opportunities for extended discussion or debate during whole-class activities (where her discourse patterns were mostly limited to review and recitation), but they did get frequent opportunities to discuss what they were learning in pairs or small groups and to write about it when working on assignments.

Lake's teaching also exemplified some of the qualities emphasized by historians and others concerned about effective teaching of history to elementary students (Gagnon, 1989b; Howard & Mendenhall, 1982). She allocated sufficient time to the subject to provide a basis for coherent curriculum and instruction, and she integrated her history teaching with her teaching of other subjects in ways that enhanced its impact. In particular, she integrated history with language arts by providing students with opportunities for authentic oral or written communication about what they were learning about U.S. history; she situated the historical content within time and space, referring frequently to timelines and maps; and she connected the information to students' lives by linking it to their family histories, local examples, or current events.

Lake "made history come alive" for her students through her use of artifacts, her own personal storytelling, and her use of historical tradebooks. Her storytelling was memorable both because she framed the stories around interesting people and events and because she told them with theatrical flair. In the process, she frequently appealed to the students' imaginations by asking for predictions about what happened next, asking them to think about how they might have responded in the situation, or helping them to visualize the scene.

Finally, Lake's teaching embodied some of the principles that are emphasized by historians and geographers who are concerned about accurate representation of their disciplines. She helped her students to understand that historical accounts are constructed by individuals who collect and synthesize information, as well as to appreciate that they could act as historians themselves. Also, she consistently embedded each new cluster of historical development within the context that she had established through frequent reference to the timeline that stretched across the front of her classroom. Rather than memorizing of dates, she emphasized the general chronology of events and the causal linkages between them. She also brought in relevant geographical and social science content when it could help students to develop understanding of the larger historical frame. These disciplinary elements were introduced informally and in language appropriate to fifth graders, so her handling of the content differed considerably from how historians would handle it when teaching high school or college students. Nevertheless, much of it was consistent with current disciplinary concerns and emphases (e.g., her inclusion of social history and the everyday lives of ordinary people).

Although Lake's teaching could be viewed as effective by all these criteria, it also could be criticized on the basis of a few others. Disciplinary historians, while likely to be pleased by the factors just mentioned, might prefer a more complete chronology than Lake offered, and they might want to see more things presented as disputed issues rather than as putative facts. Those who are especially concerned about content accuracy and disciplinary fidelity also might want to see Lake reduce her use of children's fiction and curb her storytelling in favor of greater reliance on actual historical source material or the nonfiction writings of professional historians. Revisionist historians and critical theorists, although pleased with Lake's emphasis on the history of everyday people in general and of women in particular, would likely challenge her conservatism and want to see her adopt a more critical, less Eurocentric approach to history.

Lake's teaching also might be criticized by educators who favor pedagogical approaches that are not emphasized in her classroom. Those who place a premium on inquiry, discovery, or creative expression, for example, might feel that too many of Lake's questions and activities involved repeating or applying ideas that she had told the students, and that not enough of them provided the students with opportunities to conduct inquiry on their own questions or to generate and express their own ideas (Engle & Ochoa, 1988). Similarly, educators who emphasize reflective forms of classroom discourse, although pleased with Lake's emphasis on cooperative learning activities, would want to see less recitation and more dialogue, debate, or other sustained discussion (Newmann, 1990).

Finally, educators who are concerned about challenging students to their limits, especially educators who focus on gifted and talented students, might criticize Lake for underchallenging/overprotecting her students in general and her low achievers in particular. Some might believe that her expectations generally were set too low—that she structured and scaffolded her students' work on assignments more than she needed to and that the assignments themselves were not as demanding as they could have been. Others might believe that Lake's protective and supportive approach was just what her low achievers needed, but would urge her to provide a more enriched or demanding curriculum for her higher achievers.

Given Lake's personal and academic background, the goals and historical content she chose to emphasize, and her students' limited prior knowledge, it is difficult to see how she could accomplish successfully everything recommended by those who suggest an array of alternative approaches. This underscores the importance of goal choices, and the nature of the subsequent trade-offs involved, as central to teaching elementary school American history. Lake's effectiveness, in part, can be attributed to her movement beyond the routine, perfunctory coverage of textbook facts and details for their own sake, and her adoption of a goal framework that consciously pursued a more limited chronological focus, emphasizing key themes and concepts of history and coupling them with engaging stories. In making these choices, however, she sacrificed a more inquiry-oriented, critical approach to historical study, one that would forefront directly the constructed nature of all historical accounts and their interesting, but problematic, characteristics. This trade-off places historical stories, rather than students, at the center of classroom practice. Yet, Lake was more attuned to her students and what they were learning than a teacher following an approach that focused only on textbook coverage would be. Her storytelling approach, while still traditional in many ways, was a considerable improvement over traditional textbook-based teaching.

CHAPTER 4

Qualitative Analyses of Students' Developing Historical Knowledge and Thinking

In Chapters 1 and 2, we noted the potential value of connecting curriculum content to what students know (or think they know) about the topic. This allows for design of instruction that builds on the students' existing valid knowledge and also challenges their misconceptions. To exploit the potential for applying this approach to elementary history instruction, we will need to learn more about the knowledge and misconceptions that children frequently develop about typically taught historical content.

Our research program included the largest and most systematic attempt made to date to address this need, by interviewing fifth graders before and after each of their social studies (U.S. history) curriculum units. The preunit interviews developed information about what the students knew (or thought they knew) about the unit topic via information acquired in earlier grades or through reading or out-of-school experiences. The postunit data showed how the students' knowledge and thinking had changed (or not) in response to instruction and learning activities.

DATA COLLECTION PROCEDURES

To collect these data, we returned to Mary Lake's classroom, which we selected for several reasons related to its representativeness or typicality. We knew that her U.S. history curriculum, as represented both in her own storytelling and in the textbook series used at her school, presented the traditional version of U.S. history. Because the school district's curriculum guidelines and adopted textbook series both followed the expanding communities framework, Lake's students had not been exposed to sustained, chronologically organized instruction in history prior to fifth grade. They possessed bits and pieces of knowledge about the past (Native Americans, the Pilgrims and the first Thanksgiving, Columbus, presidents and other famous Americans, and state history), but they had not yet studied systematic, chronological history.

Although greater ethnic diversity would have been desirable, we viewed this school district as a good place to begin developing information about fifth graders' historical knowledge because it was at or only slightly above average on key indicators of socioeconomic status and educational attainment (family income, years of education completed, etc.). Thus, returning to Lake's classroom provided us with the opportunity to interview relatively typical (or at least statistically average) students being exposed to the commonly taught traditional curriculum.

Two sets of data were collected before and after each of her six U.S. history units. The first set involved written KWL data as described in Chapter 3. The second set came from a sample of 10 students studied longitudinally, beginning near the end of fourth grade and continuing throughout fifth grade. The sample included five boys and five girls. Within each gender group there were two high achievers, two average achievers, and one low achiever, based on academic achievement in fourth grade. Because we could interview only 10 students due to resource limitations, we weighted the sample toward higher achievers in the expectation that this would yield more substantive responses.

Students were interviewed individually for 15 to 30 minutes in quiet rooms outside of their classrooms. Interview tapes were transcribed for analysis, using pseudonyms to identify the students. The initial interview was done in the spring of 1990 when the students were still in fourth grade. The rest were done during the 1990–1991 school year when the students were in fifth grade.

In developing questions for the interviews, we focused on key ideas traditionally taught in fifth-grade U.S. history courses. In analyzing the data, we focused on qualitative aspects of the students' responses that provided clues to their underlying historical conceptions, not on computing percentages of right answers. We addressed the data with attention to the following questions: Which aspects of the unit were already in place as prior knowledge before the unit began, and which were new to the students? Of the new elements, which were easily learned and remembered and which presented difficulties (and why)? What misconceptions did students bring with them or develop in the process of studying a unit? Were these misconceptions changed or did they persist and distort learning? What implications do the data suggest for teaching elementary social studies in general and fifth-grade U.S. history in particular?

PROFILES OF THE TEN STUDENTS
STUDIED LONGITUDINALLY

Here are brief descriptions of the 10 students whom we interviewed repeatedly. At the end of the chapter, following presentation of findings for each curriculum unit considered separately, we compare and contrast the longitudinal patterns of growth and change in historical knowledge displayed by these students.

Jason (High Achiever)

Jason's responses revealed good learning of U.S. history but limited enthusiasm for it. He usually responded tersely, either saying that he didn't know or else giving a substantive response that was brief, to the point, and accurate as far as it went (although often lacking in specific vocabulary). He began with a good sense of how people lived prior to modern inventions, and as the school year unfolded he showed good grasp of the major historical themes taught (competition for dominance in North America won by England; who came to the colonies and why; reasons for the Revolution; what might have happened if England had won the war or if another country had dominated North America; key ideas about the lives of explorers, colonists, and pioneers). Although he included Johnny Tremain in an otherwise good list of revolutionary leaders and displayed other minor confusions, he displayed no serious misconceptions, certainly none that persisted and distorted his learning. He tended to state facts and explanations briefly rather than launch into extended narratives.

Tim (High Achiever)

Tim was similar to Jason in many respects but his responses revealed more willingness to elaborate without persistent probing, more interest in history, and more empathy with the historical individuals or groups being studied. Tim's preunit responses were among the most impressive, indicating unusually strong prior knowledge. His postunit responses tended to be unusually detailed and free of naivete or misconceptions.

Mark (Average Achiever)

Although he was average in achievement level, Mark's interview responses resembled those of high achievers. He began with more (and more accurate) background knowledge than most of the other students and he did not convey naive ideas or serious misconceptions. One reason for this was that he was not willing to guess or speak freely when unsure, preferring to stick with "I don't know" responses. However, he usually spoke extensively when he was more sure of himself, providing detailed and mostly accurate responses similar to Tim's. He knew a lot about the pioneers because he had played a computer game called "Westward Ho" about traveling on the Oregon Trail. He had trouble with "no taxation without representation" and other questions dealing with government, largely because he lacked understanding about representative government (McKeown & Beck, 1990, 1994, observed this problem in many of the fifth graders they interviewed). He thought of the new nation's government as basically a dictatorship under George Washington, and even though he spoke of Congress voting on laws, he did not realize that members of Congress represent their districts' voters.

Brad (Average Achiever)

Brad provided lengthy responses to most questions even though he had less prior knowledge to draw on than the three previous boys. His responses are among the most interesting to read because he was interested in and reflective about the content and often able to assume the perspective of the people being studied. He also was willing to take guesses and speak when unsure, even though this produced many examples of confusion or misconception, especially on preunit interviews. Most of these were replaced by accurate knowledge on postunit interviews. Among other things, Brad suggested that people in the past were not as smart as we are because they didn't have modern inventions, Indians didn't have spices and didn't wear much for clothes, flint existed 10,000 years ago but no longer exists today, Indians wrote in words (although not in books like ours), explorers came to America looking for natural resources like coal and gravel, Columbus captained the Mayflower and kept going back to England to bring more people to America, black people from Africa came to America on their own and only later were used as slaves, slaves didn't get paid but made pocket money doing extra jobs for people, and the pioneers had to fight a lot because they kept running into the French, the Indians, and the British.

The latter notion was one of several that indicated persistent timeline confusion that included a tendency to conflate elements of the French and Indian War with elements of the American Revolution, to conflate information learned about Jamestown and Plymouth with information learned about the Revolution, and to conflate information learned about early pioneers crossing the Appalachians with information learned about later pioneers in the west. Finally, Brad launched into a few extended narratives and verbalized a few naive ideas, although he did not do either of these things nearly as frequently as Helen or Rita.

Ned (Low Achiever)

Ned possessed minimal prior knowledge. He said "I don't know" to a great number of questions and usually gave terse answers and minimal responses to probing even when he did offer substantive information. Most of his responses to postunit questions were accurate, although he often focused on minor details rather than key ideas. He appeared to be uninformed and mostly uninterested in history, but not cognitively immature. He did not verbalize naive ideas often and did not respond with extended narratives. Mostly he offered unimpressive responses lacking in specifics, details, or focus around main ideas.

Teri (High Achiever)

Teri was easily the most difficult of the students to interview, speaking tersely when she was willing to respond and being unwilling to guess or elaborate. Her preunit interviews featured mostly "I don't know" responses, and her postunit interviews featured terse but accurate responses focused around main ideas. Except for a few sparks of interest, she didn't seem to care much about the history she was learning. She remembered most of the big ideas, but not many names or other details. She continually responded as if being tested, sometimes saying things like, "We haven't studied that yet." She didn't express notably naive ideas or gross misconceptions, but her knowledge growth across the year was spotty relative to what it might have been if she had developed greater interest in the subject.

Sue (High Achiever)

Sue began the year with limited prior knowledge and she verbalized some naive ideas. However, she was very interested in the content, empathized with the people being studied, and typically gave impressive responses on the postunit interviews. She spoke more freely and less defensively than other high achievers, and most of her naive or inaccurate statements had changed by later interviews. Even so, her final interview included the statement that parts of the middle of the country might have remained undiscovered or at least unincorporated into any country if it had not been for the Louisiana Purchase. Thus, although she was a high achiever and made noteworthy knowledge gains across the year, Sue apparently was still undergoing development toward levels of cognitive advancement that most of her classmates had attained already.

Helen (Average Achiever)

Helen possessed high interest in history and a great deal of prior knowledge, although much of this prior knowledge was inaccurate or conflated. Hers was easily the longest transcript because she often engaged in extended narratives, frequently replete with naive conceptions and fanciful elaborations. Many of these are quoted at length later in the chapter. Other interesting features of Helen's interviews included the frequent coexistence of accurate and inaccurate ideas without recognition of their contradictions; her frequent tendency to engage in post facto attribution of motives that might explain items of historical information (such as suggesting that the Indians would not have discovered Europe because "they didn't want to go somewhere they knew there would be other people and they wouldn't get along"); her tendency to report direct conversations between people who never met and often were widely separated from one another in space or time; and her tendency to generate fanciful or otherwise unique and inaccurate content, especially when she engaged the narrative mode or conflated two or more different stories. Helen's narrative and fanciful tendencies were much more noticeable earlier than later in fifth grade, when she began to produce more non-narrative causal analyses. Even so, her misconceptions were more resistant to change and more active in distorting her learning than those of the other students.

The contrast between Helen and Teri is instructive. Helen's responses remind us that interest in the subject and willingness to talk without worrying about being absolutely accurate make for much more engaging interview transcripts, but do not compensate for intellectual or cognitive style problems that create and sustain misconceptions. Still, we suspect that many historians and many teachers (at least at this grade level) would prefer Helen's mistake-ridden but enthusiastic approach to history over Teri's tendency to learn accurately but without interest. This assumes, however, that Helen would make continued progress toward more mature historical understandings and grow out of her tendencies toward wholesale conflation and fanciful story generation.

Kay (Average Achiever)

Kay's interviews resembled Mark's in many respects, although she began with less prior knowledge. She spoke freely but without displaying much enthusiasm or empathy, focusing on main ideas without generating extended narratives. She was willing to talk and often made guesses in her preunit interviews. Typically these were sensible guesses that did not communicate naivete or misconceptions. Many of her responses focused on children and families (explorers separated from their families, families coming to the New World, families traveling in wagon trains). Also, she referred frequently to a core idea (that the settlers wanted all of the land from sea to sea and that this caused periodic conflicts with the French, the Spanish, the Mexicans, and especially the Indians), which took her a long way in answering questions in several units.

Rita (Low Achiever)

Rita was second only to Helen in length of transcripts, although hers were less narrative. An important reason for this was her family connections to the Pilgrims, which contributed to a strong interest in history. Rita makes an interesting case study because she was a low achiever who frequently expressed naive ideas and who harbored persistent misconceptions that distorted her learning, but she also possessed an unusually rich and mostly accurate fund of prior knowledge, was highly interested in the subject, and tended to empathize with the people being studied. She was less like Ned (the other low achiever) than she was like Helen, with whom she shared tendencies to produce extended and often storied responses, to insert personal commentary about or reactions to the people or events being described, and to talk at length about details or side issues instead of main ideas. However, many of these aspects of her response style had waned by the second half of fifth grade, when Rita's responses became more accurate, detailed, and analytic rather than narrative. Among the 10 students, Rita probably showed the most cognitive growth from where she began in fourth grade.

UNIT 1: HISTORY AND THE WORK OF HISTORIANS

Lake's first unit was designed to introduce her students to history and the work of historians. Key concepts included primary and secondary sources, artifacts, timelines and chronological order, the students' personal histories, and U.S. history (helping the students to realize that, just as they have histories as individuals, the United States has a history as a country that they would be learning about during the year). Students applied these concepts by developing information about their own personal histories. They interviewed their parents and other relatives, collected artifacts (birth certificates, photos, baby books, newspapers from their birth dates, etc.), then organized their information by creating a timeline that identified noteworthy events in their lives, and finally illustrated the events with documents and artifacts.

KWL Findings

For this unit, the KWL sheets instructed students to tell what they knew about history and what they wanted to learn about it. KWL data were available from three class sections.

What the Students Knew About History

Table 4.1 (on the following page) indicates that 75 of the 80 students gave generally acceptable definitions and/or examples of history: Twenty confined themselves to a general definition, 27 gave both a definition and some examples, and 28 gave only examples. The latter response is less developmentally advanced than responses that include general definitions (Estvan & Estvan, 1959). It was made by 18 boys but only 10 girls. In addition, four boys but only one girl did not know or gave incorrect answers. Thus, most students conveyed a generally accurate sense of what history means, although the girls communicated more accurate knowledge.

The most typical definitions equated history with the past ("History is a part of time—the past, not the present"), sometimes adding examples ("History is like in the past, like Christopher Columbus"). Sometimes this core idea was stated imprecisely ("It is stuff that already has been done"), and sometimes it was elaborated with noteworthy precision ("History means yesterday or back to when dinosaurs lived. History will add on every time a day passes. History means everything that happened in the past").

Students typically qualified their definitions by specifying that his-

Table 4.1 What Students Said They Knew About History as They Began Fifth Grade

	Boys (N = 44)	Girls (N = 36)	Total (N = 80)
A. *How they defined history*			
1. Gave general definition only	11	9	20
2. Gave general definition plus examples	11	16	27
3. Gave examples only	18	10	28
4. Didn't know or gave irrelevant or incorrect answer	4	1	5
	44	36	80
B. *Whether they distinguished "history" from the past generally*			
1. No qualifications: history as (study of) the past	8	8	16
2. Time qualification: history as events that happened long ago	8	9	17
3. Importance qualification: history as famous or noteworthy people or events	11	12	23
	27	29	56
C. *The examples they cited*			
1. Indians/Native Americans	10	8	18
2. George Washington/first president	6	9	15
3. Famous people (kings, presidents)	6	7	13
4. Wars (unspecified)	5	8	13
5. Pilgrims	6	4	10
6. Columbus	2	5	7
7. Particular wars (Civil, WWI, WWII, French and Indian)	3	3	6
8. Lincoln	4	1	5
9. How people lived prior to electricity, engine power, etc.	1	3	4
	43	48	91

tory refers to people or events that were particularly *important* and/or from *long ago*. Levstik and Pappas (1987) also found that fourth graders tended to specify that history refers to *important* events that happened *long ago*. They project a mythic quality to history, viewing it primarily as stories about very famous people in the very distant past (Egan, 1989). Most do not yet realize that history also includes the very recent past and the everyday lives of ordinary people.

Levstik and Pappas (1987) reported a tendency among fourth graders to cite wars, tragedies, or disasters as examples of historical content, but this was less noticeable in our KWL responses. Thirteen students did mention wars (unspecified); six mentioned particular wars; several mentioned Lincoln's assassination; and individuals mentioned the atomic bomb, Custer, and Hitler.

The majority of the examples concerned events in early U.S. history that had been emphasized in social studies units in earlier grades on Native Americans, the first Thanksgiving, pioneer life, or Columbus Day. Also, many of the responses concerned inventions (cars, baseball) or individuals who attained prominence for nonmilitary accomplishments (Betsy Ross, Ben Franklin).

Girls were more likely than boys to mention themes connected with everyday family living or people or events of particular relevance to women. Among specific individuals named, Betsy Ross was the only woman—mentioned by three girls but no boys. In addition, three girls but only one boy spoke of history as being about how people lived their everyday lives prior to key inventions; one girl mentioned women getting the right to vote as a key historical event; another girl mentioned the Ingalls family; and another girl mentioned family history as an aspect of history.

Most responses were conventional definitions or lists of examples. The following elaborated responses are worth noting because of what they reveal about the mind sets of fourth graders:

Boys
- The Indians didn't have stereos and CD players and stuff like that.
- I know about the name Pontiac, a fort. They were playing a game and they let the Indians in.
- Famous presidents who invented things. [Note conflation of presidents with inventors as categories of famous people.]

Girls
- It was a long time ago. The Native Americans had to give up some of their land.
- Long time ago. (There were no) cars and trucks and go-carts. People didn't have lots of money.
- History is about America and what happened in the past. It's about George Washington and the way to George Bush.

What the Students Wanted to Learn

Table 4.2 summarizes students' statements about what they wanted to learn about history. Most students named one or more specific things, although several did not respond, and 15 said only that they wanted to learn "everything," "a lot," or "all about" history.

Many students had difficulty answering this question. Some simply mentioned historical topics from earlier grades (Indians, Pilgrims, presidents, explorers, inventors), without identifying new topics that

Table 4.2 What Students Said They Wanted to Learn as They Began Fifth Grade

	Boys (N = 44)	Girls (N = 36)	Total (N = 80)
A. *General categories*			
1. Wars	12	9	21
2. Presidents	10	8	18
3. Everything/a lot/all about history	8	7	15
4. Indians	2	10	12
5. Dates (of specified events)	7	3	10
6. How people lived in the past	3	7	10
7. Explorers/discoveries	6	0	6
8. Inventors/inventions	3	1	4
9. Pilgrims	0	3	3
	51	48	99
B. *Specific vs. unspecified wars and presidents*			
1. Mentions wars in general	5	5	10
2. Specifies a particular war	7	4	11
3. Mentions presidents in general	3	7	10
5. Specifies a particular president	7	1	8
	22	17	39

they wanted to learn about. Others mentioned only a single, very specific item of information (what year George Washington became president, who sewed the first American flag). The majority of the most interesting and thoughtful ideas were included among the less conventional responses.

Boys

- How did history start? Why do we have history? Why did they call history *history?*
- What was the first school ever made and who made it?
- I would like to know more about sunken ships.
- I want to learn more about dinosaurs and Mother Nature.
- History about California. What made the Grand Canyon? When did California become a state?
- When did they put the faces on the mountain and a coin?
- What started the wars? Why did people take prisoners?
- Why did people have war? Why Hitler has so much power over people.

Girls

- Who was the first man in America? Were there really cave men and dinosaurs? When was history first discovered?

- How people survived when $15.00 was a lot of money. Could they make peace just by talking it out?
- People who lived long ago. Who were the presidents? What kind of things happened? How did they run businesses? How did the people farm?
- I would like to know if you had to do something famous or interesting to be in history or if it is just the way people lived and did things a long time ago. Or both? I'd like to learn about famous people.
- How people lived. What people ate for food. How people traveled.
- Why there were wars and why people are hostages. Why men had to be in the army. And women can't have jobs.
- Why did they fight at the time? What did the Indians do to the Pilgrims that made them mad? Why they invented the museum.

Interests ran to facts rather than explanations. There were a few "why" questions (mostly about war), but no curiosity about how historians gather and interpret information. A few students mentioned prehistorical times or the dawn of history, but none mentioned ancient civilizations, the Greeks or Romans, or any aspect of medieval or religious history. Girls expressed more interest in the everyday lives of ordinary people; boys more in the accomplishments of famous (male) presidents, explorers, and inventors.

What the Students Reported Learning

At the end of each unit, the KWL sheets were returned and students were asked to state what they learned. These responses cannot be treated as if they were test data because the room was still full of cues and reminders about unit content, most notably the names of key people, places, and events posted on the history bulletin board and samples of student projects displayed around the room. Many students looked at these and other cues as they filled out their postunit KWL sheets.

The postunit KWL responses mostly repeated key terms and ideas taught during the unit, so there is no need to present them in tables or discuss them in detail. Instead, we will summarize them briefly and discuss noteworthy qualitative aspects of the students' learning.

Typical responses following the first unit took one of two common forms. In the first form, the student simply listed key terms.

> I learned about a timeline. I learned what oral history is, inter-
> view, history, artifact, archeologist, secondary source, primary
> source, historian.

In the second form, the student selected some key terms and gave more
extensive definitions or statements.

> I learned that an artifact is an object from a long time ago. And I
> learned more about my own history. I also learned that a primary
> source is a firsthand experience and a secondary source is a sec-
> ondhand experience to something.

In addition or instead, some students mentioned learning about
their own personal histories or the project that involved collecting artifacts from their childhood. The following responses were noteworthy
for their completeness or the quality of their insights:

- I learned that there's a lot more to history than just wars and
  famous people.
- I learned history is more than what I thought. It can be about
  you, it can be told in oral form, which is out loud, or chronological order. It's also about wars, Indians, explorers, presidents. History isn't just famous people because I'm not famous but it can
  be about famous people.
- I learned about timelines. I learned that history can bring back
  memories and things that you did not even know. I learned that
  history can be fun. I learned more about archeologists. I learned
  about oral history and primary and secondary sources and I
  learned about other peoples and artifacts. I also learned that I
  want to be an archeologist!
- We made a timeline from the day we were born to 1990. We
  learned that a primary source is something that you saw and you
  write about. We learned that a secondary source is when I write
  about George Washington.

A few responses suggested limited or distorted learning. Some
were humorous, deliberately or otherwise (oral history is "something
passed down from the mouth"; oral history is "history told to someone
with vocal chords"; "we learned a lot of words that I can't spell"; "I
learned that if you don't turn in your work, you will get in trouble").
Several responses confused historians with archeologists, or primary
sources with secondary sources, and a few misconceptions persisted

("I learned that history is famous people and the way people lived a long time ago").

Interview Findings

We now turn to the findings from the interviews of the subsample of 10 students. Responses are presented in pairs or groups arranged to contrast the students' entry-level thinking with their thinking after exposure to the unit.

The high achievers (Jason, Tim, Teri, and Sue) generally spoke succinctly and to the point when they knew or thought they knew an answer but said little or nothing beyond "I don't know" when they did not. In contrast, the average (Mark, Brad, Helen, and Kay) and low achievers (Ned and Rita) tended to be more verbose. Usually, however, their lengthier responses were not qualitatively better than the high achievers' briefer ones. They simply took more words to say essentially the same thing that the high achievers said more economically. These findings may be related to those of Estvan and Estvan (1959), who noted a tendency for children being interviewed about social studies topics to take less time to respond, speak with more facility, and use fewer words, yet produce a greater number of ideas, when talking about familiar rather than unfamiliar topics. A second reason for the lengthier responses of the average and low achievers was that they usually were more willing to speculate if they were not sure of their answers.

Questions About History and Historians

1. *What is history?* Prior to the unit, Ned made no response and Brad guessed that history dealt with nature or wildlife. The other eight students indicated that history concerns people or events in the past, but seven specified that history refers to events that occurred long ago and four specified that history refers to noteworthy people or events.

Tim: It's stuff that happened a long time ago that's real good.
Sue: It's about what people did for our country a long time ago and the wars and stuff like that.

Following the unit, all 10 students indicated that history has to do with the past. Also, all 10 now included general definitions, not just examples. Thus, their responses were shorter, yet both more precise and at a higher level of generality (cf. Estvan & Estvan, 1959).

Only three students still said that history refers to events occurring *long ago,* and none still specified that history refers to *note-worthy* people or events. Thus, the students had acquired a more precise notion of history and most had cleared up some prior misconceptions.

Tim: Something that happened in the past. [A long time ago?] It could be a second ago.
Sue: Things that happened in the past.

2. *What do historians do?* Prior to the unit, six students could not answer, one guessed "famous people like George Washington," one said people who teach history, and two said people who study history.

Following the unit, four students gave generally correct answers (they read and study artifacts); four others gave partly correct answers but emphasized physical artifacts and confused historians with archeologists; and the other two didn't know. Two implied misconceptions were that physical artifacts, rather than written or printed materials, are the "stuff" of history and that historians work by reconstructing artifact puzzles rather than by constructing accounts from various (primarily written) sources.

Jason: Historians study history. They study artifacts. [Why? What are they trying to do?] Find out what happened. [Where do they get their information?] From books.
Helen: Historians are the people that study history, not underground. They find the stuff that's left above the ground, like an arrowhead. They look for artifacts and primary sources that they might have left over in the past.
Kay: They read and find out about the past.
Rita: They try to put the puzzle back together . . . they take the artifacts and they have more and they try to put them together. One digs and one puts the thing together.

The students' tendencies to confuse historians and archeologists might have been exaggerated by the fact that the following question preceded the question about historians in the postunit interviews.

2A. *Who are archeologists? What do they do?* All 10 students stated that archeologists dig for things that tell us about the past. All five of the boys, but only one of the girls, used technical terms (artifacts, fossils) to describe the material dug up by archeologists.

Ned: They're scientists and they study fossils and stuff they dig up from the ground.

Sue: People who find things from a long long time ago and they dig them up and look at them and see how long ago they were.

3. How do you think historians do their work—how do they find out about what happened and decide what to write? Prior to the unit, answers were generally sensible but frequently confused historians with archeologists. The higher achievers tended to emphasize interviewing and library research, whereas the lower achievers tended to emphasize physical artifacts and archeological digs.

Jason: Go looking for it where early people were. [Where would they look?] Library. Think about it and write what they think.

Sue: Maybe people back then wrote books about these people that saved their country or something, so they read some of the stuff that the people wrote and then wrote it in a book with a whole bunch of other people.

Following the unit, students showed much less confusion between historians and archeologists. Eight indicated that historians get information from written sources, four mentioned interviewing living witnesses, and only two mentioned archeological evidence.

Jason: They could look at the books.

Sue: Maybe things they dug up or things they studied from other people.

The students still tended to picture historians as interviewing people and working from primary sources more than they really do. They were vague about sources used to learn about what occurred prior to the twentieth century. Although eight mentioned books and two mentioned newspapers, none mentioned diaries, letters, or public records. Perhaps they did not yet realize how long written records have existed or the variety of such records that are available to historians.

4. Do you have your own personal history or life history? . . . When does it begin? (What was the first day of your life history?) Prior to the unit, Tim and Rita immediately answered "yes" and stated that their personal history began on the day that they were born. The other eight students initially said "no" or were unsure. However, all but Helen gave at least partly correct responses following probing. Several students seemed thrown by the notion of someone writing a history of them, and Jason initially misunderstood the question to be "Has your personal life history been written?"

Jason: No. I just have my work that my mom saves. [Stuff from school?] Yeah. [That's your life history?] Yes. [When do you think it first started?] When I was born.

Sue: No. [You don't? Why do you say no?] I don't know. [If somebody wanted to write a history of Sue, could they write one?] I don't know. [Is there anything to write?] I'm a swimmer. [If somebody was going to write your history, when would it begin?] Probably last year. [How come last year?] That's when I started really doing stuff and getting into sports. [If somebody wanted to write your total, complete history, though, even if it wasn't interesting, where would they start?] Probably when I was born.

Helen: What do you mean by that? [I'll put it this way. Do you have a life history?] I'm not really into that much. I like history, but it's not my life. [Let me see if I can rephrase that. You're how old?] Ten. [So from 10 years ago until now, there's all of that time. Is that like history, a history of your life?] I wouldn't say so. That's 10 years. History's gotta be more than that.

Three of the four students who answered Question 1 by specifying that history referred to *noteworthy* events in the past had difficulty with Question 4. Kay initially denied that she had a personal history because she didn't think that anything in her life was noteworthy enough to qualify as history, and Helen maintained this perception even after several probes. Sue initially suggested that a history of her life would begin not on her birthday but when she started accumulating sports accomplishments.

Helen's "I like history, but it's not my life" is our favorite quote from these interviews. We are not sure whether this was an ambiguously worded statement of the idea that nothing in her life as yet has been significant enough to qualify as history or, as we prefer to believe, it was a precocious expression of *fin-de-siecle* ennui!

Most of the earlier confusion had disappeared by the postunit interviews. Eight students immediately answered "Yes" when asked if they had a personal life history and went on to note that it began on the day they were born. Jason was still confused in the same way that he was in the preunit interview. Teri remained confused both about the notion of herself as a subject of history and about whether such history would begin at birth or would chronicle only noteworthy accomplishments. It is interesting that the only two students still partly confused about this question were high achievers.

Jason: No. [Why don't you have your own personal life history?] I don't really like to write. [You were born 10 or 11 years ago and since you were born up until right now, is kind of like your history. So when did it begin for you?] Ten years ago.

Teri: No. [You don't have anything that went on for you in the past?] No. [When did your life history begin?] When I made the school spelling bee. [How about when you were born?] I guess so.

Sue: Yes, in 1980.

Helen: Yes. [When did it begin?] 1980 when I was born.

Questions About the Value of Learning History

5. *Why do you think they teach history in school—why do they think you should study the past?* Prior to the unit, eight students said that history is taught "so you will know what happened in the past," without saying much about why this might be important to know. One suggested that you might need the information for school, and three that you might need it so you would not be embarrassed if someone asked you for it. Two thought that learning about history might be good preparation for jobs, but when probed about such jobs, could mention only being a history teacher or a historian.

Four students implied more general reasons for learning history than simply acquiring the specific knowledge taught. Brad suggested that it would help you to understand current events and predict the future, and Tim stated that it would help you to know more about yourself. Helen and Kay implied this same idea in stating that it would be helpful to know about the similarities and differences between your life now and your ancestors' lives in the past. Also, Sue's last idea is interesting and touching: People who did great things in the past would want modern people to remember and honor them for it, and we should.

Following the unit, most students still talked only about learning the specific information without giving good reasons why. Four basically said, "They teach it so you will know it." Two spoke of learning it in order to get good grades at school, one to get a job as a historian, and one to avoid embarrassment if people ask you historical questions.

Many of these answers were regressions from insights expressed in the preunit interviews. Brad still talked about the value of historical knowledge for projecting into the future, and Kay at least hinted about knowing the past as contributing to self-knowledge. However, Tim now said that he didn't know, and Helen spoke only about passing tests in school. The only new idea was Sue's notion that historical knowledge might help you to recognize artifacts that you discovered on your own.

Lake did not place much emphasis on the value of learning history in her initial unit. Even so, these regressions are troubling because she projected enthusiasm for history and tried to make it interesting for her students. Perhaps there is an inevitable loss of intrinsic interest in an area of knowledge once students begin to study it as a school subject.

6. How might learning about history help you in life outside of school, either now or in the future? Prior to the unit, four students could not respond even after probing. Three suggested that history knowledge might help you in a job, at school, or when others asked you questions. Brad and Tim suggested that knowing about the past might help you to understand or learn better today. Sue suggested that it might help you to recognize weaknesses or injustices that could be corrected by passing new laws.

Tim: If you were reading a book or something and you heard of this one guy, you might know about him.
Brad: I don't know . . . might help you know how you got here and how everything else got here.
Sue: Cause maybe if someone wanted something back then, maybe you could help them with doing it today. Maybe it was easier . . . if someone wanted a law in the country and it's still not here now, then maybe someone could carry it on and ask the people to make a law about that. . . . People that were important back then may have done something for our country like slaves, there are not slaves anymore, so somebody might have wanted the people not to be slaves so now there's no slaves.

Taken together, the students' preunit responses to Questions 5 and 6 indicated that most of them found history interesting and were looking forward to learning about it but had not yet come to understand that historical knowledge could give one perspective on personal identity or be useful in living one's everyday life or in thinking critically as a citizen. The typical purview was, "I don't know why we study it, but it must be important."

Following the unit, three students could not respond and the other seven once again had trouble identifying any uses for history outside of school. Mark, Brad, and Helen gave cultural literacy responses indicating that knowledge learned in school would help you to recognize and understand things encountered elsewhere (although in two cases the examples given were archeological artifacts). Brad and Kay saw at least interest value in knowing about important historical events that were linked to events in their own lifetimes. In a child-like way, they may have been groping with concepts such as identity or situating oneself in time and place.

Discussion

Most of the students viewed history as a collection of facts that might be interesting to know rather than as a subject for systematic study or personal reflection. Except for the few who had begun to wonder why people go to war or do some of the things that they do during wars, they had not yet begun to appreciate the potential of history for developing personal wisdom or insight into the human condition.

Most entered fifth grade knowing that history has to do with the past, although many thought that history is limited to the exploits of famous or important people or to events that occurred long ago, and some had trouble appreciating the notion that they themselves have personal histories. They did not know much about how historians work, tending to confuse them with archeologists and to picture them as working with excavated artifacts rather than written documents.

After the unit, their knowledge of and thinking about history was notably more sophisticated. Most now understood that history encompasses everything about the past, including the everyday lives of ordinary people in the recent past. They knew that they themselves had a personal history, having portrayed key events in their lives along a timeline. They were less prone to confuse historians with archeologists, as well as more aware of the range of sources that historians use to develop their interpretations.

However, the students failed to generate clear ideas about why they were learning history or how such learning might help them in their lives outside of school. Also, certain confusions or misconceptions persisted in some students, who still believed that history refers exclusively to events that occurred long ago, confused archeologists with historians, failed to appreciate that history is interpretive, or could not distinguish primary from secondary sources adequately.

The data suggest the need for teachers to stress two advantages to historical study that did not occur to most of these students. First, history can enhance one's quality of life. Learning about and reflecting on history can enhance one's sense of identity by helping one to "place oneself" within the broad sweep of human experience.

A second major advantage to studying history is its value as civic education. Equipped with knowledge about the probable trade-offs involved in various courses of action (based in part on knowledge about the outcomes that these courses of action have led to in the past), students will be better prepared to make good personal, social, and civic decisions.

Some interesting achievement level and gender trends appeared in the findings. Higher achieving students generally showed both more entry-level knowledge and (especially) more complete learning, although these differences were not as large as they tend to be with subjects that students have been studying for several years. Gender differences were more extensive. Boys focused more on great men and events, girls on family themes and conditions of everyday living. Students of both genders need to develop better appreciation of the fact that history is not just about famous individuals and events but also about changes in human customs, culture, and conditions of everyday living that have resulted from discoveries, inventions, and diffusion of knowledge. They also need more exposure to the accomplishments of specific females.

Along with data reported by Levstik and Pappas (1987) and McKeown and Beck (1990), our findings indicate that entering fifth graders are interested in history and already in possession of some accurate knowledge of the past. However, such children are vague about the interpretive nature of history and about the work of historians, and they need assistance in developing initial ideas about historical topics and in correcting various confusions and misconceptions. We believe that it is possible to address these problems and teach U.S. history to fifth graders in ways that emphasize understanding, appreciation, and application to life outside of school, but that doing so will require helping the students to see the value of history as a humanity and as preparation for citizenship, not just as miscellaneous facts to be memorized in case someone ever asks.

UNIT 2: NATIVE AMERICANS

Most fifth-grade U.S. history texts begin with a chapter or unit on Native Americans. It establishes a baseline for studying U.S. history by depicting the cultures and customs of tribal groups who were living in the Americas prior to the arrival of Columbus. Its content usually includes coverage of several contrasting tribal groups, selected to illustrate the variety of cultures that had developed in the Americas up until that time and, in particular, to combat the stereotyped image of Native Americans developed by most children growing up in the contemporary United States.

Ramsey, Holbrook, Johnson, and O'Toole (1992) found that 4-year-olds possessed cartoon-like (and partly cartoon-based) stereotypes of Indians, whom they pictured as wearing feathers or headdresses and often depicted as wielding tomahawks or engaging in acts of violence. These children also thought that Indians lived only in the past, and not in their hometown. The children then participated in a month-long curriculum on traditional and contemporary Native American life. This was effective in increasing the accuracy of their images of Native Americans, although they still tended to believe that Native Americans lived only in the past and not in their own town. Furthermore, some of them did not realize that the "Native Americans" discussed in the unit were the same people as the "Indians" that they had heard about in other settings. These children retained a negative and cartoon-like stereotype of "Indians" along with their newly acquired and more positive image of "Native Americans."

Also, a League of Women Voters (1975) study indicated that three-fourths of the kindergarten children interviewed described Indians as wearing feathers or animal-skin clothing, hunting with bows and arrows, or living in tipis. Twenty percent described them as mean and hostile, likely to kill or shoot people. These children also saw Indians as far removed from themselves in both space and time. Fifth graders interviewed in the same study provided much more encouraging responses, offering a more realistic view than the stereotypical images conveyed by kindergarteners. Even so, the fifth graders focused more on the past than the present, and they tended to describe the Plains tribes' characteristics as typical of Indians in general. Almost one-fourth were aware of reservations, but some thought that Native Americans were required to stay on reservations, and some appeared not to know that Native Americans also live in other places.

Lake's fifth graders usually did not have the "Plains tribes" stereotype because their fourth-grade Michigan history included study of tribal groups living in Michigan. Consequently, their prior knowledge about Native Americans was shaped at least as much by images of the Eastern Woodlands tribes as by images of the Plains tribes.

Lake's unit on Native Americans was more anthropological than historical. It set the stage for subsequent units by noting that Native

Americans have been living in the western hemisphere for at least 10,000 years, but its emphasis was on the variety of cultures found among Native American groups. Five main groups were studied: Eastern Woodlands, Northwest, Plains, Southwest, and California Coastal. For each group, information was given about one or more specific tribes and included attention to their means of addressing basic food, clothing, and shelter needs as well as unique aspects of their cultures.

Lake used dramatic re-enactment in the process of teaching students about the scientific analysis of artifacts. It was during this unit that she "discovered" the arrowhead that she had buried in a pile of sand on the floor. Then she went on to tell about how just such an arrowhead had been found by a cowboy named George McJunkin who recognized it as an ancient artifact and took it to a scientist named J. D. Figgins, who established that it was at least 10,000 years old.

KWL Findings

For this unit, the KWL sheet instructed students to tell what they knew about Indians and what they wanted to learn about them. KWL data were available for three class sections.

What the Students Knew About Indians

Table 4.3 indicates that every student made at least one substantive statement, and most made several. A few responses were confined to vague generalities (e.g., Indians lived in different groups and spoke different languages), but most communicated something specific, typically about methods of meeting basic needs through hunting, fishing, farming, constructing various forms of shelter, fashioning clothing from animal skins, or "surviving in the wild" generally. Some of these responses suggested a Plains tribes stereotype (tipis, buffalo hunting, nomadic relocations, etc.), but the majority either were phrased more generally or recognized a variety of lifestyles.

Most responses dealing with conditions of everyday life were expressed in neutral, descriptive language, but some (especially those emphasizing Indians' self-sufficiency in knowing how to live off the land) were delivered with stated or implied admiration. Positive views of Indians also were seen in some of the responses dealing with philosophy and religion, especially those that complemented Indians for being respectful of nature and avoiding waste.

Many students supplied historical information: Twenty-seven said that Indians were the first people to live in North America or that they

Table 4.3 What Students Said They Knew About Native Americans Prior to the Unit

	Boys (N = 39)	Girls (N = 35)	Total (N = 74)
A. Historical information			
1. Native Americans were the first people here/ lived long ago/have a long history	14	13	27
2. Pilgrims/Thanksgiving	5	7	12
3. Fought wars with Europeans	7	4	11
4. Lost their land/sent to reservations	0	2	2
5. Still living today	2	3	5
6. Also called Native Americans	7	4	11
7. Name "Indians" comes from "India"	4	4	8
8. Mistakenly named by Columbus	0	2	2
	39	39	78
B. Conditions of everyday life			
1. Self-sufficiency: Lived off land, knew how to survive, made everything they needed	8	12	20
2. Hunted, fished, trapped; used arrows, spears	21	22	43
3. Grew vegetables, gathered grains	7	9	16
4. Clothing simple, made from animal skins	3	10	13
5. Lived in tipis or wigwams	11	6	17
6. Lived in longhouses	3	5	8
7. Lived in log cabins, hogans, pueblos, huts, or igloos	5	3	8
8. Lived in different tribes/spoke different languages	11	6	17
9. Men and women had different roles	2	5	7
10. Were nomadic	2	3	5
11. Didn't have modern things	2	4	6
	75	85	160
C. Philosophy and religion			
1. Cherished sun, moon, and earth; believed that everything had a manitou or spirit	4	3	7
2. Ecological consciousness (avoided waste, hunted only what they needed to eat)	2	3	5
3. Believed that everything should be shared	1	0	1
	7	6	13
D. Physical features			
1. Dark skin, complexion	7	6	13
2. Red skin, complexion	3	1	4
3. Black hair	4	0	4
4. Long hair	1	1	2
	15	8	23

have lived here a long time, 12 described interactions between Indians
and the Pilgrims or recounted a version of the "first Thanksgiving"
story, and 11 mentioned that Indians were involved in wars with Europeans. Students whose responses were confined to such historical information displayed less knowledge about Native Americans than
those who talked about everyday life conditions or about philosophy
or religion.

Eight students noted that the name "Indians" comes from "India,"
although only two accurately explained the reason for this (i.e., that
Columbus called them Indians on the mistaken assumption that he
had reached the Indies). One thought that the Indians had come from
India originally, three thought that the Indians had named themselves
Indians, and the other two could offer no further explanation.

Finally, 23 responses dealt with Indians' perceived physical features: "dark," "brown," "tan," or "red" skin or complexion; black hair;
long hair.

There were no consistent differences between boys and girls in
their responses. The following are representative verbatim examples.

Boys

- They're from a long time ago. They had wars with the Englishmen. There are three Michigan tribes.
- They are called Native Americans. They live in wigwams and
  cones made out of birch bark. About manitous. They made everything by theirselfs.
- Indians talk different. They have dark skin. They use canoes.
  They hunt and farm a lot. They were friends to Pilgrims. They
  dress different and taught boys to hunt.
- Indians use canoes. They grew food. Indians only took what they
  needed. It was hard to live in the winter. They were all very different. That they ate pretty much whatever they can. They make
  arrowheads out of rocks. They build their houses out of tipis.
  They had huts for in the winter.

Girls

- Another name for Indians are Native Americans. They lived in
  tipis or longhouses. They used arrows and spears for weapons.
  They didn't have real clothes. Nothing fancy. Some didn't have
  clothes. The Native Americans are very, very old. They lived
  when the United States was just found. They killed animals for
  food and some grew crops. They had tipis or longhouses.
- Indians had to grow food, make houses, make supplies, kill their

own food. They had lots of wars and made the Thanksgiving dinner to the Pilgrims. The Indians helped the Pilgrims harvest the food.

- Native Americans used spears to go hunting for fish and other stuff. They used canoes. The boys and men went hunting and the girls and women went to pick rice and do other things. They speak in a different language. They didn't have shirts, pants, skirts, or shorts to wear. They had kind of dark skin. They didn't have any pencils or anything to write with. Lived in tipis. Lived in igloos. Lived long ago. Hunted food. Fished with sticks. Built things by hand. Made spears out of stones and sticks. Used animals for coats.

A few unique responses are worth noting.

- Most people are a little bit of Indians (i.e., have Indian ancestry).
- Most Indians live south.
- There's always an Indian chief.
- They were tricked and our government took their land.
- The children had to make their own toys and dolls.
- They believed everything had a god.
- They thought that everything had a purpose.
- They believed that everything should be shared—the wealthiest person was not the person with the most money but the nicest person.
- Some of the Indians played a game called blanket toes.
- They made glue out of deer feet.

What the Students Wanted to Learn

Table 4.4 summarizes students' ideas about what they wanted to learn about Indians. Twenty-one mentioned general categories of information (the names of the different groups, where they lived, when they lived, or how they lived), 10 the games they played or what they did for fun, six how they made their weapons, and five how they built their homes.

Responses in the first two categories of Table 4.4 suggest that many students had acquired a frame of reference or paradigm for studying cultural groups. In rationalizing the expanding communities approach to curriculum organization, Hanna (1963) recommended that students study the ways in which people in each community carry out nine basic human activities: protecting and conserving life and resources;

Table 4.4 What Students Said They Wanted to Learn About Native Americans

	Boys (N = 39)	Girls (N = 35)	Total (N = 74)
A. *General responses*			
1. As much as I can/all I don't know	6	2	8
2. Different Indian names and tribes	2	6	8
3. When they lived	1	1	2
4. Where they lived	3	1	4
5. Their customs/how they lived	3	4	7
	15	14	29
B. *Categories of basic facts*			
1. Games/recreation/what they did for fun	4	6	10
2. Their languages/how they communicated	2	1	3
3. Wars	0	2	2
4. Their homes	1	1	2
5. Their food	0	2	2
6. Their clothes	0	2	2
7. Women's clothes and jewelry	0	3	3
8. Their boats	1	0	1
9. Their holidays and celebrations	1	1	2
10. Their religion	0	1	1
	9	19	28
C. *Specific factual questions*			
1. When did they come to America?	0	1	1
2. Where did they come from?	1	1	2
3. How many were there in the 1600s and 1700s?	1	0	1
4. When did they live to? (Child does not know that Indians survive today)	1	0	1
5. How long were they in Michigan?	0	1	1
6. Did they have grandchildren?	1	0	1
7. Did they pass down information about what life was like back then?	1	0	1
8. Are any still alive today?	2	0	2
9. Where do they live today?	0	1	1
10. Do they still live in the forest in the same ways they used to?	1	0	1
11. Did they like/get along with most other Indians?	0	2	2
12. Were they mean or did they share?	0	1	1
13. What did they do when the white men came?	0	1	1
14. Did they invent the gun?	1	0	1
15. Did they use guns?	1	0	1
16. How did they become friends with the white people?	0	1	1
17. How long did the average Indian live?	1	0	1
18. What did they use for money?	1	0	1
19. What were their marriage customs?	2	0	2
20. What did they do during the winter?	1	0	1
21. How did they get seeds for planting?	1	1	2
22. Were they ever slaves?	0	1	1
23. How did they pick their chiefs?	0	1	1
24. How big were their tipis—how many beds did they have?	0	1	1
25. How did they live without stores and food markets?	0	1	1
26. Did they build huts or wigwams on the water?	1	0	1
27. Did they go ice fishing?	1	0	1
28. What events happened in their lives?	0	1	1
29. What kind of people are they?	0	1	1
30. Do they really go to the bathroom in the water?	0	1	1
31. Do they put grease in their canoes?	1	0	1

Table 4.4 (*Continued*)

32. Where did they get their utensils?	1	0	1
33. What did they do with extra animal skins?	1	0	1
34. What special things were used by individual tribes?	0	1	1
35. What did the tribe leaders do to expect effort in how the other Indians worked?	0	1	1
36. What artwork did they make?	0	1	1
	21	20	41

D. *Questions about processes and skills*

1. How did they make their weapons?	3	3	6
2. How did they start fires, cook?	2	1	3
3. How did they build their homes?	3	2	5
4. How did they make their canoes?	1	0	1
5. How did they make their clothes?	0	2	2
6. How did they make their dishes?	0	1	1
7. How did they hunt?	2	0	2
8. How did they grow their food?	1	0	1
9. How did they survive in the wild?	1	1	2
10. How did they make up their languages?	0	1	1
11. How did they write letters?	0	1	1
12. How did they make medicines/cure?	1	2	3
13. How did they teach their children?	0	1	1
	14	15	29

E. *Questions calling for explanations*

1. Why did the Indians come to America?	1	0	1
2. How did they survive so long without Americans?	1	0	1
3. Why are they called Native Americans?	2	0	2
4. How did they become Native Americans?	0	1	1
5. Why are they called Indians?	0	1	1
6. Why can't we call the people in India Indians instead of calling Native Americans Indians?	0	1	1
7. Why did they help the Pilgrims?	0	1	1
8. Why didn't they kill the Pilgrims?	1	0	1
9. Why did they have to fight?	0	1	1
10. Why did they scalp Americans?	1	0	1
11. What was war paint for?	1	0	1
12. Why did the French act so stuck up toward the Indians and why were some of the Indians not very nice either?	0	1	1
13. Why did we run them out of Michigan?	0	1	1
14. Why are there still Native Americans living today?	0	2	2
15. How did they get so good at hunting?	1	0	1
16. How did they learn to cook, build, fish, hunt—to be so intelligent?	0	1	1
17. Why did they have such strange names?	1	0	1
18. Why did they wear feathers in their hair?	2	0	2
19. Why did they worship the sun and rain?	1	0	1
20. Why did they have rain dances?	1	0	1
21. Why did they migrate south in America?	1	0	1
22. Why did they have totem poles?	2	0	2
23. Why did they have chiefs?	1	0	1
24. Why did they decide to name November 22 as Thanksgiving Day?	0	1	1
25. Why are they dark tan colored?	0	1	1
26. Why did they wear such odd clothing and do such odd things during celebrations?	0	1	1
	17	13	30

producing, exchanging, and consuming goods and services; transporting goods and people; communicating facts, ideas, and feelings;
providing education; providing recreation; organizing and governing;
expressing aesthetic and spiritual impulses; and creating new tools,
technology, and institutions. Similarly, Fraenkel (1980) suggested that
systematic study and comparison of societies could be facilitated by
asking who the group of people were, when and where they lived, what
things they left behind that tell us something about them, what kinds
of work they did and where they did it, what objects they produced,
what they did for recreation, what family patterns they developed, how
they educated their young, how they governed and controlled society,
their customs and beliefs, their problems and how they attempted to
deal with them, and the special events, individuals, or ideas that they
are known for. Most of these categories of information about societies
listed by intellectual leaders in social studies were represented in the
students' questions. Apparently, several years of social studies instruction had developed in some students paradigms for organizing their
thinking and gathering of information about cultural groups.

The questions in the remaining sections of Table 4.4 range from
the naive and occasionally humorous to the well informed and occasionally deep. Some reveal confusions or misconceptions. At least one
student believed that Indians had become extinct, and several wondered if any Indians survive today. One did not realize that people in
India also are called Indians, and another believed that the Indians decided to name November 22 as Thanksgiving Day. Others knew that
some Indians have survived, but did not know about how they live
today or wanted to know more about how they survived without modern inventions and conveniences.

Several students wanted to know more about the reasons for conflict between the Indians and various European groups. Underlying
several of these questions was a concern about why people frequently
are not able to solve their conflicts without escalating to wars.

What the Students Reported Learning

Postunit KWL responses were more differentiated and better organized
(around the notion of five main groups that lived in different areas and
had contrasting customs). The students had learned to think about Native Americans within the context of their own times and cultures,
not just in terms of how they interacted with Europeans or how their
everyday life conditions contrasted with those of today. Conspicuously
absent from the *L* responses were mentions of the Pilgrims, Thanksgiv-

ing, or wars with Europeans. The only non-Indians mentioned were McJunkin and Figgins, by students who retold the flint arrowhead story.

Almost three-fourths of the students noted that there were different groups of Native Americans, and the majority named the five groups and talked about their artifacts or practices. Most of what they said was valid as far as it went, although it rarely included explanations for the artifacts or customs. For example, only a couple of students mentioned that shelter construction methods were influenced by the climate and natural resources of the region, and none mentioned that tipis were well adapted to the nomadic lifestyle of the Plains tribes.

Historical information was provided by 22 students. Seven repeated the flint arrowhead story. The rest stated that Indians had migrated over 10,000 years ago, had come from Asia, or had crossed an ice bridge.

Finally, 15 students spoke about Native Americans today. Ten mentioned that they had learned that Native Americans still survive today. Six said that modern Native Americans live the same way as everyone else, but one said that they "are all a lot different than us."

The following are illustrations of the students' *L* responses.

Boys

- I learned that there are five different Indian groups: Plains, Northwest, Southwest, Eastern Woodlands, California Coastal. George McJunkin found the first flint arrowheads and gave them to J. D. Figgins. The flint arrowhead proves people were alive 10,000 years ago.
- Not all Indians live in tipis. Only Plains. There is five groups of Indians. Not all Indians are dead. Indians are just like you and me.
- They crossed the ice bridge. There were five regions. Wampums were a kind of currency. They made seed medallions. Chinook tribe was named after Chinook salmon. They told lots of legends. They were here 10,000 years ago.
- I learned that Indians used a lot of animal skin. I learned that the Eastern Woodlands made wampums. The Indians' canoes came out of birch bark. I learned that they came from India and traveled over the ice bridge. I learned that there are five different regions and a lot of different tribes in each region. I learned Indians would thank the animals and thank the spirits when they shot an animal. They would worship spirits, but when there wasn't any food or rain they knew the spirits were angry.

Girls

- They lived in longhouses, tipis, thatched huts, pueblo and ho-
gans. They were separated in regions. There was the Southwest,
Northwest, California Coastal, Plains, and Eastern Woodlands.
The Indians that lived in our area mostly hunted for deer.
- I learned that there are five different tribes. They made seed medallions and that the Indians still live today. They make up legends. The Eastern Woodlands lived in longhouses. Plains used
travois and lived in tipis.
- I learned that they made their canoes out of birch bark and I
learned the names of some of their tribes. And acorns was some
of their favorite foods. Some of them made totem poles and during the ice age they crossed over the Bering Strait.
- I learned that Native Americans got here by crossing over the
Bering Straits and about George McJunkin finding the flint arrowhead. And about the Plains living in tipis. The California
Coastals ate acorns, made baskets, and made necklaces out of
shells. The Chinook tribe lived in the plank houses, ate the Chinook salmon, held potlatch festivals, and made totem poles. The
Eastern Woodlands made wampums and were farmers.

The following unique comments are worth noting:

- The Indians weren't ever slaves.
- Indians are very interesting–neat. They made all kinds of things.
- I bet if all the groups went together, the whites would never have
taken America from the Indians.
- I thought they were interesting people.
- Guns were thunder to the Indians. That's why all the game was
gone.

One student identified herself as Indian. Her KWL responses show
that she expressed pride in her heritage before the unit began and that
the information she learned during the unit reinforced and enriched
her positive ethnic identity.

K: I know most Indians lived in longhouses and eat deer mostly. I
know they were the first people in America and taught Pilgrims
how to plant corn and trap game. How to build homes.
W: How they learned to cook, build, fish, and hunt and how they
were so intelligent and why they helped the Pilgrims and why
they had to fight.

L: The Indians really did live a very exciting life and lots of things they did were similar about them. They had a form of money called wampum. It was also used as a decorative belt and very beautiful indeed. They made beautiful totem poles in many different ways. I'm also Indian and it is exciting to learn what Indians did long ago. It helps me to know what they did long ago. Some kinds of homes they lived in were tipis, longhouses, plank houses, thatched houses, and adobes and many other kinds I like.

Interview Findings

Questions About the Timeline

We now turn to the interview data from the subsample of 10 students.

1. How long have the Native Americans lived in North America? Prior to the unit, six students responded. Three guessed between 150 and 600 years ago and the other three guessed 1,000 or 2,000 years ago.

In the postinterview, all 10 students said "10,000 years" or more, although it is not clear how meaningful a concept of 10,000 years they possessed.

2. We know that Native Americans have lived here for at least 10,000 years, but how *do we know that? What is the evidence?* Prior to the unit, Teri couldn't answer and Tim guessed that people have passed down history from those who lived 10,000 years ago. The other eight students spoke of finding and dating artifacts. These responses implied at least four theories of the dating process: Scientists could tell how old the artifacts were by using machines (unexplained further), by the degree to which bones were fossilized, by the degree of fragility of bones, or by writing found on the artifacts. None of the students specifically mentioned arrowheads.

Postunit answers to this question testify to the power of the teacher's dramatizing as a way to help students remember key historical facts. Eight students recounted the essence of the flint arrowhead story. The other two mentioned arrowheads among artifacts that provide information about how long Native Americans have lived here. The students still were vague or confused about how artifacts are dated. Three thought that flint existed 10,000 years ago but no longer exists today, and one guessed that scientists could tell how old an arrowhead was by "researching it and by the marks and stuff that's on it."

Brad: From an arrowhead they found that existed 10,000 years ago. George McJunkin found it and J. D. Figgins told him that. [How did they know the arrowhead was that old?] Flint existed 10,000 years ago and the arrowhead was made out of flint.

Helen: There was a cowboy and his name was George McJunkin and he found the first flint arrowhead and he took it to this scientist J. D. Figgins and he found out it was 10,000 years old. So there must have been people here 10,000 years ago. [How did they know the arrowhead was 10,000 years old?] The scientists have a research center and they tested it.

Questions About Native American Culture and Customs

3. What do you know about the Native Americans—about how they lived, what they did? . . . Tell me what you know about them. Prior to the unit, eight students reported a variety of beliefs. Most of these were valid and implied respect for or empathy with Native Americans along with some knowledge about them.

Most responses dealt with food, shelter, and conditions of everyday living, noting that Native Americans lacked modern conveniences but crediting them for their skillfulness in living off the land. Even students who mentioned conflicts with Europeans described Native Americans neutrally or in ways that indicated empathy with their point of view. None projected negative or cartoon-like stereotypes.

Jason: They lived here a long time ago. They weren't as greedy as we were.

Mark: When the Pilgrims came, they showed them how to grow corn and some other stuff and they brought food for the first Thanksgiving.

Brad: They were in tribes and they hunted a lot for their food. They didn't have houses like us. They had to make everything themselves out of what they had there and there wasn't any electricity when they lived and they carved things and lived in little tipis. They didn't have warm clothes like we do. [What were their clothes like?] They didn't have much for clothes. They had moccasins that were hand sewn together and they had little shorts and things.

Teri: Well, they lived in longhouses and some other places and they had this big banquet and they hunted a lot for food and for skins. They never hunted for fun and they lived long ago.

Kay: They planted lots of fields of corn. They had canoes. Tipis. They made their food by themselves. They didn't go out to the store and buy it. [Did they have stores?] No. Not like we have stores. [So they'd have to make everything themselves?] Yeah, gather it and make it and grow it.

Rita: I read a book about them, *The Sign of the Beaver*. The book said they built things out of wood and then they'd hunt and the girls wouldn't be able to eat until the men were done eating. [Why was that? Why did they have to wait?] Because the men told them to and the men thought that was right. On TV they said that they would chop off their scalps. [Who chopped off whose scalps?] The Indians chopped off the white men's scalps. And then they put it on their belts and stuff. [Why did they do that?] Just for victory, I guess, plus the white men were stealing their land. [Oh. Stealing the Native Americans' land?] Yup. [And the Native Americans were there first?] Yeah. And they said, "This is my land." They were cheating them too. [Who was cheating whom?] The white men were cheating the Indians. [How were they doing that?] They were saying "Just sign right here," and they'd put an X and then the white men would steal the land then. If they got the guys to sign it, then they could have the land. [You said before that they built different things out of wood. What did they build out of wood?] They built fences for their villages and they built tipi poles and then they built things . . . there's this one book that I read and it said that some of the Indians used to find a fork, a branch with two things . . . they'd find two of them and then they'd find a straight stick and then they'd put it in between the forks and then you can build a fire and put a pot, hang it on the thing, then you can cook whatever.

Only five students supplied the word "tribes" in response to probing, and only three could name specific tribes (mostly tribes mentioned in their Michigan history unit in fourth grade). None could make specific comparisons between tribes.

Tim: They had different chiefs, different families—like one family would start their own tribe.

Mark: Some might live in huts and some might live in tipis. They might have different legends about things.

Kay: Some had different ways of living. They probably hunted different kinds of meat that they liked, so they hunted different kinds. Some probably grew lots of corn and food and some probably didn't grow as much because they didn't have enough.

Rita: Some eat some foods, some go after buffalo, some just go after the beaver. Some are vegetarians, I think. Some are just normal. [What's normal?] They didn't move. They stayed and ate whatever they could find and they grew, just like everybody else.

The students studied five tribal groups during the unit, but we did not ask them to compare all five groups in the postunit interviews. Instead, we asked them to focus on the two largest groups (Eastern Woodlands and Plains). The Eastern Woodlands group included the Michigan tribes that the students had studied in fourth grade. The Plains group included the tribes whose customs provided the basis for the Indian stereotype projected in movies and television programs about the Old West.

Except for Rita, who got mixed up and started talking about the customs of the tribes of the Pacific Northwest, all of the students supplied at least two facts about the Eastern Woodlands tribes. They understood the main point that these tribes farmed, fished, and hunted locally but did not migrate to follow buffalo or other game animals. Even so, five included incorrect notions (that they lived in tipis, used totem poles, etc.).

Ned: They made birch bark canoes ... they made baskets or totem poles. [What else?] Maybe clothes and maybe hunting. [What did they hunt for?] Birds and deer.

Helen: They lived in longhouses and they made canoes out of birch bark wood and they fed on corn and stuff from crops and if they wanted an acorn, they'd have to chop down a tree with some kind of tool made from horns of an animal. They'd chop it down and make canoes and their houses out of it and tools out of the birch bark.

Sue: The Eastern Woodlands Indians used canoes to get around and the tribe was the Iroquois tribe and they built longhouses that could fit up to 10 families of Indians.

All 10 students supplied at least one fact about the Plains tribes, and five supplied at least four facts. Five students (four of them boys) also made incorrect statements. Only Mark, Brad, Kay, and Rita understood the major point that the Plains tribes hunted and followed the buffalo.

Tim: They lived in the middle of the U.S. .... it was just flat land and they did a lot of farming.

Mark: They lived in tipis so they could move with the buffalo and they built travois to carry their goods on. [What's a travois?] It's something that they made out of two long sticks and buffalo hide. [How did they work?] The Indians took one end and dragged the other end so it would move. [What did they move with it?] Their food. [Why did they move around a lot?] They hunted buffalo.

Helen: The Plains Indians lived in North Dakota and South Dakota area. They had things called travois and they moved to another area and they'd put their stuff on travois and then they could carry it along with them. [Why were they moving?] Like if the Europeans came over and destroyed their land, they'd want to move somewhere else. [What were the travois?] They were two sticks and buffalo skin in between. They shot buffalo and ate that. That was their favorite food—buffalo.

Rita: They used travois to carry their goods. [What are travois?] They're two sticks and a piece of leather holding them together and they can put their food and all their belongings on that. They lived in tipis and they hunted buffalo. They put different kinds of paint on their tipis to make their gods happy.

Some incorrect responses reflected reasoning based on the "Plains" designation for the tribal group. Tim took the term to mean flat lowland, so he assumed that the Plains tribes were farmers, perhaps in Iowa or Nebraska. In contrast, Ned assumed that the Plains tribes lived in Montana, Colorado, and Wyoming, so he suggested that they hunted mountain leopards or moose.

Even most of the students who showed awareness of the importance of the buffalo to the Plains tribes still thought that these tribes engaged in at least some farming. They did not yet understand hunting and gathering societies, so they often suggested that tribes moved because their land was farmed out or because of pressure from Europeans, rather than primarily because they needed to follow the buffalo. The following conversation with Brad illustrates how gaps in understanding and misconceptions were frequently in evidence even when the students were discussing topics about which they had acquired considerable knowledge.

They lived in tipis because they did a lot of traveling. [Why did they travel so much?] The land didn't have much on it and if they used what they had, they'd go to another place and use that. [Where did the Plains Indians live?] If you folded the United States in half, the Plains Indians would be right on that fold. [How is the land different from the Eastern Woodlands area?] The

Eastern Woodlands had a lot of trees and stuff and didn't have clear land but the Plains you might see 20 trees or so in the area and they didn't have much for growing stuff and they used every part of the buffalo. They'd use the skin for clothing, or afghans or covering when they're sleeping and sometimes they'd use it for a pot. They'd put four sticks in the ground and they'd make a little pot. They'd use the bones for necklaces and tool handles. They also followed the buffalo from one place to another because the buffalo had to go to a new place to get their food, too. . . . There were a lot of buffalo and one could last for 3 weeks for three families. There's a lot of meat. [How would they hunt them?] Bows and arrows and spears. [Did the Plains Indians have other kinds of food too?] They'd have deer and wild berries and I'm not sure, but I think they gardened a little bit. . . . [What was special about tipis?] They could use tipis because they're compatible. You can take the sticks down and roll them up and put them on your horse and you can always get more sticks to put it back up. If you had something like a longhouse, it takes time. You carve your totem poles out and you cut the wood and put them together and cut the joints out. Longhouses were really big. They held like eight families. [Why didn't the Eastern Woodlands Indians use tipis?] They might have. There's two kinds of tipis. One you put skin around and one where you use bark. [So they could have used the kind with the bark?] Yeah. [How did the Plains Indians get around?] They'd walk or ride on a horse. [Did they always have horses?] They might have rode the buffalo too.

4. *Some Native American groups lived in the same place all the time, but others packed up and moved to a different place several times each year. Do you know why they kept moving?* Prior to the unit, eight students supplied 10 substantive responses: four that the tribes moved to find new or better land, three that they were forced to move by Europeans, and three that they sought more animals or better hunting. None mentioned following the buffalo, although Rita suggested that "the animals" (unspecified) would move south for the winter and the tribes would follow them.

Nine students responded following the unit. Six mentioned following the buffalo as the reason for nomadic movements, but seven (including four of the first six) mentioned moving to find new or better land. The students had learned that the Plains tribes followed the buffalo, but several of them still thought of them as farmers in addition to or instead of buffalo hunters.

Tim: The Plains Indians made tipis because they traveled a lot. [Why did they travel a lot?] Probably to go find more farmland. [Did the buffalo have anything to do with them living in tipis?] Yeah, because they had guys just to go out and hunt herds of buffalos with spears and horses. [What did that have to do with the tipis?] If they were hunting for a couple of days, they'd have a place to stay. They were easy to tear down and you could just pack them like tents.

Mark: The Plains Indians had to move and they didn't want to build new houses. They had tipis and they could just take those down and go and move. [Why didn't the Woodlands Indians move around?] Because there were a lot of forests and the deer kept coming in and different game stayed there.

Helen: For the buffalo. [Why did the Woodlands stay in one place?] For the deer.

Kay: Their crops might have died and they wanted a new place to grow ... the Woodlands had trees and stuff that they could take food from but the Plains Indians had a big piece of flat land and not many trees, so they moved around to get new crops and find more food. [They also ate the buffalo?] Yeah. [Would they also go to new places to find buffalo?] Well, the buffalo I think stayed in one place, but they wanted new crops, so they'd move around.

5. How did the Native Americans get to the next place when they moved? Prior to the unit, nine of the students mentioned horses, and three mentioned canoes. None mentioned travois.

Following the unit, five students said that the Eastern Woodlands tribes used horses and six that they used canoes. Four said that the Plains tribes used horses and seven that they used travois. Thus, the students had learned that the Eastern Woodlands tribes relied heavily on river travel using canoes but the Plains tribes mostly traveled over land using travois. Only Tim, Teri, and Rita realized that the Native Americans had to get along without horses until they were introduced to the continent.

Tim: Wagons with horses pulling it. [Any other ways?] Just a bunch of horses. [What about the Woodlands Indians?] Just horses. [Did the Indians always have horses?] No. [How did they get around before they had horses?] Walk.

Rita: The Plains got around with the travois before the white men came and they'd drag it behind them. The Eastern Woodlands, they just walked. [If the Eastern Woodlands Indians wanted to go farther, did they have any way of getting from one place to another besides walking?] Not before the horses came.

6. Why did some Native Americans live in tipis instead of other kinds of homes? Prior to the unit, only Brad and Kay stated the key idea that tipis were easy to put up, take down, and transport. Ned had part of this idea but did not connect it to travel. Tim and Mark also offered guesses.

Tim: Maybe to store food and stuff and then they used the huts in the winter.
Mark: Tipis have open tops, and if you wanted a fire in one, the smoke wouldn't linger around in the place. It would just go through the top.
Brad: They didn't have the things that we have to make bricks and carved-out wood and stuff. They didn't have machines. The tipis would probably be easy to put up and when they moved, they could probably take them down pretty easy.
Ned: They're smaller and you don't have to use as much animal skin and wood. [Any other reason why they would want to have tipis instead of longhouses?] No.
Kay: Because they could take it down and take it with them.

Following the unit, seven students stated that tipis were used because they were easy to put up and take down. Three of the girls suggested instead that the Plains tribes lacked lumber or knowledge about how to construct longhouses. Jason (and perhaps others) thought that these tribes felled and trimmed new trees to use as lodge poles each time they moved, not realizing that the lodge poles doubled as travois supports and thus were moved too.

Ned: Because they traveled on big hunting trips and they traveled around a lot. [Why was the tipi good for that?] Because it's smaller than a longhouse.
Sue: The Plains lived in tipis. Maybe they didn't have the lumber to build other houses or else they never heard of those and were used to making tipis. [Did tipis have any special kinds of features that helped the Plains Indians?] They drew something on it to tell a story.
Kay: They could move the tipis around. They could just take the sticks down and get their leather and move easier for the Indians

who moved a lot. Indians who lived in longhouses usually stayed in one spot.

Questions About Legends

The unit emphasized the importance of legends, both to Native Americans themselves (as mechanisms for passing on religious and philosophical traditions) and to historians (as sources of historical and cultural information).

7. *Tell me what you know about Native American legends.* Prior to the unit, six students stated the essential idea that legends are stories passed on from long ago, and Tim had a partial understanding of this notion. The other three students could not respond.

Jason: Something that happened a long time ago.
Tim: Somebody that does something, like a hero . . . he does something good. . . . [Is it a book or a story or . . . ?] It's a person.
Mark: Stories that have been passed from generation to generation.
Sue: Well, they're things that are maybe true or partly true.
Kay: It's something that people say happened long ago.

Following the unit, eight students described legends as myths or stories passed along from one generation to the next. Ned and Helen confused legends with totem poles, because they had been taught that the carvings on totem poles represented symbols or historical events associated with the family.

Jason: They were myths. It's what the Indians thought were true. [About what?] Like the sun and the stars.
Mark: There was one legend about the stars in the sky. There was one about how corn grew and there was one about the North Star.
Sue: Well, they didn't understand some of the things, so they just came up with some things that would explain it. Our teacher told us something about the stars and the moon, where this guy had crystals and he put them in stars to make the Little Dipper and the Big Dipper. The fox always wanted to trick them, so he took the rest of the little ones and threw them up there and the next night the guy that put them up there couldn't find any of the shapes he put up there before, so he went to bed and then the fox came again and he had a last big crystal and he threw it up there and it was the moon.

Kay: The legends were for what the Indians thought. Thunder—they thought the gods were mad. They told what they thought and they told everybody what they thought it was.

8. *Why were legends important to the Native Americans?* Prior to the unit, six students offered tentative responses or guesses. Four interpreted legends merely as entertainment, and none described them as vehicles for maintaining cultural traditions.

Brad: Something they'd do for spirits or sometimes they'd do it for fun.
Ned: So people could tell them how to make bows and arrows, and hammers and axes.
Sue: Because they didn't have TV back then and the only thing they did for entertainment was tell stories.

Postunit responses indicated considerable growth in knowledge about Native American legends. Four students still described legends as entertainment, but five mentioned their role in providing explanations for natural phenomena.

Mark: Because when they told legends they thought that's how the stars and North Star and corn got there.
Brad: To kind of tell us and themselves how they got there.
Sue: Because they didn't understand some things and they didn't have TV, so they had to tell something to entertain themselves.

8A. *Tell me what you know about totems and totem poles. Why were they important to the Native Americans?* This question was asked only following the unit. Responses differed in degrees of accuracy and detail, but all 10 students understood that totem poles were not merely decorative but functioned to preserve family or tribal history. However, none connected this with the lack of written language.

Jason: They told the history of the family.
Brad: The Northwest Indians used totem poles to tell a story about a good hunt or their family. [Why was this important to them?] I'm not sure. Just for design or something.
Ned: They tell stories or legends about Indian tribes or families. They might carve animals in it or maybe masks.
Teri: They built them right next to their houses. They told about what

happened in their life, and they bring back the past or something like that.

Sue: They told a legend or a story. Each family would build one of them in front of their house and it would tell a story or legend about the family that lived in that house.

Questions Calling for Comparisons of Native Americans with Europeans

The next set of questions addressed the students' knowledge about the similarities and differences in cultures and life conditions of the Native Americans and the Europeans "back then." In the preunit interview, the students were asked a single open-ended question inviting them to compare Native Americans with Europeans. In the postunit interview, this question was replaced with a series of questions that called for more specific information. We were interested in the degree to which the students were aware of the following differences: (1) Europe was densely populated and included many large cities, but America was thinly populated; (2) Europeans had books and libraries but the Native Americans did not (because they did not have written language); and (3) Europeans tended to practice monotheistic religions and go to churches, whereas the Native Americans practiced pantheistic religions and conducted ceremonies in their homes or outdoors.

9. How were the Native Americans different from the Europeans who came to North America later? Prior to the unit, eight students mentioned differences in skin color, language, or religion that were described neutrally (i.e., simply as differences, rather than as advantages held by one group over the other). In addition, four mentioned European advantages in clothing, ships, or housing construction, and two mentioned Native American advantages in farming or survival knowledge.

Tim: They dressed different. The Indians didn't really wear a lot of clothes and the English would wear fancy clothes. The Indians would wear something made of skins. . . . They had black skin and white skin.

Mark: The Pilgrims and the Indians dressed a lot different and their boats were different. The Indians had canoes and the whites had big old ships.

Kay: The Europeans came to America and they didn't find any food and they didn't know how to grow anything. The Indians helped the Pilgrims get food and stuff and then they had Thanksgiving dinner and they had a lot of wars.

Rita: They were white and those were tannish. It didn't really matter, but it mattered to them. They wanted to tell them, share their gods with them. [Who?] The settlers. They wanted to show their god to the Native Americans because they didn't think they had gods. But they did.

9A. Were there any Native American cities? Following the unit, nine students stated that the Native Americans lived in small groups or villages rather than in cities. None cited reasons such as the development of specialized occupations, money-based economies, or trade. Instead, they suggested that the Native Americans lacked the knowledge or materials needed to construct large buildings, that different tribes could not communicate or get along with one another and thus preferred to live apart, or that the Native Americans liked to live in the open spaces or needed hunting grounds and thus could not stay in one place.

Mark: No, but they might now. There weren't cities back then. [Why not?] They didn't have the right materials. [What were they missing?] Steel. [Any other reason that they didn't make cities?] I think it was the California Coastal that if certain tribes went off into other tribes' grounds, they'd get shot or killed. They had to stick in their own villages. [How big were the villages?] Not very big. [Thousands of people?] Less than that.

Brad: No, they didn't have cities, they had villages. [Villages are what?] A tribe would live in their homes. They wouldn't have stores to go to, so it really wouldn't be a city. . . . [Why didn't they all live together like we do?] They just separated themselves from their own kind.

Teri: No . . . they just lived in scattered places. [Big groups or small groups?] Big groups in scattered places. [Why didn't they live in cities?] I guess the Indians just wanted to have more space to grow crops or something.

Helen: Not that we studied about. [Why don't you think they had cities like we have today?] There were no such things. No stores, no fashion clothes, no streets. [Why not?] Because only Native Americans lived back then and there were no schools and you had to go to school to learn about this stuff. [Why didn't they just make cities?] They didn't have the right equipment. They needed paint and they had to know how to make chimneys. . . . [Why didn't they put a bunch of longhouses together and make a city?] They liked their space. The tribes didn't mix together very well.

Rita: No, there would be one group and then another group and then another group. All the people would talk different languages, so if they wandered into the next village and tried to talk to somebody, the people would say, "What are you talking about?"

9B. Did the Native Americans have libraries? All 10 students knew that the Native Americans did not have libraries, but only six said that this was because they did not have written language. Mark and Kay stated that there were no books back then, so that the people had to rely on their memories. It is not clear whether they realized that the Native Americans did not have written language or instead thought that they did not have books simply because the technology for producing books had not been developed yet. Brad and Rita believed that the Native Americans had books, although they knew that they did not have libraries.

Jason: No. [Why not?] They didn't know how to write.

Mark: No, they didn't have books back then. [Where did they keep their information?] They had to remember it.

Brad: No. They didn't have the right tools. They kind of did, but they didn't know that they could. They had the materials but they didn't know how to use them. [So they didn't have books?] They may have had some, but they weren't like ours. We have plastic covering and painting. They'd use berries and stuff for their paintings. [How did they write, or didn't they write?] They could use a feather or a stick. [Did they write in words or did they make pictures or what?] They wrote in words.

Sue: No, they didn't know how to read. That's how the Europeans tricked them. They made them sign something and they didn't know what it was.

Helen: No. They didn't know how to read and there was no way to build a library.

Rita: No. [Why?] Because that would lead on to a city. [Could they have a small part of a longhouse be a little library?] No, because they needed that for people to store stuff and to live in. [What did they do with their books?] There was a storage place underground. [So they had books?] Yeah, like a diary we write sometimes. [Did they have books like in our libraries?] No. It would be in their language and no one else can read it except if they had an Indian interpreter.

9C. Did the Native Americans have churches? The students recognized that the Native Americans did not have large places of worship resembling modern churches, synagogues, or mosques but did have religious beliefs and ceremonies.

Tim: They didn't have churches but they had dances that present spirits and stuff like that. A fire in the middle and then they'd dance around it.

Mark: If somebody died, they'd have a ceremony. They would bury them and then they would make a circle or some different way of forming something and the chief would be in the middle, saying something about the person who died. [Was this outside or in a building somewhere?] Outside.

Rita: They might have, in the middle of the village. They might have a round place that could be like their church . . . they might have a place set off where they buried people who died. They just might have that place and that's where they go if they need to pray to their gods and stuff.

9D. How were the Native Americans' religious beliefs different from the Europeans who came to North America later? Responses to this question were rather vague, although six students suggested that the Europeans had one or a small number of gods but the Native Americans had a large number of gods or spirits. Three suggested that the Europeans worshipped masters or kings whereas the Native Americans worshipped chiefs or spirits.

Jason: Europeans had churches. The Indians worshipped spirits. [What were spirits?] Hunting spirits. [Why did they worship them?] So they could bring home a deer or two.

Brad: The Native Americans had a god for everything. They'd have a god for trees, flowers, water, paint, berries. [How about the Europeans?] They may have had some great spirits, but I don't think they had as many as the Indians did.

Rita: The Europeans had to worship a certain god and that god was probably the king and if they didn't do that then they'd die. But the Native Americans, they worshipped spirits. They were kinda religious.

Questions About Contemporary Native Americans

10. Are there any Native Americans still around today? Prior to the unit, six students said yes, two said no, and two weren't sure. Four stated that contemporary Native Americans live just like everyone else.

Jason: Yes. [Where do they live and what do they do?] Probably live like normal people now.

Tim: Yes. . . . Right now they usually live in Arizona and Mexico.

Mark: Yes . . . they live in all different spots. [Do you think they are still living in tipis?] No—just living in regular houses.

Rita: Not the same ones, but they are still around. But they don't dress like that and they live exactly like us. Sort of like us. [Do they live anywhere specific?] Maybe in the country, because then they can have their own property and do what they want on that property.

On the postunit interview, all 10 students stated that Native Americans survive today, and nine added that they live like most other Americans. Rita related a negative interpretation of life on the reservation that she had picked up from her mother.

Jason: Yeah, some live here and all over. They live like regular people. [What happened to their old way of life?] They wanted to fit in.

Tim: Yes. They live mostly out west, the same way we do. They dress the same.

Sue: I know someone in fifth grade that's part Indian. [Do they still live in tipis?] No, they live just like us today.

Rita: Yes, but they were shoved onto Indian reserve things. [Reservations?] Yeah. [Who shoved them on there?] The government. It's not fair that they have to stay there. [Where did you learn about this?] My mom. She said she used to live in an Indian reservation thing and I told her that I wanted to live there. She goes, "Rita, no, you don't, because they're kind of poor and they drink a lot." I said, "Forget it, mom."

Except for Rita, the students believed that contemporary Native Americans had been completely assimilated into modern American society. Apparently, they did not know about Indian reservations or about differing points of view among contemporary Native Americans on the issue of assimilation versus maintenance of tribal traditions.

11. Why do we call them Native Americans? What does this term mean? Only three students answered the question correctly. Jason immediately said that Native Americans are so called "because they are native to this land," and Mark and Kay thought that the term means that these people were the first ones in America. Sue and Rita could not respond, and the other five students gave incorrect responses.

Tim: They're not really from America. They came from another country over to here so they're Native Americans.

Brad: Americans are white people and natives . . . I think I know what the word means, but I forgot. I think it's long ago.

Ned: Because they were free. They didn't have anyone to boss them around except maybe the chief.

Helen: First they lived in the area of the plains or the native area and then they came over to America, so they had two homes. [So what does Native American mean?] They are part American, part native. Part American and maybe something else.

Tim and Helen apparently believed that Native Americans are just one more type of "hyphenated" Americans—immigrants from somewhere else who can be distinguished from other Americans by using an ethnic prefix. Perhaps the term "Native Americans" meant something like "early Asian-Americans" to these two students.

Discussion

The students' knowledge about Native Americans had become both more differentiated and better organized (around the notion of five main tribal groups who lived in different parts of the continent and had contrasting customs). The minority who were still operating with a generalized stereotype of Native Americans as living in tipis and hunting buffalo learned that this undifferentiated image of Native Americans fit the Plains tribes much better than it did the other four groups. Students who already understood that there were different tribal groups with different customs learned much more about the similarities and differences among tribal groups and could now use the notion of five main groups as a way to organize their knowledge.

The most obvious development and solidification of knowledge occurred with respect to the Eastern Woodlands tribes, about whom the students entered the unit with the most prior knowledge. The process of comparing and contrasting five tribal groups helped the students to develop a deeper understanding of the implications of saying that the Eastern Woodlands tribes were farmers who raised crops on good farmland and hunted in game-rich forests. Most indicated appreciation of the fact that life conditions were much more difficult for the Plains tribes than for the Eastern Woodlands tribes, and some were aware of geographical reasons for this.

There were many instances of naivete, learning gaps, and misconceptions, even in the postunit interviews. Many responses revealed good knowledge of concrete details such as the specifics of the construction of tipis and travois or the use of totem poles, but only limited grasp of abstractions such as the notion of a hunting and gathering society or explanations such as the reasons why nomadic tribes kept moving or lived in tipis.

Perhaps covering five tribal groups created information overload and the students might have profited more from studying only two or three. However, this would have meant omitting some important geographical areas and tribal adaptations. This is but one manifestation of the ever-present breadth versus depth of coverage dilemma that is so acute in social studies. All three of the teachers profiled in this book felt time and coverage pressures related to this dilemma, both in their initial unit planning and in their decisions to scale down these plans as their units unfolded.

Incorrect associations (e.g., thinking that tipis were used by the Northwest tribes or that the Plains tribes made totem poles) are to be expected whenever students attempt to learn a great deal of new information. However, many students' learning was distorted by certain persistent naive conceptions or confusions. Many did not realize that the Native Americans did not have horses until they were introduced by Europeans, or were unclear about when this occurred vis-a-vis other historical events. Some images of Native Americans were rooted in the Ice Age and pictured Native Americans migrating to a continent that contained animals but no people, whereas other images were rooted more in the eighteenth or nineteenth century and depicted Native Americans retreating westward ahead of an advancing frontier. Several students entered the unit believing or wondering whether Native Americans were people from long ago who no longer exist. All students learned that there are still Native Americans around today, although some assumed that assimilation had progressed to the point that full-blooded Native Americans were extinct.

Many students began (and some remained) confused about the names "Indians" and "Native Americans." Some thought that the Native Americans had given this name to themselves. Some thought that the term is reserved to refer either to the original migrants who crossed over on the land bridge or to the east coast tribes who interacted with the first European settlers. Subsequent interviews on the colonies and the American Revolution revealed that some students used the term

"Native Americans" to refer to the European immigrants who settled in the English colonies. These students spoke of the American Revolution as a fight between the "Native Americans" and the British. Given the different ways that the term is employed, the students' difficulties with it are easily understood.

Students found certain things hard to imagine (a purely hunting and gathering society that did not do any farming; a society that lacked written language). In other cases, they had little difficulty understanding that something was true, but great difficulty explaining why it was true (the fact that Native Americans tended to live in small groups rather than in large cities).

In some respects, the students showed a great deal of the kind of empathy that Dickinson and Lee (1984) have emphasized as important in providing a basis for understanding people from the past in their own terms. For the most part, they had learned to see the details of Native American lives and customs as sensible adaptations to their times and environments. Most of the students credited the Native Americans for their inventiveness and accumulated knowledge in farming, hunting, and other survival skills and for their "ecoconsciousness" in respecting nature and avoiding waste.

The students showed less empathy in talking about Native American religious beliefs and customs. Apparently these had not been explained in terms that would allow the students to relate them to modern religious beliefs and customs, so they seemed strange or pointless. The students often viewed legends purely as entertainment. They did not make connections between the Native Americans' pantheistic practices and modern monotheistic practices such as blessings of crops or prayers of supplication or thanksgiving (e.g., for good weather or a good harvest).

When attempting to explain some custom that they did not understand, students often said essentially that Native American groups did what they did because they wanted to (e.g., they lived in small, scattered groups rather than in cities because "they liked their space"). This tendency to attribute behavior to acts of will or expressions of personal preference has been reported frequently in the child development literature. It is to be expected when students lack the knowledge that would allow them to view certain cultural practices as adaptations to the time and place in which a group lived.

There were some noteworthy minor trends but no major differences related to the genders and achievement levels of the students. The girls were more likely to mention arts and crafts, clothing, jewelry, or women's roles. The boys seemed to have a better grasp of the reasons for the nomadic lifestyle of the Plains tribes, whereas the girls had a better grasp of specifics such as the construction and use of travois.

There was some tendency for higher achieving students to demonstrate both more entry-level knowledge and more complete learning. However, the degree of knowledge displayed in the preunit interview appeared to be related more to the students' personal experiences and reading interests than to their achievement at school.

UNIT 3: EXPLORERS

In the previous unit, the students learned that the Native Americans fanned out all across the Americas, differentiating into tribal groups with different customs and cultures. These communities were in place long before the first European explorers arrived.

Within this context, the teacher's explorers unit developed the following key ideas:

1. The Vikings had explored to the west and even reached North America, but they apparently did not realize that they had encountered an entire continent and did not keep coming back.
2. Improvements in shipbuilding and navigation eventually made ocean sailing around Africa an attractive alternative to overland transportation between western Europe and the Far East.
3. However, the western European nations were looking for shorter routes.
4. They knew that the world was round and deduced that "the Indies" might be reached by sailing westward.
5. This led Spain to commission Columbus (and other western European nations to commission other explorers) to sail west.
6. These explorers did reach land but not the expected Indies, and eventually it became clear that there were continents previously unknown to Europeans.
7. Several European nations claimed dominion over parts of the New World, explored these areas, and began exploiting their resources and later colonizing them.

The unit was taught prior to the development of special instructional resources connected with the Columbian Quincentenary, so its content reflected a relatively traditional (i.e., Eurocentric) point of view. Most learning activities were based on selections from children's literature or articles from *Cobblestone* magazine.

Lake frequently referred to the use of flags (sailing under flags, planting flags) to help students understand that most explorers sailed and claimed land on behalf of the nations that sponsored their expeditions. The students heard stories about various explorers, studied their expeditions with reference to timelines and maps, and discussed the question, "Was anything really discovered?" They also wrote compositions describing which of the expeditions they would liked to have been on and why, wrote "historical profiles" of Ponce de Leon and Amerigo Vespucci, and worked on an "explorers contract" that called for them to use textbooks and encyclopedias to write profiles containing at least six facts about each of three explorers chosen from a list of 14, and a short story (illustrated with artwork) describing an imaginary exploration of their own.

KWL Findings

The KWL sheets instructed students to tell what they knew about the discovery of America and what they wanted to learn about it. KWL data were available for one class section.

What the Students Knew About the Discovery of America

Table 4.5 shows that all 22 students expressed a belief about who discovered America, although most were guessing. Two said the Pilgrims, but the other 20 gave defensibly accurate answers (Columbus, Indians, Vikings). Two recognized that the answer would depend on how one defined "discovered." A few students elaborated their responses in interesting ways.

- Christopher Columbus discovered America. He is an explorer and he was looking for an easier way to the land and he came from southern Arabia.
- I think it was someone whose last name was "America" because Columbus landed in Cuba.
- I think the Indians discovered the U.S., but it was named "land."
- I think Columbus discovered America because though the Indians were there first, Columbus had never been there, except the Native Americans would never know about it.
- The Pilgrims. They went to Plymouth Rock. Christopher Columbus went to the Bahamas.
- I think it depends on how you use the term "discovered." It could

Table 4.5 What Students Said They Knew About the Discovery of America Prior to the Unit

	Boys (N = 11)	Girls (N = 11)	Total (N = 22)
Who discovered America?			
1. Columbus	3	5	8
2. Indians	3	2	5
3. Vikings	1	2	3
4. Pilgrims	1	1	2
5. Someone whose last name was "America"	1	0	1
6. Someone who came before Columbus	1	0	1
7. Columbus or the Indians, depending on how you define "discovered"	1	1	2
	11	11	22

be the Indians, but they didn't find it, or maybe it could be Columbus.

What the Students Wanted to Learn

Table 4.6 summarizes what students Wanted to learn. Five wanted to learn "everything" or "more" about explorers and 10 wanted to learn who really discovered America (and thus to verify the accuracy of their guesses). Some of the more unusual or elaborated responses were the following:

- I want to know who he is and how he got here and what made him come.
- How they came? How many people came? Did they meet the Native Americans?
- I want to know what Mr. America's first name was.
- I want to know how, where, and because, and if I am right.
- I want to know who discovered America and I want to know more about the person.

Compared to the W responses for other units, these responses are rather limited and mundane. Perhaps this was because the question focused specifically on the discovery of America rather than on the more general topic of voyages of discovery and exploration.

Table 4.6 What Students Said They Wanted to Learn About the Discovery of America

	Boys (N = 11)	Girls (N = 11)	Total (N = 22)
A. *Generic or minimal responses*			
1. No response/don't know	1	2	3
2. Everything/more about explorers	2	3	5
3. Who really did discover America/whether my guess was correct	6	4	10
	9	9	18
B. *More substantive questions and comments*			
1. How he (they) came/did it/got here	5	2	7
2. Where in America the discoverers (Indians, Vikings) landed or lived	1	1	2
3. The discoverer's motivation (What made him come)	1	0	1
4. More about the person who discovered America	0	1	1
5. When the discovery was made	0	1	1
6. How many people came?	1	0	1
7. Did they meet the Native Americans?	1	0	1
8. What Mr. America's first name was	1	0	1
9. What they ate and drank	0	1	1
	10	6	16

What the Students Reported Learning

Following the unit, the students knew a great deal about the European discovery and early exploration of the New World. Three confined their remarks to explorers in general (e.g., the countries that they sailed for). The other 19 named specific explorers and supplied facts about them or their discoveries. The following examples are typical:

- That Christopher Columbus had seven ships on one of his voyages. That there were three main countries exploring them: France, England, Spain. Henry Hudson had Hudson Bay and a river named after him. Jacques Cartier discovered the St. Lawrence River. Francisco Coronado believed that there were seven cities of gold. Leif Ericson's dad's name was Eric the Red because he had red hair and a red beard. Christopher Columbus discovered Cuba.
- Leif Ericson was the first explorer to land in the New World. We say Columbus discovered it because he was the one who spread

the news. Even though people call it America because Amerigo Vespucci made a map of the land and signed it "Amerigo," which in Latin means "America." Spain, England, and France were the countries exploring.

Several students supplied more personalized responses that provide interesting insights into their thinking.

- Vikings discovered America but Columbus gets the credit. Who did the exploring, what countries were sending people to explore, and a lot about Columbus's part. New places, people, and events, shipwrecks, who discovered other places. Mysteries, and about people.
- I learned that Leif Ericson discovered America but didn't call it America. Columbus found it and called it America. Amerigo Vespucci discovered it too, but Leif Ericson really discovered it and didn't know it. The reason why is Leif Ericson was the first one there and he named it a different name, though. I learned a lot about explorers and I enjoyed it.
- I found out that the Vikings found America but it didn't really matter. America came from Amerigo Vespucci. Christopher Columbus discovered the Bahamas. I found out that exploring could be fun and interesting. Being an explorer could really change someone's life.
- I learned that Leif Ericson really discovered America but everyone thought Columbus did because Leif Ericson didn't say much about it. I learned that America was named after Amerigo Vespucci who followed Columbus around and he drew maps of whatever land Columbus found. I learned that Ponce de Leon discovered Florida and unlike many other explorers he stayed at the land that he discovered. I also learned that Francisco Coronado met two men named DeVaca and Esteban who were looking for the Seven Cities of Gold and he sent them out to look for them. While they were there they shook a gourd that they thought meant peace to the Indians, but to one Indian tribe it meant war. I also learned that Henry Hudson discovered the Hudson River and that the three main countries who sent out explorers were England, Spain, and France.

Some responses indicated confusion about the timelines involved or about related developments in societies and communication systems. Several implied that certain explorers were contemporaries in close contact with one another, and several depicted voyages of exploration as undertaken on behalf of individuals (the king and queen of Spain) or small groups, rather than as sponsored by very large nations. The students were clearly more comfortable with the notion of Columbus serving the queen of Spain or Drake serving the king of England than with the notion of large nations competing for hegemony in the New World.

Several students were confused about the naming of discovered lands. One thought that the Native Americans had named America "land" (i.e., using the English word) when they migrated. Others thought that America was named by Columbus. Among those who understood that America was named after Amerigo Vespucci, one thought that Vespucci accompanied Columbus and another thought that "Amerigo Vespucci was French for America."

Interview Findings

Questions About the Timeline

1. When did the first Europeans discover America? Prior to the unit, only Tim, who said "In the 1400 or 1500s" answered correctly. Two students could not respond, two guessed recent dates (1812 and 200 years ago), and the other five guessed 3,000–10,000 years ago. The latter students were thinking about Native Americans coming across the land bridge. Some did not understand that the term "Europeans" referred to different people.

Following the unit, no one said "1492" and only half gave "correct" answers: Sue said it was the Vikings around the year 1,000 and four other students said "1496," "about the fifteenth century," "in the 1500s," and "sometime in the 1500s." Two could not respond, one said 10,000 years ago, one said 1607, and one said 1872.

These students at least had moved beyond "In fourteen hundred and ninety-two, Columbus sailed the ocean blue." They had learned that the "discovery" of America was actually a series of encounters that took place over many years at many different locations. However, only half of them could locate these events in time reasonably accurately.

2. America was there the whole time. Why do you think it took the Europeans so long to discover it? Prior to the unit, seven students suggested the following reasons: The Europeans were not looking for America because they didn't know it was there (4), it was a long and difficult trip (3), they had no motivation to look for new lands (1), and they feared falling off the end of a flat earth (1).

Tim: It was hard to get over here, so they probably didn't think there was any land over there.
Kay: They just knew there were two pieces of land because they kept on going back and forth to those. They didn't go any farther.

Surprisingly, the postunit responses were not much better. Only five students answered the question asked. They gave the same reasons mentioned prior to the unit, except that Helen added the idea that these Europeans were slaves who had been waiting for a chance to escape from their masters. Others told how the Europeans discovered America (accidentally in the process of looking for shorter routes to the Far East) but could not say why it took them so long to do so. They remained relatively unclear about European developments in geographical knowledge, sea travel, and international trade and rivalries that set the stage for the discovery.

Questions About Explorers and Their Voyages

3. What was it like to be an explorer? Prior to the unit, 7 students gave 12 reasons why being an explorer was hard or dangerous. Some were thinking about the French exploring Michigan rivers in canoes, others about explorers sailing across the ocean and sighting land.

Tim: They came through rivers and stuff in boats. They'd stay close to shore so they can come ashore and sleep and find food.
Teri: Hard. [Why do you think it was hard?] Well, just sailing around on the ocean and having barely anything to eat. They probably had to go through a lot of storms. Some people got sick and died, I think.
Helen: It'd be pretty hard to be an explorer because they didn't have a Burger King to go to so they had to make their own food with crops and stuff.

Following the unit, all 10 students said that being an explorer was hard or dangerous, citing 31 reasons. These postunit responses re-emphasized the danger of storms or dying at sea and added comments about other hardships of sea travel (e.g., the ships were crowded and dirty). Seven students now mentioned attack by other humans—unfriendly Indians or rival Europeans. Three noted the lengthy separations from one's family. Finally, Mark noted that the queen might get mad at you if you failed to accomplish your mission.

Some students were aware that exploring was not just hardship and danger. Jason (preunit) and Ned (postunit) mentioned spontaneously that it was exciting to experience the thrill of discovery. In addition, following the unit some students were asked if there were positive aspects to exploring (after they listed negative aspects). Three mentioned monetary rewards. Two others mentioned fame.

Mark: It would be pretty hard because like Christopher Columbus was looking for a shorter way to Asia and he ran into there and he thought it was Asia and it wasn't and some of the Indians were nice and some weren't and some didn't really like him. When he went back the queen might have gotten mad at him or something.

Sue: If you were coming across, a lot of the ships weren't very good. They were small and they had a lot of people on the ships. . . . And they didn't have motors like we do. [Why was life hard?] Food and storms and the ocean. [Was it better when they got to land?] They had Indians and some weren't friendly and it was dangerous.

4. Where were the explorers going and why? Prior to the unit, eight students suggested 16 possible destinations or reasons: Six, shorter routes to the Far East; five, new lands; three, riches or prized goods (fur, spices); and two, a place where they and their people could live in freedom. At this point, few if any students understood the explorers to be agents commissioned by governments. Some viewed them as individual entrepreneurs or even as casual hobbyists.

Tim: They partly were looking for gold . . . they wanted to go to India. I think they were just trying to find India to trade with them. Instead of just travel on land, they decided it was better to travel by boat.

Ned: They floated a boat. [What were the boats like?] Canoes or sailboats. A whole bunch of people would go and spread out and say, "Meet back here in 25 days" or something. They wanted to be free.

Following the unit, all 10 students stated at least one motive for the explorations, and six stated at least three. This time, nine named riches or valued commodities; seven, new lands; five, shorter routes to the Far East; and five, freedom. The search for shorter routes to the Far East apparently had faded into the background as the students learned specifics about Columbus, Ponce de Leon, and other individual explorers.

Jason: They wanted to find a quicker way to get to Asia. . . . Because they wanted to get away or they didn't want to be bossed around by the king. [Were they looking for other things besides freedom?] Yeah. Gold and riches and fur and stuff.

Tim: The kings wanted to be a rich country and so they sent you and they would give you a certain amount of money or something. [What would the king get?] More land and they'd be a richer country. They were looking for more land and gold and stuff that would make them a richer country.

Ned: For furs and gold.

Teri: If the king and queen told you to go out and get some gold, they would pay you something. . . . They were looking for gold and silver and stuff like that.

Kay: They went to search for land. [What did they do when they found land?] They'd stick a flag in the land and claim it for the king and queen. [Where were they going?] They didn't know where they were going. They were just trying to find land and money and to claim land for the king and queen. . . . They came for gold and religious freedom.

5. Who paid for the men and ships and the equipment needed for these explorations? Why did they pay for this? Prior to the unit only three students realized that these explorations were paid for by governments, and only Tim and Rita understood why.

Jason: Because they were getting paid to find new spices. [Who paid them?] The king of England or Europe. [Why?] I don't know.

Tim: I think the head kings and queens. [Why were they willing to pay for this?] Because if they found gold or something, they'd be a richer country. Each king and queen was trying to rule the world.

Brad: You'd have to raise money. [Where would you go to raise money?] They'd get a job. . . . If you were sent out by somebody, they'd probably help you with it. [Who would send you out?] A boss or a company.

Rita: The king of the Europeans. [Why did they pay for this?] So they can go out and claim the world for their king. So the king could move his people over there and have some people here, and here, and here. All over the world. And he would own it.

Following the unit, all 10 students said that the trips were paid for by monarchs who wanted new lands or riches. However, most referred only to the personal motives of the monarchs, not to the national interests of the countries they headed.

Mark: Usually the king or queen got the ships for them. [Why?] Because if they're the ones who needed something, they should supply the ships. [What did the king and queen hope to get?] They were greedy and wanted gold and more land, and sometimes they wanted jewels and different things.

Rita: The king and queen. [Why?] It's overpopulated and they wanted to kick some people off their land and they'll get recognized . . . say I'm a queen of England and you're the king of Spain and I have more land than you do, but you have more money than I do. So you give some of your money to these men and they find this huge bunch of land. And I send some of my men with some money and I find bigger land than you, so you'd recognize me because I have more land than you do.

6. *Once they got to America, what did these explorers do? Why?* Prior to the unit, five students pictured the explorers looking around to see what the new land was like. The other five confused the explorers with the settlers who came later. They pictured the explorers building houses and beginning to farm the land.

In the postunit interviews, all 10 students knew that the New World was initially explored by explorers and only later settled by colonists. All 10 also said that the main thing that explorers did was plant their flag and claim the land for their king or queen. Two still did not distinguish between initial explorers and later colonists. Jason said that the explorers would check to see if the land they had claimed was a good place to live and "then go back and tell the people, so more people would go over there." Kay initially said that the explorers would go back, get their families, and "bring them back to this new land and make houses."

These responses, like others given throughout both interviews, indicate that some students' learning was distorted by failure to appreciate that more than 100 years elapsed between Columbus's initial discoveries and the founding of Jamestown. These students pictured direct, personal linkages (the explorer would go back to his country and tell his friends and other people about the discovery, then lead a group of settlers to the new land).

Several misconceptions concerned the motives of explorers. Prior to the unit, the majority of the students believed that the explorers were looking for land for people to settle. Some thought that they were acting on behalf of the future settlers themselves (people seeking to escape slavery, oppression, or crowded living conditions in Europe). Others knew that they worked in the service of monarchs but thought that the monarchs were seeking places to send some of their people (to relieve overcrowding or to expand the country's land holdings). Related misconceptions concerned the colonists. The majority of the students viewed the immigrant settlers as groups of slaves, Pilgrims, or people seeking a better life and acting on their own initiative. They had not yet learned about the concept of a colony or about why monarchs or organizations such as the British East India Company would recruit people to establish colonies in the New World.

*Questions Calling for Comparison of Europeans
with Native Americans*

   7. *What was similar about the Europeans and the Native Americans? What was different?* Prior to the unit, seven students named 15 similarities. Some were trite (both were human, alive, could talk). Most noted primitive living conditions (both had to make their own houses and grow or hunt for food). Other observations were that both wanted the same land and that both wanted "to share their gods with the other people so their god will be stronger." All of the students named at least one difference between the two groups.

Tim: They were different because they lived in buildings instead of tipis and huts, the Indians. I don't know any way they were the same.
Sue: Maybe their houses were the same. [What about differences?] The boats they sailed in. The Europeans had like ships and the Indians had canoes.
Helen: They celebrated differently. The Indians might have sacrificed something and the Americans might just have a party or something.
Rita: They both used everything from nature and they both wanted to share their gods with the other people so their god will be stronger. [What about differences?] The Indians wanted to be friends. They didn't want to hurt your feelings, but the Europeans wanted to get the furs and take the land away from the Native Americans. The Europeans wanted to hate and steal the land. The Indians just wanted to be friends.

The students struggled with similarities even more following the unit. This time five could think of no similarities and the other five mentioned only seven similarities among them. Two were trite (both human, both ate food), and two noted that both groups wanted to live on the same land. The other three were that both groups did some exploring, wanted to be free, and included some people who were mean.

All 10 students named at least two differences, producing a total of 32. Nine mentioned skin color; five, housing; four, clothing; three, languages; and three, morality or values (the Indians didn't just kill animals for fun, the Indians were friendly whereas the Europeans were mean, and the Indians just wanted to use the land but the Europeans wanted to possess the land and everything on it). Other observations: Both groups traveled but in different ways and for different reasons; the Indians had chiefs and tribes whereas the Europeans had kings and colonies; the groups came from different countries of origin; the Indians had better survival skills; the Indians had lived in the New World much longer; and unlike the wasteful Europeans, the Indians used all parts of the animals they killed.

Tim: They had dark skin and the Europeans had white skin. They lived differently. The Europeans lived in castles and stuff and the Native Americans lived in huts and tipis, nothing that big. They dressed different. The Europeans had fancier clothes. They had different languages. [What was the same?] I can't think of anything.

Sue: I don't know. [How were they different?] The Indians knew how to live in the wilderness and grow their own food but the explorers probably knew how but not as well as the Indians. [How else?] Clothing . . . skin color. The Indians were dark colored and the Europeans were white.

Kay: They both wanted the land. They both wanted to live there. The Europeans or explorers wanted all the gold and stuff and the Native Americans wanted some of that too. [How were they different?] The Native Americans wanted the land to live on, but the explorers wanted the gold and everything on the land. [How else were they different?] They had a different language and Indians lived in camps but Europeans wanted to build big houses.

Rita: I don't know. [How were they different?] They were different color. The Indians used everything . . . if they had a deer, then they would use everything on the buck. The Europeans would use what they needed and throw the rest away. The Europeans were wasteful. [Any other ways they were different?] The Native Americans were real nice and the Europeans weren't. "Get off my land. Move over!" Like that.

8. *What did the Europeans learn from the Native Americans?* Prior to the unit, seven students suggested that the Native Americans taught the Europeans farming, hunting, or wilderness survival skills. Other suggestions included "how to use more natural resources and maybe how to use smaller boats," Native American languages, and "that the Native Americans liked to love." The last comment was from Rita, who viewed the Europeans as mean, hostile people and the Native Americans as peaceful, loving people, and surmised that some of each group's traits might have rubbed off on the other.

After the unit, seven students (the same ones) again mentioned farming, hunting, or other survival skills. This time, however, one boy and all five girls mentioned other things in addition or instead: house-building techniques (2), tobacco (2), the symbolic meaning attached to shaking a gourd (from a story about DeVaca and Esteban), recipes for cooking corn, and "to be nice, sort of" (Rita again).

9. *What did the Native Americans learn from the Europeans?* Prior to the unit, three students suggested technological knowledge and skills (making and sailing large ships, making and using stronger tools, sewing European-style clothes). Other suggestions included learning European languages and learning "how to fight" (Rita).

Ned: Probably their language. [What else?] The Indians probably told them where some of the best spots are for fishing and planting food. [What do you think the Europeans taught the Indians?] Their language.

Sue: I think the Europeans learned to survive in the wilderness from the Indians and maybe some other things. [What do you think the Indians learned from the Europeans?] Maybe how to carve things and make things . . . tools. They learned to make stronger tools.

Helen: The Europeans learned from the Native Americans how to survive, how to grow crops and stuff and how to survive out in the wilderness without food besides corn and stuff like that. The Europeans taught the Native Americans how to sew clothes and stuff or make clothes out of birch bark and stuff. [Who learned the most from whom?] I think it was pretty equal. Native Americans didn't know as much as the Europeans about living and slaving out where there was food and apples and stuff that you could just pick. Europeans didn't know how to live out in the wilderness where there's animals and how to fight them and stuff. So they were both pretty equal.

Rita: The Native Americans learned how to fight and the Europeans learned that the Native Americans like to love.

Responses to the postquestion were similar. Three students again mentioned technological knowledge (how to make and sail large ships, shoot a gun, and make European-style clothes), and Rita once again suggested that contact with Europeans had taught the Native Americans "how to fight, how to be mean."

Mark: They learned how to grow crops and how to survive by using things from the wilderness. [What did the Europeans teach the Native Americans?] I don't know.

Ned: They taught the Europeans how to plant food. [What else?] How to build houses. [What do you think the Native Americans learned from the Europeans?] How to shoot a gun.

Helen: They taught them how to cook corn and sell tobacco and how to grow corn and vegetables and the Americans taught them how to sew with wood and bark and stuff like that—how to make clothes.

Kay: How to survive and live off the land. [What else?] How to get their food and how to get materials to make houses. [What did the Indians learn from the Europeans?] I'm not sure.

The students' attempts to describe how the two groups influenced each other were hampered by their lack of knowledge about the Europeans. They had studied the Native Americans and could talk about how they taught the Europeans how to grow food and survive in the wilderness, but they didn't have much of an image of the Europeans beyond that they sailed over on large ships and didn't know how to survive in the wilderness. Brad thought that Columbus sailed on the Mayflower and Helen thought that the Europeans were slaves and that they made clothes out of birch bark.

The postunit responses included some new details (tobacco, guns, the gourd story), and most misconceptions expressed earlier had disappeared. Nevertheless, these responses still conveyed remarkably little awareness of the knowledge and inventions that the Europeans brought to the Encounter: large domesticated animals used for food, transportation, and work; wheeled vehicles; manufactured tools made of metals; guns and other weapons; written language and maps. If students are to more fully appreciate the "Encounter" aspects of this unit, they will need more information about life and times in sixteenth- and seventeenth-century Europe. Possession of such a context in which to embed their learning would support the development of more sophisticated historical conceptualization, imagination, and empathy with the people being studied (Brophy, VanSledright, & Bredin, 1993; Dickinson & Lee, 1984; VanSledright & Brophy, 1992).

Questions About the Discovery of America

10. Who were the first Europeans to discover America? In the preunit interviews, none of the students spontaneously mentioned the Vikings. Rita knew that "the first ones were the Native Americans and then there was someone before Christopher Columbus," but she could not identify the "someone."

When asked about the Vikings, Jason said that they "wore hats," Tim that they were "big guys," Teri that she had heard of them "on cartoons," Helen that she thought that they came from Russia, and Rita that "the men would wear skirt-like things. They were fur traders, I guess, and their skirt-like things would be made out of fur and they had hats and it had like a rhinoceros thing. And they had rocks on their hat." Thus, the students' ideas about Vikings were confined mostly to images associated with cartoons. They did not know the Vikings as Scandinavians who explored the Atlantic long before Columbus did.

Following the unit, seven students mentioned the Vikings as the first Europeans to explore America. Six stated that they were from Norway, Iceland, or Greenland, two that they were Europeans, one that they were from France and England, and one that they were from England, Spain, and France.

Concerning what the Vikings did once they reached America, four students stated that they did not establish permanent colonies or claim land in the name of a king or nation. Four others were unclear about this. Sue thought that the Vikings had settled here, and Helen thought that they had planted a flag and claimed the land.

Mark: The Vikings. [Where did they come from?] Norway. [What did they do when they found America?] Leif Ericson's dad got kicked out of Norway and they moved to . . . I can't remember, but then Leif went out exploring for himself and first he bumped into a place that was all ice and he called it Iceland. Then he moved on and he found an island that had trees and stuff on it and Iceland didn't have any trees at all, so he kept on going and he found it and

named it Vinland. Him and his mom and dad went to live in Vinland for a year and then they ran out of supplies or something and
went back to Norway. [Did the Vikings have colonies?] No.

Kay: [What about the Vikings? Do you know where they were from?]
I think Greenland. They really discovered part of America, but they
never put anything in the ground or anything to prove they were
there.

Except for Mark, the students did not display much interest in the
Vikings or connect them to the eventual encounter between the Old
and New Worlds. No one noted that the Vikings did not realize that
they had encountered an entire continent, or mused about how history
might have been different if they had.

*11. Christopher Columbus usually gets credit for discovering
America. Do you know why this is?* Prior to the unit, five students
said because Columbus supplied proof of his discovery (planted a flag,
returned with journals and maps) or publicized it upon his return. Teri
could not respond, Brad and Rita made responses that contained inac-
curacies but recognized that Columbus's discovery had important effects, Kay thought that Columbus was the first to explore what is now
the United States, and Helen supplied another fanciful narration.

Tim: Because the Vikings didn't come back. Columbus came back and
told the people about it.

Sue: Maybe because the Indians never really told anyone and Columbus did.

Helen: He discovered America. If he didn't come here, then Amerigo
wouldn't have been here. He might have died or something before
anybody got to America, so if Columbus didn't come here, this
wouldn't be a city. If nobody was here, this would still be flat land.
[Do you remember I said the Vikings discovered America?] Yeah.
[Why do we give so much credit to Columbus?] He lived in
America the longest. He didn't discover America first, but he lived
in America when Amerigo died and all the Vikings died, because
they were on America long before Columbus. When Columbus
came to America, nobody was there except for the Indians. The
Indians died and when everybody started coming to America, they
found Columbus and no one else, so they named that date "Columbus Day."

Kay: He was the one that actually had been around the United States
. . . but we should give some credit to the Vikings.

Following the unit, nine students stated that Columbus got the credit because he documented and/or publicized his discovery. Helen once again spun a fanciful narrative.

Mark: Because when Leif Ericson found it, he didn't go back and brag about it and Christopher Columbus did.

Brad: He was the second one to come to America and actually discover it and he had a big mouth. They knew he was going out to explore and I think he took all the ships just to America and he kept on going back and bringing more people. [What do you mean "he had a big mouth"?] He went back and told the king and queen and told everybody else at his village and the word got spread. The other ones kept it to themselves.

Teri: That depends on who was there first. The Indians didn't really know that they discovered anything and the Vikings didn't really care. [How did Christopher Columbus get the credit?] He planted his flag.

Helen: The person that sailed there first lived there for a long time, but that person obviously didn't survive. So when Christopher Columbus found America and stayed there, he didn't die for a long time, and by that time people recognized him and knew him. [How did they learn about him?] He lived in Spain before and he sailed to America and found America and he said, "Come to the new land." So they started coming over and saying, "Christopher Columbus found this land. He's the explorer who found this land, so it belongs to him." And the rumors went on and on and he got all the credit even though he wasn't the first one to discover it.

The students pictured communication about the discovery as proceeding through word of mouth at the village level, not through mass communication to thousands of people in many nations. Teri's response summarizes what the students had been taught. The references to Columbus "bragging" or "having a big mouth" reflected language that the teacher had used in telling stories about Columbus. Several students pictured him less as a commissioned agent of the government and more as an independent entrepreneur involved in recruiting and transporting colonists for the New World (i.e., someone akin to Sir Walter Raleigh).

Questions About the Origins of Names

12. *How did America get its name?* Prior to the unit, none of the students knew. Following the unit, all 10 knew that the name had

come from Amerigo Vespucci, and seven provided an essentially accurate explanation.

Jason: Amerigo Vespucci made maps and put his name on them all. He gave them to a mapmaker when he came back and they put "America" on it.
Sue: From Amerigo Vespucci. He was drawing maps and always put his name on it and the guy that would really draw the maps, but Amerigo in a different language was "America." The people were mad because they wanted it to be Columbus.
Helen: Amerigo Vespucci. [Why didn't we call it Columbia?] Well, Amerigo Vespucci made a lot of maps and on it he put "Amerigo," but the guy that gave the maps out, he spoke French, so French for "Amerigo" is "America." That's how they got the name America.

13. How is it that the Native Americans got to be called Indians? Prior to the unit, none of the students could answer. Even after the unit, only five could give substantive responses. Mark and Ned knew that Columbus named them Indians because he thought he had reached the Indies. Brad was vague and uncertain. Teri's and Rita's responses mixed accurate with inaccurate elements.

Mark: Christopher Columbus thought he was in India or Asia so he called them Indians.
Brad: I think some of them were from India. [Who thought that?] I'm not sure.
Ned: Because Columbus thought he landed in India, so he called them Indians.
Teri: Indiana. [Are you guessing?] Yeah. I think it was from Christopher Columbus because he thought they came from India, so we just called them Indians.
Rita: I think it was Columbus—no Ponce de Leon. Ponce de Leon thought he was in Asia or China or wherever and at this one place that I'm talking about, the people who live there are called Indians. [That's India.] Yeah. He thought he was in India and he called them Indians.

*Questions About the Voyages of Exploration
and Their Aftermath*

14. After the explorers had gone back and told their home countries about what they had found, what happened next in America?

Even prior to the unit, nine students said that settlers began coming to live in America. Six added that the settlers displaced or fought with Indians when they got here.

Tim: A lot of people started coming over here from Europe and started battling the Indians and eventually they were a country.

Teri: A whole bunch of people came to live here. [From where?] England and France. [What did they do?] They probably built homes and cities.

Kay: They brought all the other people over and then more people came and the Indians got mad and had a fight. [What happened?] I don't know. I think the Indians lost.

Following the unit, all 10 students noted that people came over to settle in America (some of them referred to starting colonies), but only two now mentioned that these settlers displaced or fought with the Indians. The Native Americans had begun to fade into the background as these students began learning about the Europeans.

Tim: Spain took Mexico and Florida. England discovered West Virginia and New England and France discovered Canada. [What happened then?] They had wars and stuff to get more land once it was all explored. [Did more people stay?] They started to stay.

Sue: More settlers started to come and they started building colonies.

Kay: People started coming over for religious freedom and gold and land. They were colonists and they built colonies.

Discussion

Most of the students developed an understanding of the personal motives and goals of explorers and of the monarchs who commissioned their voyages, but they had difficulty placing these voyages within the larger context of the global rivalries occurring at the time. Also, along with the many minor confusions expected when students are presented with a great deal of new information, there was evidence that learning was distorted by persistent naive conceptions or misconceptions.

The students had learned about the Vikings as precursors of Columbus, about Columbus's life and discoveries, about other New World explorers, and about rivalries among England, France, and Spain in establishing claims in the New World. However, they remained vague about the timelines involved and the scope of the communities affected. Some pictured explorers who lived in different places and times as contemporaries in direct communication with one another, and some pictured news of the discoveries as being passed by word of mouth from the explorer to people in his village but not as being circulated internationally through the news media of the times. Barton (1994) noted a similar tendency in the fourth and fifth graders that he interviewed to compress the time and space dimensions of history when they encoded historical events as elements in a connected narrative.

Prior to the unit, the students understood that America was mostly undeveloped wilderness inhabited by Indians. During the unit, most came to understand that its "discovery" actually was a series of encounters that took place over many years at many different locations, and that it took the Europeans some time to determine that they had encountered new continents.

Prior to the unit, some students viewed the explorers as individual adventure seekers or even casual hobbyists. By the end of the unit, most understood that the explorers sailed on behalf of the governments who commissioned their voyages.

Prior to the unit, the students emphasized the search for shorter routes to the Far East and the desire to claim new lands as the primary motives for exploration. Following the unit, they placed more emphasis on the search for riches or valued commodities (gold, fur, spices). The latter half of the unit focused on explorers such as Ponce de Leon, Coronado, and Esteban and DeVaca who began exploring the land itself, usually in search of riches. As a result, the desire of European nations to find shorter routes to the Far East faded into the background of the students' attention.

Helped by the visual image of planting flags, the students understood the European notion of claiming newly discovered lands, although some personalized it to the monarchs involved without yet appreciating that these land claims established the Old World nation's hegemony over the claimed area in the New World. These students may not have appreciated the fact that Columbus claimed land on behalf of the nation of Spain and that these claims continued even after the deaths of Ferdinand and Isabella.

Some students showed confusion about the timelines involved or conflation with prior knowledge, especially about the Pilgrims and the first Thanksgiving. Prior to and even in some cases following the unit, some pictured the explorers as scouting promising locations for settlements, then going back and bringing "their people" to the New World as a way to escape slavery or religious persecution. They had not yet learned about why European nations wanted to establish colonies, but they could understand the notion of a small group (perhaps a few hundred people) commissioning an explorer to find them a place where they could move to establish a better life for themselves.

The students had difficulty, even following the unit, with questions about what the Europeans and the Native Americans, respectively, brought to the Encounter. Through their fourth-grade unit on Michigan history and especially their fifth-grade unit on Native Americans, these students had acquired considerable information about the Eastern Woodlands tribes in particular and about four other major tribal groups. They viewed the Native Americans with a degree of empathy and a good deal of respect, praising them for their inventiveness and accumulated wisdom in learning how to get food through farming, hunting, and fishing and how to fashion homes, clothing, and tools from natural materials. Some students even had acquired a romanticized notion of Native Americans as people with a finely tuned ecological consciousness who never wasted anything or as peace-loving and generous people who got along well and cooperated with one another.

The students did not have richly detailed images of the Europeans of the times, however, and many elements of the images they did have were negative ones. Some stereotyped the Europeans as greedy and otherwise immoral people who practiced slavery, confiscated other people's valuables, and murdered anyone who tried to stop them. These students had difficulty in identifying similarities between the two groups. They had much less difficulty in identifying differences, but these differences were focused on the two stereotypes described above. The students had not yet learned much about, nor come to appreciate the implications of, the cultural exchanges that changed both the Old World and the New World in so many ways as a result of the Encounter.

These findings suggest the value of culminating units on the discovery and exploration of America by studying the major features and implications of the Encounter. This would help students to appreciate how both the Old and the New Worlds were affected, for both good and ill, by the infusion of previously unknown elements. Charts that pull together this information often are included among instructional materials developed in connection with the Columbian Quincentenary, so perhaps they will become commonly used in elementary social studies curricula.

The students learned that Columbus's discovery was publicized and led to what became the Encounter. However, their understanding of the Encounter and its implications was limited. Most apparently learned something like "Leif Ericson never told many people about Vinland, but Columbus told the king and queen about his discoveries and bragged about them all around town." Some students' understandings included at least a partial grasp of the implications that the European elites of the time drew from Columbus's news, but none of them said anything as connected and sophisticated as "Columbus's first voyage stimulated several European nations to commission explorations for a westward route to the Indies, and this in turn led to recognition that previously unknown continents lay between Europe and the Far East, which then led to establishment of land claims and colonies."

The students' learning was insightful in many ways but also replete with naive conceptions that serve as reminders that fifth graders are children whose cognitive structures are still developing. This raises questions about the degree to which it is desirable and feasible to replace oversimplified and romanticized treatments of these topics with more realistic and analytic ones. Egan (1988) and others, noting children's responsiveness to stories that feature romantic elements such as heroes fighting for good against evil, have argued that the elementary curriculum should emphasize such stories, including not only conventional history rendered in story form but also myths, folk tales, and history-based fiction. Traditional applications of this approach to "the age of exploration" have featured Washington Irving's version of heroic Columbus sailing westward to fulfill his dreams, keeping his head when all about him were becoming hysterical with fear of sailing over the edge of a flat earth. More recent romantic versions have emphasized the scourges visited upon gentle, nature-loving Native Americans by evil, greedy European conquerers. We recognize that such stories are interesting and memorable. However, we believe that they can encourage the development of misconceptions about the Encounter and ought to be replaced, or at least balanced, by more realistic treatments that reflect what is known about the motives and information available to the historical actors in question, and neither heroize or demonize them. Guidelines adopted by the National Council for the Social Studies (1992), along with recently developed instructional materials (Davis & Hawke, 1992), provide a good start in this direction.

Finally, the persistence of certain misunderstandings and difficulties in making historical connections suggests that in order to appreciate the Encounter more fully, the students need information not only about Native Americans but about fifteenth- and sixteenth-century Europe. This would include not only information about advances in sailing and global trade via sea routes that would help them to understand the motives behind voyages of discovery and the establishment

Table 4.7 What Students Said They Knew About Colonies Prior to the Unit

	Boys (N = 29)	Girls (N = 24)	Total (N = 53)
1. Don't know/no response	11	16	27
2. Group of people, village, small settlement	9	5	14
3. Eastern seaboard, first 13 states, Pilgrims, English	5	3	8
4. Founded by explorers, first people to live here	2	0	2
5. Big piece of land	1	0	1
6. An area of land claimed by a country	1	0	1
	29	24	53

of colonies, but also information about the conditions of everyday life in these times. Recently developed curriculum materials, especially lists of what the Old and the New World brought to the Encounter that did not exist in the other world at the time, would be especially useful for this purpose (Wooster, 1992).

UNIT 4: THE COLONIES

The colonial unit picked up the story of the establishment of the United States as a nation by noting that England established 13 colonies on the eastern seaboard of North America. It was taught much as Lake taught it previously, as described in detail in Chapter 3.

KWL Findings

The KWL sheets instructed the students to write what they knew about colonies and what they wanted to learn about them. KWL data were available for two class sections.

What the Students Knew About Colonies

Table 4.7 indicates that about half (27) of the students were unable to report anything about the colonies. Substantive responses were recorded by the other 26 students, 18 of the 29 boys but only 8 of the 24 girls.

Only one student supplied a precise definition of a colony ("an area of land claimed by a country"). Fourteen described a colony either as a group of people or a small settlement, and eight mentioned that the original colonies became the first 13 states, that they were located on the eastern seaboard, or that they were settled by Pilgrims or people from England. However, none of these responses mentioned the relationship between the colony and the mother country. The following are representative examples.

Boys

- There were different colonies. The Pilgrims were from the colonies. The first 13 states were called colonies.
- Explorers came over and made colonies.
- All I know is that colonies was where people first lived.
- Colonies are groups of people who are making settlements.
- Indian houses in a group were colonies.
- I know that a colony is an area of land claimed by a country.
- There were 13 colonies by the Atlantic Ocean.
- There were seven of them. People in the colonies came from England.
- There were groups of people. A colony was like a region. George Washington was in one of the colonies. Many people live in colonies.

Girls

- I know that there are groups. People made them. They are history.
- A colony is like a village with a lot of people living in it.
- A colony is a village that is going to get bigger.
- Englishmen were in the English colonies.
- Not much. The Pilgrims lived in a colony.
- There were 13. America fought England for them. The Pilgrims settled in them. They were along the east coast of the U.S.A.
- I know that colonies are a group of people that are the same in some way. Like an example of a colony is a big family.

KWL data obtained the previous year showed similar trends. In that data set, only 22 of 73 students were able to provide a substantive response, and only one supplied a precise definition ("It's a country that another country rules"). Four of those students confused the colonies with the continents ("There are seven colonies in the world—they are land."). This same confusion probably explains the fact that one student in the current study stated that there were seven colonies, and another said that "the colonies are a big piece of land."

What the Students Wanted to Learn

Table 4.8 summarizes what students Wanted to learn about colonies. One said that he didn't know, and 15 that they wanted to learn "everything" or "all about" colonies. The other 37 students recorded a total of 74 questions. At least 17 of these indicated complete unfamiliarity with the term "colonies" ("What are colonies?"). For two students, the term referred to people rather than to settlements, and thus was akin to terms such as "Pilgrims" or "Indians."

However, most questions were about colonies or the people who founded and lived in them, indicating that the students had at least a general idea about the meaning of the term. The gist of what most students said is reflected in the categories in the table. The following responses contain interesting insights, elaborations, or misconceptions.

Boys

- What it was like living in the colonies. Was there any famous things in the colonies?
- Who are they? And why are they named that?
- Who are the leaders of the colonies? Why they made colonies. Did they have wars with each other? Did they have leaders? How long did they stay as colonies? What they lived in?
- I want to know where they were, what they did, how they did it, when they were here, what were the people like, and what countries they came from.

Girls

- I want to know what they are and what they have to do with explorers and are they places people live?
- I want to know how people knew about the colonies. How come they came there. What a colony is like and is it a nice place to live and why we don't have them anymore.
- What are they? Were there 50 of them?

What the Students Reported Learning

In their *L* responses, about half (23) of the students mentioned things learned about colonies in general: There were 13, they were small villages or settlements, they were owned or governed by other countries, they had their own leaders, or their people had come from England.

Table 4.8 What Students Said They Wanted to Learn About Colonies

	Boys (N = 29)	Girls (N = 24)	Total (N = 53)
A. Vague generic responses			
1. Don't know/no response	1	0	1
2. Everything/all I can learn	7	8	15
	8	8	16
B. Responses indicating unfamiliarity with the term "colonies"			
1. What are/were colonies?	5	7	12
2. Who are they?	1	1	2
3. Are they places that people live?	0	1	1
4. What do they have to do with explorers?	0	1	1
5. What was famous about them?	1	0	1
	7	10	17
C. Questions about the people who founded/ lived in the colonies			
1. Who were the people/where did they come from?	3	2	5
2. What were the people like?	3	0	3
3. What language did they speak?	1	0	1
4. Who were their leaders?	1	1	2
5. Why did they come/start a colony?	2	3	5
6. How did people know about the colonies? (i.e., How did they learn of the existence of colonies as a place to move to?)	0	1	1
7. When did they come?	1	0	1
8. How did they start the colonies?	2	2	4
9. What was life like in the colonies?	2	1	3
10. What were their houses like?	1	0	1
11. What was their habitat?	0	1	1
12. Did they have wars with each other?	1	0	1
13. How did they make peace with the Indians?	1	0	1
	18	11	29
D. Questions about colonies			
1. Where were the colonies?	2	3	5
2. How many colonies were there?	2	4	6
3. How big were they/how many people?	3	0	3
4. Which was the first colony?	2	1	3
5. Which was the biggest colony?	1	0	1
6. How long did the colonies last?	1	0	1
7. Why are there no colonies now?	0	1	1
8. Why were they called colonies?	3	0	3
9. Who owned/claimed the colonies?	1	2	3
	15	11	26
E. Other comments			
1. I would like to see some of the colonies long ago	0	1	1
2. About the War of 1812 and who signed the Declaration of Independence	0	1	1
	0	2	2

Ten mentioned reasons why people came (mostly freedom and/or gold).

Twenty-three students commented about hardships and problems in the first colonies, especially hostile Indians, lack of fresh water, cold winters, limited food, and people refusing to do necessary work because they were obsessed with finding gold. Some of these comments conflated elements that had been taught about different colonies. What came through to most students was not the specific hardships endured at particular colonies, but the more general notion that the first colonies had hard times, especially during the winters, until they "made friends" with local Indians and learned to grow their own food.

Twelve students focused on the hardships faced by children in the Puritan colonies: getting up early and working all day, not speaking to adults unless addressed first, eating standing up while the adults sat at the table, sleeping on straw-filled mats instead of beds. Many of these ideas were acquired from the book *Sarah Morton's Day.*

Twenty-eight students supplied information about Jamestown: John Smith was the leader, it was founded in 1607 or was the first colony to survive, Pocahontas saved Smith's life, it was named after King James, and its government was called the House of Burgesses. Twenty-three made statements about Plymouth: William Bradford was the leader; it was governed by the Mayflower Compact; Squanto and Samoset helped the colony become established; and settlers came on ships named the Godspeed, the Susan Constant, and the Discovery. Nineteen made statements about Roanoke Island: The colony had mysteriously disappeared, John White was the leader, on his return he could only find the word "Croatoan" carved on a tree, and Virginia Dare was the first English baby born in the New World.

Slavery was mentioned by 18 students. These responses focused on its horrors: crowded conditions in slave ships, hard work, cruel treatment, or poor housing and clothing. Finally, two students mentioned that tobacco became an important crop and 14 reported unique observations: Not every colony had a fleet of ships; most colonies are started where a country puts their flag on a piece of land; some are still around and are states with the same names; colonists made tin lanterns and corn bread; there were famous things in colonies like Phyllis Weatby [sic: Wheatley]; some colonists were searching for the cities of gold; Maine was called Massachusetts back then; Indians don't get along with people and might even kill them; the Pilgrims' village was dull and boring; the slaves came over here on their own but then were taken over by white men; Sarah Morton and her friend Elizabeth played a game called a knicker box; most of the time people looking for something did not find it; a set of comments and questions about slavery (quoted below); and the statement that "I'm glad that people are not slaves anymore."

Except for a few of these unique observations and a few instances of confusion or misconception, the students' statements reflected what the teacher had taught. Most of the confusions involved mixing up John Smith with John White or events that occurred at Jamestown with events at Plymouth.

Our interviews the previous year had revealed misconceptions about slavery: that the slaves were white people from Europe rather than black people from Africa and/or that slavery involved voluntary acceptance of low-paying and undesirable work (for lack of better opportunities), without understanding that it involved kidnapping and forced labor (Brophy, 1990a). This time, Lake spent more time on slavery and addressed those misconceptions more directly, with successful results.

Boys were more likely to talk about the colonies in general and to recount information about Jamestown, Plymouth, or Roanoke Island. Girls were more likely to talk about hardships and problems faced in the early colonies (especially by children), about slavery, and about female individuals (Pocahontas, Virginia Dare, and especially Sarah Morton). Representative responses follow.

Boys

- I learned why they came. They came for gold. Some people came for religious freedom. There was an island called Roanoke Island. It was found but they ran out of supplies, so the captain went back to get supplies. When he came back there was no one in sight, not even one person, so John White the captain said, "Maybe they went to the other side of the island." So they went over to look, but no one was there. He said, "Maybe they went to another island." So they went to another island, but no one was there and then John saw something on a tree that said "Croatoan," and on another tree he saw "Croa."
- The kids could not do very much. They could not sit at the table or talk unless spoken to. I learned about England's King James and the history of America. I also learned why people came to America and what it was like here. I learned about slaves, how they got here, and how they acted and how they were treated.

Girls

- I learned that they are part of a country that is separated from another part. I learned that some colonies have mysteries to them like Roanoke Island. I learned about slavery, how some slavemasters were mean and cut their heads off if they do something. That slaves had to work all day and only on special days they would get to have a gathering with their family and tell stories. I learned about Jamestown, where they were dying and getting killed by Indians and their leader left Jamestown. They had laws and named Jamestown after the leader John Smith.

- I learned that the colonies were ruled by other countries like Spain. Sarah Morton had to do a lot of chores and had very little breaks. Sarah couldn't talk without her parents talking first. Sarah's parents sat at the table and she had to stand up. Sarah had a friend and her name was Elizabeth. Sarah and Elizabeth played with a knicker box.

A few other responses contained more personalized comments.

Boys

- I learned a lot about how Jamestown got its name. Indians were involved. I also learned how women came later as colonies grew. I learned that Indians don't get along with people. They might even kill them.
- I learned that living back then wasn't easy. I'm glad I wasn't a kid back then or I couldn't talk without being talked to. You had to get up at 4:00 a.m., you had to stand up eating if you were a kid, if you talked without being talked to you would get the stick. You had to wear a big rag over your shoulder when you ate. So basically what I am saying was, life then was a nightmare come true.

Girls

- Slavery is very cruel even mostly to blacks. I say this because I like black people. Some are just like white people. What I'm trying to say is what's wrong with blacks? Why were they slaves? Why did the whites fight with the blacks? I want to know.
- Most of the time, people are looking for something and don't find it. For example, the Pilgrims were looking for Jamestown but they landed at a different place and the people in Jamestown were looking for gold but they didn't find gold but they started a colony. They worked very hard and didn't have a soft bed and children were used like slaves. Many people died on the way to the place and some people died after. They had a very hard life. I'm glad that it paid off! Slaves were black and most people mistreated them like when they shipped slaves they packed them

right next to each other. It always stunk because of the sweat that stinks and I'm glad to see that people are not slaves anymore!!

Interview Findings

Questions About European Colonization of the New World

1. Why did Europeans start coming to live in the New World? Prior to the unit, nine students suggested 13 reasons. Five said that the people simply wanted to see and explore the new lands, and two each cited desires to acquire gold or riches, to acquire natural resources (minerals, trees), and to escape overcrowding in Europe. Brad thought that some came to seek the Fountain of Youth and Helen that the first European immigrants were slaves who sought freedom. Some of these responses (the search for riches, natural resources, or the Fountain of Youth) reflected information learned in the previous unit. Others were inferences that students developed on their own.

Tim: Because it was new and there was a lot of gold you could find and people hadn't found out a lot about it yet, so they'll try to explore more and because it's just new and they want to see what it's like. [Who were the people who came over?] Spain, England, and France.

Brad: There was more land here and more, I forgot what it was called—minerals they get from the ground, natural resources. I'm pretty sure that's why. And the Indians would tell some stories and told an explorer from Spain about the Fountain of Youth in Florida. That might be part of the reason why they came.

Helen: Well, in Europe, they were slaves for the king and they thought if they went to a New World where the Indians were, they wouldn't be slaves anymore. They thought, "You want to be free, come over to America."

Kay: They wanted somewhere new to be and it wouldn't be as crowded. It was new and more things were there, like trees and stuff to make houses with.

Following the unit, emphasis had shifted from a desire to explore to a desire for riches, land, or religious freedom. In addition or instead, three students suggested that Europe was overcrowded and Helen persisted in her belief that the immigrants were escaping slavery.

Brad: There was new land here and they wanted the land and resources. [Why couldn't they find them in Europe?] People had been there for a long time and they've got most of the things from over there.

Ned: They wanted to get away from the king. [Were there any other things they wanted to get?] Gold.

Sue: Because they were exploring the new land and they wanted to see what was on the new land and see if there is anything valuable. They came here to live and make colonies for the kings of their country. [Why?] So the king would have more land. [Why would that be good for the king?] Because the more land you have, the richer you are. [Who were some of these people who came?] John Smith, William Bradford, John White. [They were from what country?] England.

Kay: They were after gold and some were after religious freedom. [Any other reasons?] Fur trading.

Rita: Because they didn't want to live under the king's rules. [Any other reasons?] It was too crowded over there.

2. Many of the people who came over lived in colonies. What does that mean? What are colonies? Prior to the unit, six students could not respond, three said that colonies were villages or settlements, and one said that they were states. None mentioned anything about colonies being owned or governed by another country.

Following the unit, all 10 students made substantive responses. Four said that colonies were communities (villages, settlements, cities) but did not say anything about how they were governed. Two described colonies as independent states or nations. Finally, four described colonies as communities owned or ruled by another nation (or its king).

Several students suggested that colonies were small villages or cities. This is one of several indications in our data that study of the early colonies led students to think of them as very small settlements (probably surrounded by stockades). This image persisted in certain students' later learning about developments between 1607 and 1776. Some did not realize that, by 1776, the colonies had become large and populous precursors to today's eastern seaboard states.

Tim: It's sort of like a state or group of people. It's sort of like a country and they have their own government and they just live separately from the other colonies.

Mark: It was a group of people that lived away from the English, but they were still ruled by King James.

Helen: It's like a village with not a lot of people and it's not a big piece of land—it's really small—and a lot of people live in it. It's really broken down. There aren't any fancy houses or anything.

Kay: A colony is a little village that has many houses and the person who brought them there would be the king or ruler of that colony. The colony was along the Atlantic Ocean.

3. Native American Indians were already living here when the English came. So how could the English explorers claim the land for England? Prior to the unit, this question produced a variety of responses. Among students who focused on the English, two suggested that they did not know that the Indians were there or that the land belonged to them, but one noted that the English took the land by force and three stated that they were greedy, arrogant, or lacking in respect for the Indians. Among students who focused on the Native Americans, three suggested that they did not know that they had discovered land and could lay formal claim to it and three that they did not realize what the English were doing until it was too late to stop them. Sue was the only student to describe a fundamental difference between the English and the Indians in ideas about land ownership and use. Brad made an extended attempt to grapple with the question by reasoning from limited prior knowledge.

Jason: They might not have seen them at first.

Brad: The Indians weren't exploring when they found the United States. You kind of need people there or something there to discover. So the Indians didn't really discover it. . . . I don't think the Indians marked it off. They marked it off in tribes, like the Plains Indians, South Central, Northwest, and they kind of stayed in their own groups, but they didn't say, "This is my tipi, stay out of it." They kind of shared. They didn't know basically how big the United States were and when Christopher Columbus discovered the Bahamas and then came back on a second voyage, I forgot his name, he went off, and an Indian told him about the Fountain of Youth in Florida. The way it sounded to me, there basically wasn't any Indians there. You just put a flag there and it would kind of be yours as far as you could see. Spain was doing most of the exploring then and then France and England came and did some more exploring. They thought America should be Christopher Columbus's because he discovered it first, but really he discovered the Bahamas. I'm not really sure how they could just come and take the land.

Sue: Well, some of the Native Americans didn't like it because it was no one's land. It was just there so people could walk on it. [The

Indians didn't stick their flag in the ground and say, "This land is ours," is that what you mean?] They did do that but the Native Americans just wanted it to be everyone's land. But the English wanted to claim it for their king or queen.

Kay: They didn't think much of the Indians. They just thought, "I found it, it's mine." Plus, the Indians probably didn't know they were there until a couple of months after they were there, or maybe a couple of years.

Following the unit, the students placed more emphasis on how the English took the land by force and were arrogant in not respecting the Native Americans.

Jason: They signed a treaty. [Who?] England with the Indians. [What did the treaty say?] It said that "you are giving us this land."

Tim: They just didn't really care. The English just took it. None of them cared. [How could they just take the land?] Sometimes they'd just have treaties and if the Indians moved out, they'd give the Indians land and just leave them alone, but they just kept taking the Indians' land and the treaties didn't really mean anything.

Sue: They didn't care what the Indians said about it. They just wanted to claim land for their king.

Kay: They just put a flag on it and said it was theirs and the Indians didn't have a way of claiming it.

4. Why do you think England started sending people over here to live in these settlements that we called colonies? Why did England want to have colonies? Prior to the unit, three students could not respond, two suggested that England wanted to relieve overcrowding, and the other five suggested that additional land would enhance English power, wealth, or prestige.

Following the unit, only one student could not respond, three spoke of relieving overcrowding, and six spoke of enhancing power, wealth, or prestige. Some of the latter students pictured a personal rivalry between *monarchs* seeking to outdo one another, rather than a competition between *nations* for hegemony in the New World. None said anything about colonies as sources of raw materials or as markets for finished products.

Jason: It was good to have colonies because it made them more powerful. [How did it make them more powerful?] They thought the more you had, the richer you were.

Mark: King James wanted the first people that came over to get gold plus more land. [How did gold and land help the king?] It made him richer.

Helen: More land for the king. He had only this little bit of land and he didn't think that was good enough for him. He wanted to have all of this land.

Rita: For the land. [Why?] Because it was overpopulated and whatever is on the land, the king owns.

Questions About the Early Settlements

5. *Have you heard of Roanoke Island? (If yes: What do you know about it?)* Prior to the unit, no student knew anything about Roanoke Island. Following the unit, all 10 knew that it had been the site of the "lost colony," and most recounted the story at some length. The majority explained the gist correctly, although four referred to the leader as John Smith (rather than John White). Helen conflated Roanoke Island with Jamestown, creating an expanded story that included some charming commentary about life at the time as she understood it. An interesting gender difference appeared: Four of the girls but none of the boys mentioned Virginia Dare.

Brad: Yes, it's a lost island. They came from England and they had a fort there and they ran out of supplies. John Smith had to go back to England and get more supplies. There was a war and they said he had to stay there and help. It was 3 years before the war was over and when he went back, there wasn't anything left on the island. It's a mystery.

Sue: John White took his family over there and his daughter was married, so they took her husband along and she was ready to have a baby and they ran out of supplies and he had to go back. He went to get more supplies and there was a war going on and he couldn't leave for 3 years. The lady's daughter was named Virginia Dare. Anyway, John White came back and no one was there and all he could find was a tree that said "Croatoan." [So what happened to Roanoke Island?] It just disappeared. The fort was ruined. Nobody knows what happened.

Helen: King James sent three ships over and they were called the Godspeed, the Susan Constant, and the Discovery. He sent the ships from England and the captain of the ship was John Smith and these ships were really dirty. They got there and they lived really good. There were Indians. It was a good clean life. John Smith's daughter was Virginia Dare and she was pregnant at the time and the father was John White. John White went back to England and there was a war going on and at Roanoke Island the Indians started to get real mean and then John Smith went on the Indians' land and the Indians caught him and the Indian chief's daughter, Pocahontas, told her father not to do that. Back then when a daughter sticks up for another person, it means that Pocahontas owned him because she saved his life. Meanwhile, John White went to England and there was a war going on and when he came back with all the supplies and right before John White left, Virginia Dare had the baby. He went back and Roanoke Island and all the people were gone. People didn't know what happened to it. I think that something happened between the Indians and the Americans and the Indians killed them all.

6. *Have you heard about Jamestown? (If yes: What do you know about it?)* Prior to the unit, seven students had heard of Jamestown but only Rita could say anything about it. She related story of John Smith and Pocahontas, but conflated it (or at least the name of the Indian woman) with the story of Hiawatha.

It's Hiawatha. Her dad was chief of the Native Americans that lived there. Then Hiawatha fell in love with this one guy. He was one of the Pilgrims. They went to Jamestown and went over and found this land. It was real nice land to live in, so they named it Jamestown and then the Indians . . . Hiawatha would go over there and spy on them, and they were trying all this stuff to grow corn and how to fish, and Hiawatha told them how to fish and stuff. Everybody in Hiawatha's village had to work and Hiawatha's dad didn't have her work. She got to play all the time and she was playing and she saw these guys and she fell in love with this one. She told her father about it and she said if they didn't hurt them, then they'd let them stay. Then these guys found Hiawatha's village and they started taking corn away from them and nobody seen it and Hiawatha was walking over there and she seen it, but she didn't tell her father because she loved this guy. [Is this guy's name John Smith?] Yeah. Finally her father found out about it because everybody told him about it. The girls in the village seen them. So Hiawatha's father sent troops over and John Smith got captured and so during this, everybody got dressed up because Hiawatha's father was going to sacrifice him to this god.

Following the unit, nine students supplied at least two facts each about Jamestown. Six mentioned that it was named after King James, three that John Smith was the leader, three that the colony was helped by Pocahontas, two that Jamestown was the first colony to survive, and two that it was governed by the House of Burgesses. The students also provided unique responses: The colony was surrounded by a stockade, many men died during the first year, some concentrated on finding gold rather than on doing needed work, the colony later became Virginia, and the people grew tobacco. Rita once again related the John Smith-Pocahontas story, this time naming Pocahontas correctly but referring to John Smith as John White.

Mark: The main reason they went there was to find gold but they didn't find it and nobody was helping build up the colony because they wanted to find gold. A lot of them knew they wouldn't find it and John Smith made up a rule that said if you didn't work, you didn't get to eat or have any shelter. Jamestown was the first surviving colony. [Anything else you can think of?] Pocahontas was one of their friends. She was an Indian girl.

Rita: Pocahontas helped them to survive. Pocahontas was an Indian princess and there was Powhatan and he wanted to kill John White and Pocahontas saved him twice.

7. Have you heard about Plymouth Rock or Plymouth Plantation? (If yes: What do you know about it?) In contrast to their preunit ignorance of Roanoke Island and Jamestown, all of the students had heard of Plymouth Rock (but not Plymouth Plantation) and nine could supply information about it. Seven stated that Plymouth Rock was where the Pilgrims landed, two that it was in Massachusetts, and one that the first Thanksgiving was held there. Kay thought that the Pilgrims literally sailed into Plymouth Rock and had to stop there because the boat was damaged. Several other students said that the Pilgrims landed "on" (rather than "at") Plymouth Rock, so they might have shared this misconception.

Jason: It's where the Pilgrims landed.
Mark: The Pilgrims landed on Plymouth Rock.
Kay: I think the Pilgrims first came and hit that rock and that made the boat stop. They got off onto the United States.

Following the unit, Kay still thought that the Pilgrims had slammed into Plymouth Rock. All 10 students supplied various facts about the Plymouth colony. Eight said that it was founded by the Pilgrims, six that they had come for religious freedom, three that William Bradford was the leader, and three that their ship had been blown off course. Two mentioned the Mayflower Compact and two that the colony was located in Massachusetts. Individuals said that the first Thanksgiving was held in Plymouth, that it was a very small colony, that Sarah Morton lived in it, that most of the time the colonists got along with the Indians, and that they were helped by Squanto.

Tim: William Bradford and a bunch of guys went over. William Bradford was the leader and they were Pilgrims. They wanted their own church so they came over from England and started to build a colony in America. . . . Plymouth Rock was one of the first colonies. It was small.

Sue: The Pilgrims came over and William Bradford made them sign the Mayflower Compact. They had to sign it or be shipped back to England. It said they had to work and stuff. It was like a promise. [Do you know why the Pilgrims came to the colony?] They were really going to Jamestown but the wind took them to Plymouth.

Kay: The Pilgrims sailed across the sea and came ashore and hit this one big rock and they named the colony Plymouth. They were going to find new land for religious freedom.

Rita: The Pilgrims went to Massachusetts. It's rough and cold in the winter and the Indians taught them how to plant corn. Squanto helped them. [Who were the Pilgrims?] They came from England and they came because they didn't want to follow the king's rules because he told them what church to go to. The Pilgrims thought that wasn't fair so they went to the new land.

Questions About the People and Life in the Colonies

8. Do you know anything about groups of people who decided to leave England and come to live in the New World? (If student names a group, probe this initial response and then ask about other groups.) Prior to the unit, only two students were able to respond. Teri characterized English emigrants as "people who wanted to live somewhere else," and Jason described the Pilgrims as seeking to escape the mean king of England.

Following the unit, all 10 students identified at least one reason why people left England for America. Seven mentioned gold or riches; seven, religious freedom; four, land; one, a better life; and one, escape from overcrowding. Most did not realize that people of the times usually worked on farms. Four mentioned people coming for land, but Tim assumed that most came for other reasons and Helen thought that people became farmers only if they could not get better jobs.

Tim: A lot of them were people who wanted to find gold. They came over here for the gold. [Were there some farmers?] I'm sure there were some, but not a lot. [Any other kinds of people?] Just people that wanted more land. They came here because there was a lot of land.

Sue: They wanted religious freedom. The king made them go to his church and they didn't want to do that so they came over for religious freedom. [Why did other people come to the colonies?] To build a better life and to discover gold and stuff.

Helen: They came for religious freedom and to get away from people. [What kind of people were they?] Back then, there weren't a lot of jobs. You couldn't expect to be a truck driver. It was hard to get a job and they didn't have jobs, so they planted corn, so I guess you can call them farmers. They just grew crops and other stuff.

9. Why did the Pilgrims decide to leave England and come to America? Prior to the unit, five students could not respond and one guessed that the Pilgrims were searching for riches. The other four indicated that the Pilgrims wanted to escape the king, but only Rita understood that the problem focused on religious freedom.

Mark: They wanted to be free of the king. [Why?] Because they didn't really like what he wanted them to do. [What did he want them to do?] I don't know.

Rita: The king was forcing them. They had to believe a certain way and they said, "I don't want to believe this way." So they tried to pack up their stuff but they could only take one cat and one dog. So they got on these ships and went to Plymouth Rock. They wanted to believe how they wanted to believe. [Are you talking about believing in God?] Yes. The king told them they had to go to a certain church and they had to do this and that. If they didn't, they'd get killed.

Following the unit, eight students stated that the Pilgrims came for religious freedom. Brad said for new land and Teri could not respond.

Jason: They wanted their own church. . . . The king said that they had to go to a certain church.

Helen: This man built a church and said if you live in England, you go to my church and the people didn't think that was fair. They wanted to believe in God but not the way that he did.

10. How do you think life in the colonies compared with life back home in England? What were some similarities and differences? Prior to the unit, nine students generated 15 comparisons. Four suggested that the colonies were mostly wilderness whereas England had developed houses and roads; three that the colonies had few people but England had a dense population; two that the colonists enjoyed freedom but the English had to submit to the king; and two that the colonists had to adjust to unfamiliar geography and life conditions whereas the English enjoyed familiar settings and routines. Individual students indicated that the English could buy what they needed at stores but the colonists could not, and that there were more animals, wars, and dark-skinned people in the colonies.

Tim: It was sort of different because there were a lot of trees and England was just a bunch of buildings—not a bunch but some. [How else was it different?] Here you'd have to sleep in tents and there you'd have a little house.

Brad: In the colonies, you were just learning things and they had a few wars and they were just getting settled. But back home they knew where everything was and they had friends. You know where you're at.

Kay: It was different because there was more trees and wild life here. In England it was more developed and had more houses and villages and cities and stuff.

Following the unit, all 10 students responded, generating 22 comparisons. These were mostly the same ones noted prior to the unit, but with a different emphasis. Seven students now noted that the English could purchase food and supplies in stores but the colonists could not, and five that the colonists were not under tight control by the king. These popular postunit responses reflected themes emphasized during the unit.

Three students now mentioned that the colonies were a wilderness but England was more developed, and individuals mentioned that the colonists had to cope with the unfamiliar rather than rely on familiar routines, that the New World had a small and isolated population, that the colonists did not have medicine, that the colonies did not have the right materials to allow them to make the supplies that were manufactured in England, that there were jobs in England that did not exist in the colonies, that there were Native Americans in the colonies, and that the colonists had to fight or learn to get along with the Native Americans.

Tim: Here there wasn't a lot of people or houses yet and over there, they were all settled and they were ruled by kings and queens. They just had leaders of different groups of people like the Pilgrims.

Ned: It was easier in the colonies because they weren't being bossed around. It was harder because the colonists had to find their own food. They didn't have stores where you can buy stuff.

Kay: In the colonies you had to do everything on your own but in England the king would tell you to do things, but everything was already made and you could just buy it.

Rita: Life was different. It was harder because you had to fight for your food because of the animals. You couldn't go to the 7-Eleven or other stores. They had stores in England.

Questions About Colonies' Locations and Their Implications

11. *Most of the early colonies were located near water—either right on the seacoast or on rivers. Why was that?* We expected that students would emphasize the need for fresh drinking water and the importance of boat travel at the time. These were the two most common themes, both before and after the unit. However, few responses communicated clear understanding that water is vital to life or that water transportation was crucial to the colonists. Most depicted the colonists' behavior as a matter of convenience rather than necessity.

Prior to the unit, seven students generated nine reasons for location of colonies on the seacoast or on rivers. Four emphasized that people traveled by boat then, three that they needed water to drink, and two that these locations made for convenient fishing or swimming.

Tim: Because that's pretty much the only way you can get water. If you lived out in the middle of nowhere, you couldn't get water.

Mark: So they would have more to drink.

Ned: So they can fish. [Any other reasons?] Get around in boats.

Sue: Maybe they liked the water. [Why?] On a hot day, they could go swimming or something. [Any other ways it might have been good for them to be by the water?] To drink the water . . . fish.

Following the unit, all 10 students provided at least one reason. Five mentioned that people traveled by boat in those days, and four mentioned the need for drinking water. Individuals said that location on the seacoast made it possible to see resupply ships coming from Europe and that location on rivers would make it easier to fish, to hunt animals who came to drink there, or to find one's way back home in the wilderness. These postunit responses still indicated only limited understanding of the necessity for fresh drinking water and for travel by boat.

Jason: They wanted to be close to the water so if they wanted to go back, they wouldn't have to walk through a lot of woods and stuff. They didn't want to get lost.

Tim: I'm not sure. Probably so they could go back and forth to the big ships.

Mark: So they'd have more water to drink, but they stopped drinking it because the salt water was dehydrating their bodies. [This refers to what he had learned about Jamestown.]

Teri: They lived near the water because if there was a ship coming, they would know about it. [Why would they want to see a ship?] Because maybe more people would be coming or more supplies. [This reflects an incident in the Sarah Morton story.]

Sue: They didn't have enough water, so they lived on the shore. [They depended on that water for drinking?] Well, for cleaning and for washing clothes and cooking.

Helen: I don't know—no faucets. Deer and buffalo and stuff went to the river to drink and the colonists could catch them by the water for lunch or breakfast.

Questions About Slaves and Slavery

The previous year, in the process of teaching about plantations, Lake had mentioned the difficult lives lived by slaves. However, she had not said much about who the slaves were, where they had come from, or how they had come to America. Consequently, many students emerged from the colonies unit believing that the slaves were a subset of the people who had come from England, perhaps as indentured servants or as people who accepted low-paying, unpleasant jobs because they lacked better alternatives. This year, Lake made it clear that the slaves were black people from Africa who had been forcibly kidnapped and sold into slavery, transported to America in crowded slave ships, and then forced to work for their owners.

12. *What is a slave?* Prior to the unit, all 10 students knew that slaves were people forced to work for others against their wills. Two added that slaves were owned and sold as property. Thus, their knowledge of slavery was much greater than that of the previous year's fifth graders.

Jason: People that were made to do other things . . . they do things they might not like to do. [Are they paid?] No. They were forced to do things.

Rita: It's a black person who has to work for someone else and do whatever they say or they'll get whipped or something. [Do they get paid?] No, they don't. They might get a treat, like molasses.

Following the unit, the students again described slaves as people forced to work for others against their wills, and seven now added that slaves were owned and sold as property.

Mark: It means that somebody would hold a person against their will and make them do stuff they don't want to do. They had to do everything for the people that bought them. They had to grow fields, tobacco and cotton and different things.

Sue: A slave had a hard life because they had to do everything, but they didn't get paid. They'd only get clothes they needed and a little tiny room. If they talked back, they'd get a warning or get a lashing.

13. *Where were the slaves from originally?* Prior to the unit, only Brad mentioned Africa, and even he was not sure. Four did not know, and the other five suggested that the slaves were from Europe, from South America, or from the colonies themselves. Three described slaves as black people.

Following the unit, eight students stated that the slaves were from Africa. Helen still thought that they were from Europe. Brad's response indicated continued uncertainty about whether all the slaves were black people from Africa, as well as difficulty in distinguishing slaves from paid servants.

A slave is the property of someone. People from the colonies and England would go to Africa and kidnap them and bring them over on ships and sell them to people who wanted to buy them. You could do whatever you wanted with them. They used them for farm work and housecleaning work and cooking their food and serving it. Sarah Morton tended the fireplace and polished the copper. I'm not sure if she was a slave or not. I think she was. I think she lived in Plymouth. [Did you know most of the slaves were in the southern colonies?] No, but it makes sense, because it's closer to Africa. They'd use slaves for pulling the plows or planting. Some people would have their own groceries, so the slaves would do other things. [How much did they pay the slaves?] The slaves didn't get paid, but they could earn money by going to someone else and doing extra jobs for them. [What's the difference between a slave and a servant?] A servant would just do your dishes and I think they could get paid and they'd serve you. Kind of like a maid or a butler. A slave would do the really hard work. Mostly slaves just do what they're told or they'd get whipped by a whip.

Questions About Colonial Governance and the Revolution

14. How were the colonies governed? Prior to the unit, only three students could respond. Kay suggested that the people who discovered the land exercised authority over the colonies. Jason and Rita suggested that the colonists elected their leaders.

Following the unit, all 10 students responded. Seven suggested that leaders were elected and/or laws were adopted through town meetings or other democratic voting procedures. In addition or instead, six suggested that monarchs or appointed leaders exercised authoritarian control of the colonies, five mentioned the House of Burgesses at Jamestown, and three mentioned the Mayflower Compact at Plymouth. Most described these governmental structures as mechanisms for exercising authority over the people. Children commonly describe governments and laws as coercive, serving to keep people from behaving badly and thus preventing chaos (Sinatra, Beck, & McKeown, 1992; Torney, 1977). However, at least one student viewed the House of Burgesses more as a mechanism for democratic self-government.

Tim: They usually didn't have one person rule everything like they did back in England. They'd work out a government and vote on everything.
Mark: Jamestown had the House of Burgesses and they made up the rules. Plymouth had the Mayflower Compact that said they'd work together. [What does it mean, the House of Burgesses?] It was just

people that met to make the rules . . . people from around the colony that people voted on.

Sue: Jamestown had the House of Burgesses and they made up the rules and before they had that, John Smith made up a rule that if you don't work, you don't eat. The other rule from Plymouth was the Mayflower Compact.

Helen: They had leaders, kings, queens. [How did they get laws?] House of Burgesses, Continental Congress. [What was the House of Burgesses?] It was this place and they made the laws there and it was like the government and you couldn't disagree with them.

Discussion

As they began the unit, most students knew that the Pilgrims had landed at Plymouth Rock, but they did not have information about the settlements at Roanoke Island, Jamestown, or Plymouth Plantation. They did not know much about the events that transpired, either in Europe or in America, between 1607 and 1776. They thought of colonies as small settlements (e.g., villages surrounded by stockades), usually without knowing much about why mother countries wanted to establish colonies. Except for the few who remembered that the Pilgrims came for religious freedom or to escape a mean king, they did not know much about who came from Europe or why they decided to come. Some thought that they were escaped slaves or wanted to leave Europe because it was too crowded.

By the end of the unit, the students had acquired a good deal of information about Roanoke Island, Jamestown, and Plymouth, as well as the institution of slavery. With the help of stories drawn from children's literature, they developed appreciation of the early emigrants as people: who they were, where they came from, why they came, and what their lives were like in the colonies. Because so much of this information was new to them, they frequently confused things (John Smith with John White, events at Jamestown with events at Plymouth) and overgeneralized from specific examples (thinking that all colonies were small settlements surrounded by stockades or that all colonial children lived like Sarah Morton). They also remained fuzzy about the timelines involved and about the development of the colonies into 13 sizable and populous political entities. Still, it was clear that the students had developed initial ideas that enabled them to understand such things as the distinction between the early explorers and the later colonists, the fact that European countries established colonies on land that they had explored and claimed earlier, and that they took by force lands occupied by Native Americans.

Much of what the students remembered and emphasized in their responses were key elements in the stories that they had heard during the unit. Stories tend to focus attention on particular incidents and details. One side effect of this may be to minimize attention to important historical concepts and generalizations. The tendency to think of colonies as small villages or to think that all colonial children's lives were like that of Sarah Morton have already been mentioned. Other examples include tendencies to think of governments primarily as ways to force people to work for the communal good (based on what the students had learned about John Smith's rules and the Mayflower Compact), that Europeans did not know how to farm (based on the traditional Thanksgiving story), or that most emigrants came to engage in fortune hunting rather than farming (based on stories about early Jamestown).

To the extent that the students' ideas about the colonial period remained rooted in what they had learned about the earliest settlements, their later learning about the American Revolution would tend to be limited. That is, they would tend to think of the Revolution as a squabble between King George and a few villages, rather than as an attempt by a populous confederation of sizable colonies to secure political independence from a leading imperial nation.

The students were fuzzy about the geographical aspects of colonial life. Even though unreliability of a fresh water source had been emphasized as one of the problems at Jamestown, most students failed to indicate significant appreciation of the need to secure access to fresh drinking water or the importance of inland waterways as transportation routes. In contrast to the previous year, these students did learn a great deal about who the slaves were, how they had been brought to America, and how they lived and were treated on plantations.

The data suggest the need to help the students place this learning into larger contexts. First, prior to beginning instruction about U.S. history, a few lessons might be invested in teaching key information about world history and about the organization of society and the conditions of everyday life in Europe in the fifteenth to the seventeenth centuries. It would be helpful for students to know, for example, that life in Europe during the fifteenth and sixteenth centuries was modern in many respects but still lacked engine-powered transportation and electronic communications; that cities and towns had developed but Europe was not overcrowded; that there were streets and roads but only horse-drawn vehicles; that there were books and newspapers but no

radio or television; and that most people still lived and worked on
farms.

Students also will need help in connecting the early settlements
to the forward march of history. They will need to learn that over 150
years elapsed between the founding of Jamestown and the American
Revolution, and that during that time the meaning of the term "colony" shifted from a small settlement to a much larger and more populous collection of communities that operated in many ways like a modern state (but was still under the dominion of England). This would
help them to appreciate the scope and geopolitical aspects of the American Revolution, so they would not view it as nothing more than a
few villages telling King George that they were not going to listen to
him anymore.

Finally, the students might be helped to appreciate that the colonists did not simply recreate England in North America. The development of colonial cultures and customs was influenced by what emigrants from several European nations and slaves from Africa brought
with them from their countries of origin, as well as by what the colonists learned from their interactions with various groups of Native
Americans. The blending of these influences produced unique patterns
that gradually differentiated colonial world views and lifestyles from
those prevalent in England, creating uniquely American cultures and
customs.

UNIT 5: THE REVOLUTION

In the American Revolution unit, the students learned how conflict
over taxes and other issues eventually led the colonies to unite and
declare independence from England, then to secure that independence
through the Revolutionary War. Key content included: King George
faced debt problems as a consequence of the French and Indian War;
he attempted to service this debt by imposing taxes; and the colonists
resisted these taxes, setting the stage for armed conflict. Much of this
was taught using the book *Can't You Make Them Behave, King George?*
(by Jean Fritz and published in 1977 by Coward, McCann, & Geohegan,
New York).

The unit then covered selected events leading up to the actual conflict: the Stamp Act, the Boston Massacre, the Boston Tea Party, the
Intolerable Acts, and the activities of the Sons of Liberty and the
Minutemen. Students learned about the phrase "no taxation without
representation" by writing songs and making posters. Lake read *My*

Brother Sam Is Dead (by James Lincoln Collier and Christopher Collier and published in 1974 by Four Winds Press, New York) to illustrate how the conflict divided the colonists into groups that either were loyal to the king, were bent on forming their own country, or were uncommitted to either of these factions.

Using additional tradebooks, historical fiction accounts, and her own storytelling, Lake profiled a number of revolutionary leaders, including John and Abigail Adams, Sam Adams, Paul Revere, Ben Franklin, George Washington, Thomas Jefferson, Nathan Hale, Crispus Attucks, and Francis Marion (the "Swamp Fox"). Her coverage of the war itself focused on the key battles at Trenton, Valley Forge, Yorktown, and Charleston. She featured women important to the revolutionary effort by using the book *Patriots in Petticoats* (written by Patricia Edwards Clyne and published in 1976 by Dodd, Mead & Company, New York), which described the activities of women such as Deborah Sampson, Lydia Darragh, and Sybil Ludington. Each student researched one of these women and made a product (e.g., poster, game, video, etc.) that featured her accomplishments.

Students also wrote a historical fiction account as if they were actual participants in the Revolutionary War and a point-of-view paper that required them to distinguish the perspectives of King George, the British soldiers, and the American patriots. Lake mentioned the signing of the Declaration of Independence and the writing of the Constitution but did not get into either document in any detail, leaving that for later grades.

KWL Findings

The KWL sheets instructed students to write what they knew about the American Revolution and what they wanted to learn about it. KWL data were available for three class sections.

What the Students Knew About the American Revolution

Table 4.9 shows that almost half of the students knew nothing specific about the Revolution. Nine students indicated (probably intuitively) that many died, six that it was a big war, four that it happened a long time ago, one that it was important, and one that many people were involved.

More specific details appeared in 38 responses. Four students knew that the war was fought over independence, three that the "Bluecoats won," and three that women participated. Only a few students in-

Table 4.9 What the Students Said They Knew About the American Revolution

	Boys (N = 40)	Girls (N = 31)	Total (N = 71)
A. No information			
1. I don't know anything	19	18	37
B. General Ideas			
1. Many died	4	5	9
2. Happened long ago	2	2	4
3. Big war	2	4	6
4. Important to history	0	1	1
5. Many people were in it	0	1	1
6. I know lots	1	0	1
	9	13	22
B. Specific details and Ideas			
1. Happened in the 1800s	1	0	1
2. Happened in the 1700s	0	1	1
3. Fought against British	2	0	2
4. Fought for freedom/independence	3	1	4
5. Began in 1775 and ended in 1783	2	0	2
6. Fought between England and 13 colonies	1	0	1
7. Bostonians threw tea in the bay	1	0	1
8. Paul Revere's ride	1	0	1
9. Bluecoats fought the Redcoats	1	0	1
10. Eight-year war	1	0	1
11. Cannons were used	1	0	1
12. King George was part of it	1	0	1
13. Bluecoats won	1	2	3
14. Fort Washington	1	0	1
15. Fought for Georgia and Alabama	1	0	1
16. Women served/helped men	1	2	3
17. War took place in the southern and northern states; fought for black freedom and slavery; Lincoln was president; north won/south wanted slavery	1	1	2
18. Constitution was written	0	1	1
19. Took place in the north central states	0	1	1
20. Fought in the New England states	0	1	1
21. Fought between France and us	0	1	1
22. Lasted 4 years/long time	0	2	2
23. Guns, tanks, cannons, missiles were used in ground war	0	2	2
24. Fought over whether the king should rule in the New World	0	1	1
25. Fought by the Great Lakes	0	1	1
26. Molly Pitcher	0	1	1
	20	18	38

cluded details such as references to Paul Revere, the Boston Tea Party, King George, Molly Pitcher, the Constitution, or the fact that the war was fought against the British. Two described details about the Civil War, one said that the war was fought between France and "us," and one mentioned that it was fought near the Great Lakes. The latter two responses reflected what students had learned about the French and Indian War in fourth-grade state history.

McKeown and Beck (1990) reported similar responses by fifth graders asked to tell what they knew about the Revolutionary War. Lacking specific knowledge, most students drew on an "empty war schema" to say that there were battles, many people were killed, and so forth. (Beck & McKeown, 1994). Only a few had specific knowledge that the war was fought for independence from England, although many guessed that gaining freedom had something to do with it. About half confused the Revolutionary War with the French and Indian War, the Civil War, or other wars.

What the Students Wanted to Learn

Table 4.10 outlines students' responses to the *W* section of the KWL form: 27 wanted to learn "everything," "all I can," or "a lot"; the rest asked questions that we have grouped into what, who, why, where, and when categories. These fifth graders most wanted to know about the people of the period (39 questions), why the war started or seemed necessary (25 questions), and the details, events, and terms of the war period (22 questions).

What the Students Reported Learning

The students' *L* responses made reference to a wide array of events, terms, names, and key words: Nineteen mentioned Paul Revere's ride; 17, the Boston Tea Party; 12, the first battle at Lexington; 13, the surrender at Yorktown; and 16, that the colonists won the war. Frequently mentioned people included Paul Revere (34), Francis Marion (32), King George (32), Sybil Ludington (12), and Molly Pitcher (8). Twenty-four students mentioned the Sons of Liberty; 22, the Boston Tea Party; 22, the Boston Massacre; 16, the Redcoats; 11, the French and Indian War and Lexington; and 10, the Stamp Act, Yorktown, and Concord.

A number of students drew cause–effect inferences: Fourteen suggested that the harassment of the Redcoats by colonists was a primary cause for the Boston Massacre; 10 related the efforts of Francis Marion to the retreat of British troops from the southern colonies; 10 noted

Table 4.10 What the Students Wanted to Know about the American Revolution

	Boys (N = 40)	Girls (N = 31)	Total (N = 71)
A. *Vague generic responses*			
1. Everything (or all I can or a lot)	14	13	27
B. *"What" questions (events, terms, concepts)*			
1. What happened?	5	2	7
2. What was the Revolutionary War?	2	0	2
3. What does "revolutionary" stand for?	1	0	1
4. What weapons were used?	3	0	3
5. Cost of weapons	1	0	1
6. Different battles	2	0	2
7. How many people died?	2	3	5
8. How did people survive the war?	0	1	1
	16	6	22
C. *"Who" questions (people)*			
1. Who started the war?	4	2	6
2. Who won the war?	4	3	7
3. Whose side were we on?	1	0	1
4. Who fought in it?	2	8	10
5. What did they want from the war?	1	0	1
6. Were Indians involved?	1	0	1
7. Did women die in the war?	1	0	1
8. Who was president?	1	0	1
9. What famous people were in the war?	2	3	5
10. What famous people died in the war?	1	0	1
11. Who was the war with?	0	4	4
12. Who were the women in it?	0	1	1
	18	21	39
D. *"Why" questions (reasons)*			
1. Why did the war start?	11	4	15
2. Why were they fighting?	3	0	3
3. Why did we have the war?	0	6	6
4. Why was the war important?	0	1	1
	14	11	25
E. *"Where" questions (location)*			
1. Where did it take place?	6	3	9
F. *"When" questions (chronology)*			
1. When did the war take place?	3	3	6
2. When did the war end?	2	0	2
3. How long did the war last?	1	0	1
4. What year did it start?	1	0	1
	7	3	10

that the Stamp Act, the Quartering Act, and the Intolerable Acts led to the Revolutionary War; 18 wrote about how the French and Indian War debt created circumstances that eventually turned many colonists against England; and seven described the work of the Sons of Liberty and the Boston Tea Party as tied to the British tax on tea.

Girls were more likely to talk about the Boston Tea Party; boys about Francis Marion, the colonial victory, and details of the war (key figures, battles, and weaponry).

Interview Findings

Questions About Events Leading Up to the Revolution

1. How did the United States become an independent country? Why? Prior to the unit, three students could not respond. Jason said by winning the Revolutionary War, Helen that the colonists had a constitution and were after religious freedom, Sue and Rita that a war was fought for freedom, Mark and Kay that people fought over the land (without elaborating). Teri related ideas about settling the New World. Thus, only Jason had specific prior knowledge.

Following the unit, the students answered with ease. Four noted that the patriots fought the British and won the Revolutionary War, five spoke of winning freedom, and six mentioned the tax issue. Helen mentioned the signing of the Declaration of Independence, although she included Johnny Tremain among the signers.

Tim: King George started to tax the colonists on tea and started to send his British soldiers over here to make sure they were doing OK. Then King George said the soldiers had to move in with the colonists. If they knocked on your door, you had to let them in and let them live with you. There were taxes on about everything. [What effect did that have on the colonists?] They were mad about it. They had to pay taxes for the war even though they didn't really fight in the war. King George decided to tax people on tea and have them pay for the war.

Sue: They were sick and tired of the king taxing them and the Redcoats killing people because of the Boston Massacre. They had a war and the last war was in Yorktown and the colonists won so they were free from King George so they could live like they wanted to.

Helen: I really don't know how that happened for sure. I know John Hancock and John Adams and Johnny Tremain, and someone else,

I can't remember who, but they signed the Declaration of Independence and that meant that our country was free from England. [So just by signing that piece of paper, that meant they were free?] Yeah. Before they signed the paper they had to win a war first.

2. Colonists changed their minds about being under British control. Why? Prior to the unit, only Rita approached an accurate idea, and she seemed unsure of herself.

Brad: I'm not sure, but it doesn't seem like it would be fun to be ruled around. They probably wanted their own way and their own lives.
Rita: I think the king wanted too much. [Too much what?] Too much gold and stuff like that from the colonies and they said, "We're no longer yours. We're not going to follow your rules or anything."

After the unit, all 10 students stressed the taxation issue, which several connected with the French and Indian War. The following were mentioned by one student each: the Boston Massacre, the closing of Boston Harbor, the Quartering Act, and the Stamp Act.

Mark: Because after the French and Indian War, the colonists thought that King George should pay for it because it was his land they were fighting on. [What did King George think?] He thought they should pay. He didn't want to pay the bill so he started taxing a number of items.
Sue: Because he was taxing them and it was getting out of hand because he was taxing them so much they were going poor and he sent over Redcoats and King George made them knock on a door and the people that lived there had to shelter them and give them food whether they wanted to or not. I would think King George wasn't a very fair king. [Why was the taxation thing a problem?] He was taxing everything, even tea. Then he sent over stamps on things which was called the Stamp Act and they still had to pay more taxes and they were finally getting sick of it. [Why did he want to tax them so much?] Because he couldn't pay for the war. [What war was that?] The French and Indian War.

2A. What were the problems caused by the French and Indian War? This question, asked only after the unit, produced a range of responses. Five students told about how the British had won the war and thereby protected colonial territory, then asked the colonists to help pay for the war through increases in taxes. Helen told a fanciful story of the French and Indians winning the war, subsequent anger by King George, and his resolve to win the territory back through the Revolutionary War. Kay also became confused and attributed victory to the French and Indians.

The latter responses are reminders that the French and Indian and the Revolutionary Wars need to be taught carefully, lest students develop misunderstandings. This is particularly important because students often must wait until eighth grade to deal with this material again in any systematic fashion.

Tim: The taxes were sort of because King George taxed the colonists for the French and Indian War. He could have paid for it himself but he didn't want to, so he just decided to let the colonists pay for it. [Was there some reason he wanted the colonists to pay for it?] Not really. He just didn't want to pay for it. [Who was fighting whom?] The French and Indians were fighting against the British in the territories and unknown lands—the western part. [Were the colonists really involved in this war?] No. [What were they fighting about?] I think the Indians and the French wanted the western part and the English fought them off so they could get it right now. [Who won that war?] The British. [Did fighting that war benefit the colonists?] Yeah, because if they hadn't, the French and Indians could have took over the colonies.

Brad: The colonists didn't want to pay for it and the king taxed them, mainly tea and some other products used in everyday life, and then he sent over the Redcoats because the colonists went under self-control. [What does that mean?] Getting out of hand. The Sons of Liberty dumped the tea into the harbor and that got out of hand, so they sent over Redcoats and the Redcoats shot somebody because he got hit with a snowball and those are some of the problems that were caused by that.

Helen: The colonists kept moving over and over in this area where the Indians were. Well, they moved into the Indians' land and said, "This is my land now. It belongs to King George." Well, the Indians and the French people all lived there and the French and Indians got together and fought King George. [Why did this French and Indian War cause problems?] That was one of the things that led up to the Revolutionary War. [Explain that to me. How do you mean?] The French and Indian War took place about one year before the Revolutionary War, so the French and Indian War happened and I think the French and Indians won, but King George didn't like it and he said, "How can they win? We're stronger." So they fought and that led up to the Revolutionary War which took place for 9 years. [Why did the French and Indian War lead up to the Revolutionary War?] It made King George mad.

Kay: The French came to the new land and the Indians were there and the Indians got mad and wanted to fight a war, but the French won because they had guns and knives and stuff. [Were the British also involved in the French and Indian War?] Um hum. [What side were the British people on?] Probably the French. [So the British won too?] I'm not sure. [Do you know some of the problems that were caused by the French and Indian War?] No.

3. What does "no taxation without representation" mean? Prior to the unit, no one knew. Guessing, Helen told a story about taxes and concerns about the rising cost of tea sold door to door, and Rita told a story of an unnamed king, taxes for land, and colonists "going on strike." McKeown and Beck (1990) reported a similar lack of knowledge, but ability of some students to make educated guesses, in response to a similar preunit question about "no taxation without representation."

Helen: I'd probably be guessing at it. [Take a try.] Before, when Lincoln was president they sold tea door to door and they kept raising the taxes and people fought against it, that the taxes were so high. [Did you study this?] Part of it is from my knowledge and part of it, I was just guessing.

Rita: No. Maybe the king wants tax for the land. [It says, "No taxation without representation."] They were going on strike. Maybe they don't want the king to own that land and they're not going to pay taxes for it. What was the other part? [Representation.] I don't know what that means. I think it means you represent something. You're special.

After the unit, Jason and Teri still could not respond and Mark could only guess. Helen's misconceptions continued. Tim also had trouble with the phrase.

Tim: "Don't tax us without . . . (pause)" [What does it mean to have representation?] Like no taxation without . . . they didn't get much out of that war, so they shouldn't have to pay taxes for all of it. [Is that phrase confusing?] Yeah. [Are you sure you understand it or is it difficult to understand?] I know what they're saying but . . . [How did they decide to make taxes? Not why, but how did they go about making tax laws for the colonists? Who made those laws?] King

George and people like that. [What did the colonists want?] They wanted supplies to be shipped to America.

Helen: I think it means you can't have . . . if you don't represent King George, I think you can't get a certain product. I think it was tea. I think you couldn't get tea if you don't represent the king.

For Brad, Ned, Sue, Kay, and Rita, the question posed less trouble. Each attributed the phrase to the idea that it was "unfair" to tax the colonists if they had no say in the imposition of those taxes. Jason, Mark, and Teri had been absent during the discussion of the phrase. If they had been present, they probably would have been able to explain it as well.

It is noteworthy that even half of these students could explain accurately "no taxation without representation." McKeown and Beck (1990) found that only two of 37 sixth graders could explain the phrase accurately. We do not know whether the five students quoted below would have been able to produce similarly accurate explanations a year later, but their responses to this postunit question suggest that, with careful teaching, abstract phrases and their conceptual underpinnings are not beyond the understanding of fifth graders.

Brad: They were saying it was not fair for King George to tax them when they can't share their feelings and say what they have to say. It's kind of like a vote. If we got a president and we didn't get to vote what we wanted—it was just government, that wouldn't be fair. That's what King George was doing. He was taxing them without them having their share of comments on it.

Ned: The colonists didn't want to be taxed without voting on it.

Sue: You can't tax us without us voting on it. [Was this because they were mad at the king?] Yeah. [Did the colonists want to be able to vote on the new taxes?] Yeah. They really didn't want the taxes but if he was going to tax them, they wanted to vote.

Kay: No taxes without us making it be right or declaring we want taxes.

Rita: They say that King George can't tax them without them voting on it. The colonists wanted to be able to vote on what taxes they would pay. They probably wanted that England would pay some taxes too.

4. What was the Boston Tea Party? Prior to the unit, six students did not know. Of the others, only Teri described the event as colonists dumping tea into Boston Harbor.

Mark: They were going around selling tea and they had too big of a tax on it.

Brad: I think it was a get together so one group of people like their leader could show how brave and powerful they were. [Can you tell me more about that? What happened specifically?] I think the town's king wanted to show how big and powerful he was. I think he made presents and gifts and would give them to the people that came. [Where did you learn this?] I'm kind of guessing but I think it's like the Indians over in the Northwest region.

Teri: I know! I know! There was a ship and it carried a lot of tea to Boston and some people went down to the ship and started throwing all the tea over. [Why did they pitch the tea overboard? Why didn't they just take it home with them?] Well, there was this one guy that was selling it for too much. [Were they mad about that? Was that the idea?] Yup. [Where did you learn about this?] In a book, something like "John Adams" and I got it out of the library.

Helen: They took tea door to door. [Who's they?] I don't know what they're called . . . not the president but an assistant or whatever they called them back then. They took tea door to door and they sold the tea and they kept raising the taxes because they weren't getting enough money for it so they kept raising the taxes and . . . [Who was raising the taxes?] The president, or the people that were selling it. They raised the taxes because they weren't getting enough money so the people didn't think that was fair, so they kind of went on a strike or they wouldn't buy tea unless the taxes went down.

Following the unit, all 10 students narrated the account of the Sons of Liberty dressing as Native Americans, boarding a British frigate, and dumping chests of tea into the harbor in protest against "unfair" taxes.

Tim: The Sons of Liberty were a secret club, Americans, and they were a club that was against King George and one night they decided to get on the British ships and dump all the tea. [Why didn't they just steal the tea instead of dumping it into Boston Harbor?] It was to tell them they didn't like what they were doing. They were so angry they just dumped all of it. [Do you think that was a good idea?] Yeah. [Why?] They knew what they were doing, but then King George closed down Boston Harbor and it was where they got all their supplies from.

Brad: The Sons of Liberty were . . . [Who were the Sons of Liberty? Were they Redcoats?] No. They were on the colonists' side. They were a secret group and they met at the Liberty Tree. There weren't too many people in the Sons of Liberty and they decided to go dump the tea instead of having to pay taxes. [Why did they want to dump the tea?] It's basically what was in the harbor and it was what he was mainly taxing them for. They did it to get back at King George. [Why didn't they just take it home with them instead of just dumping it in the harbor?] I'm not sure. If they took it home, they could get caught and then the Redcoats would know who took it. But when they dumped it, the king couldn't find out who specifically dumped the tea. It would be kind of obvious if they took a lot of tea home. [Do you think it was a very good idea to do that?] No. [Why not?] At the time, it seemed kind of a reasonable thing, but there could be more reasonable things to do besides that. I don't think they should have done it. I wouldn't know that King George would close down the harbor, but he would probably do other mean things, like when he sent over the Redcoats, he told them to tell the colonists to share their homes with them and to feed them and clothe them and give them shelter.

Sue: It's where the Sons of Liberty dressed up like Indians and when England sent over ships of tea, they went over and cut open the crates and threw the tea into the Boston Harbor. [Why did they throw it into the harbor instead of just taking it home with them?] Because people would have to pay taxes for it. [Why didn't they just steal it?] I don't know. [Who were the Sons of Liberty?] The colonists. They were getting mad at King George so they would have meetings to discuss what they should do about it. [Do you think it was a good idea for them to throw the tea into the harbor?] With what happened after, no. [What do you mean?] King George did this "Intolerable Act" where he closed up Boston Harbor so no ships could get in or out so the colonists couldn't get food.

As the quotes above indicate, we sometimes probed students' attitudes concerning the wisdom and morality of the colonists' protest actions. Most students judged the act by its effects (e.g., practicality) rather than by applying moral or ethical principles.

Questions About the Declaration of Independence and King George's Response

5. *What was the Declaration of Independence?* Prior to the unit, Jason identified the Declaration as a document declaring freedom from British rule. The remaining students gave vague and only partially ac-

curate responses or else guessed inaccurately. Tim and Helen confused the Declaration with the Constitution. McKeown and Beck (1990) reported that only 26% of the fifth graders they interviewed could explain the Declaration of Independence. Another 39% produced "document stew" responses that confused the Declaration with other documents. The fact that students know less about Independence Day than other national holidays can be attributed to the fact that it falls during the summer when they are not in school.

Jason: It was declaring that we weren't ruled by the English anymore. [Who is we?] The 13 colonies. [Did they write it on the wall or where was it put down or did they just go around saying to each other?] It was written on paper. [Do you know who wrote it?] Benjamin Franklin, John Adams. [Do you know when it was written?] I can't remember.

Tim: I get it confused with the Constitution a lot. [Could not elaborate in response to probes.] [Do you know when it was signed?] 1776. [Do you know what day?] July 4.

Sue: It's for people's freedom. [What people's freedom?] Slaves and ours. [Do you know when it was signed?] July 4.

Kay: It's when the president signed a paper making us the United States, I think. [Do you know when it was signed?] I don't know.

Following the unit, six students noted that it was a document separating the colonies from British control. Sue noted that it involved the rights of the colonists. Ned and Teri were still unsure. Jason thought that it involved the English signing independence for the United States (as if it had been a treaty concluding a war).

Jason: It was where the English signed the United States independence and it was free. [The English signed this or the Patriots?] Both.

Tim: It was written and it was so that they'd be one country. They wouldn't belong to England. They would be Americans. It was a document written by all the leaders from all the colonies.

Mark: It was a document that was declaring their freedom from King George. [Do you know who signed it or who wrote it?] John Hancock, Samuel Adams, but I'm not sure about anybody else that signed it. I don't know who wrote it or anything.

Sue: A whole bunch of people signed it and it just says that we have rights and it's just the rights we have on a piece of paper. [Can you tell me about what it says in there?] No.

Helen: John Hancock, John Adams, Paul Revere, and Johnny Tremain all signed a piece of paper and it said that our country is free. They all signed a document that our country was free from New England.

Kay: The Declaration of Independence was where a group of men that signed a sheet that told that we had freedom in the United States.

6. *What was in the Declaration of Independence?* This follow-up question emphasized the word "in," to see if students could describe the content of the Declaration. Prior to the unit, only Jason produced an accurate characterization. Four students knew or guessed that it said something about freedom but were not able to elaborate. Two described it as a document that brought the colonies together as a single country. These responses were better suited to the Constitution than the Declaration.

Mark: It said people would work together to make it a better country and that they could be free to do whatever they wanted.

Brad: I think it's something about freedom and getting their share of the land.

Helen: It says, this paper means that you are free and you can live in peace and you don't have to do what other people say, unless they're your parents or something because you are now free. Blacks are not slaves anymore and they have a right. John Hancock signed. [Did other people sign it too?] I don't think so.

Following the unit, eight students knew that the document declared freedom from Great Britain. Teri could not respond and Sue confused the Declaration with the Bill of Rights.

Tim: It says they were now free from England and we need to join together and be one country, American, not England. And they should join together because they were sort of separate before.

Kay: It says something like the United States of America has a freedom and the right to do anything they want. [So they were free from . . . ?] King George. [Who signed it?] George Washington, Samuel Adams, Paul Revere.

Rita: It probably said, "We declare our independence from England and we don't have to go by any of those rules."

These responses compare favorably with those reported by McKeown and Beck (1990). Of the sixth graders they interviewed, only 36% unambiguously described the Declaration as a proclamation of freedom. The other 64% produced "document stew" responses that confused the Declaration with other documents such as the Constitution or the Bill of Rights. The students we interviewed may have developed more of these "document stew" responses as they began to learn about other famous documents. McKeown and Beck reported that the frequency of such confusions actually increased from fifth grade to sixth grade because the students had been exposed to more information but had not yet sorted it out. Many students undergo confusion before developing stable understandings of the Declaration as the initial statement of independence from Britain, the Articles of Confederation as the document establishing our first form of government, the Constitution as the document that established the government that has endured since, and the Bill of Rights as the first 10 amendments to that Constitution.

7. *What did King George think about the colonists?* Prior to the unit, five students could not respond and the other five speculated that the king was probably upset or angry with the colonists.

Tim: That they were being unfair to him because he supplied all the ships and all that. They never gave him anything in return.
Brad: I think he was thinking he was going to get a lot of land and when they started arguing with the king over in the colonies, the King of England was probably getting pretty angry and probably wanted to start a war. [What would a war do for the king?] It might give him more land.
Sue: He might have been mad. I don't know.
Rita: He probably didn't have any feelings for other people and just said . . . he's probably selfish. [Did he have any reason to be upset with the colonists?] He might have been upset, but he didn't have any reason because it's his fault that they don't want to listen to him, because he asks too much.

Following the unit, all of the interviewees were able to assume a degree of empathy for King George. Lake had taught them about the different points of view surrounding the taxation issue, even though her point of view favored colonial separation and resistance to British policy.

Tim: He just thought, "Hey, we fought your war and so you should pay all the taxes and shouldn't be complaining about it." [Do you think he thought they were bad people?] Yeah, just sort of greedy.

Mark: That they were misbehaving and he sent his soldiers over to tell them to behave because King George didn't think they were. The soldiers were supposed to straighten out the colonists to make them pay their taxes.

Brad: He probably thought they were dumb to leave him because they wouldn't know what they would get in the colonies. At home they know what they were going to get and they have the supplies. He probably thought they were smart leaving him, but he was probably mad at them.

Teri: Well, he was thinking the same things they were thinking except for . . . I don't know. He didn't like the stuff they were doing. They were going against his rules.

Sue: That they were mean to him but he was really being mean to them. He thought it was just a great idea to tax them. He thought the colonists were crazy because they didn't like what he was doing.

Kay: He probably thought they were people who took land and they wanted to get away from him and that they were a group of selfish people not giving it to him.

Questions About the Revolution and Its Aftermath

8A. Eventually the Revolutionary War started. What happened and why? Probes: Where was the war fought? How long did the fighting go on? Who won? This question was asked only in the postunit interviews, after the students had acquired significant knowledge. All 10 students pointed out that the colonists won the war, giving us the United States. Tim, Brad, Helen, Kay, and Rita provided lengthy accounts. Six students mentioned Lexington; five, Concord; five, other battles; six, the Boston Massacre; two, the surrender of Cornwallis as the end point; and one, the Boston Tea Party as the origin.

Sue: The Patriots were getting mad at the Redcoats so the Redcoats decided to attack. Paul Revere and this other guy—William Dawes—they waited for the church lights to go on. Two if by water and one meant by land. Two were on so it meant by water so they rode to Lexington but they got caught by English officers, so this doctor went to warn Concord that the Redcoats were coming and they hid and then attacked them. [Who won at Concord?] The Patriots. [How long did the war go on?] Nine years I think. [After it was all done, who won?] The colonies.

Rita: The Boston Massacre happened. Some kids were throwing snowballs at the Redcoats, Lobsterbacks, whatever. At first the soldiers didn't mind but then they started shooting and they shot Crispus Attucks—one of the colonists—and then that's what really got the colonists mad. Then they won more of the Tories over to the Patriot side. Then it started getting bigger and bigger. They finally said, "We're fed up with you. Leave us alone. We're not a part of you." [What do you mean things got bigger and bigger.] More and more things happened so the colonists got more and more mad. [Can you explain that?] The Boston Massacre happened and that's what really got them going. Then the Stamp Act happened. . . . [What happened with the Stamp Act?] King George put his stamp on everything and that made the price go even higher just for him. Then he let the soldiers stay with the colonists and the colonists didn't like that. The Tories didn't mind. [How did the fighting start?] They got fed up and they said, "King George, you went too far," and they started shooting. That's called "the shot heard around the world."

9. Who were some of the leaders of the American Revolution? Prior to the unit, five students had no answer. Three boys mentioned George Washington and Tim also mentioned Thomas Jefferson and John Quincy Adams. Mark noted William Bradford and John Smith, and Rita also named Bradford. The students were unable to say much about those they did name.

Following the unit, the list grew substantially. Seven students mentioned George Washington; six noted Paul Revere and Francis Marion; and two each told of John Adams, Johnny Tremain, John Hancock, Sybil Ludington, and Molly Pitcher. Only Ned was unable to recall anyone. The other nine students provided details on at least two of the people they mentioned.

Mark: Francis Marion. He started his own army. General George Washington, Paul Revere, and I can't remember. [Tell me a little more about Francis Marion.] He started his own army and he was with the Patriots and he knew his way around the swamps so well that people called him the Swamp Fox. He knew his way around and could get out of them. The Redcoats followed him into the swamps and they got lost and he made it out. He hurt his ankle doing that and had to stay at home. He thought, "I'm going to do something about this war," and he started up his own group of farmers. [Why is he so important as a leader?] Because he lost some of the Redcoats plus he fought for the Patriots with a group of farmers. [Why did he come to your mind first?] He's the one I read the most about. [How did that happen?] Mrs. Lake read a short part about him out of a book and I just started reading about him. [What do you know about George Washington?] He was the main leader of the Patriots and he made most of the decisions. [Why is he thought to be so important? Because he made all the decisions?] Yeah. [Were there other reasons?] He was in the Sons of Liberty and he fought against the Redcoats.

Teri: George Washington. [Who besides George?] That's all I can think of. [Tell me about George. Why was he important?] He was the general of the colonists. He was also the first president. I remember the Swamp Fox. [What's the deal with him?] There was a war and most of the Patriots got captured. He had to go home because something happened to his ankle and he couldn't fight anymore. When he thought it was healed, he heard about all the Patriots being captured and so he made up his own secret Patriots. They were farmers and they had to bring their own things and they would attack from the swamp and they drove the British crazy. [Why did that story stick in your mind?] She told it to us just a few days ago.

Helen: Paul Revere, John Hancock, Johnny Tremain, John Adams— that's all I can think of. [Pick one and tell me about that person.] Paul Revere was a famous and strong Patriot. He was a silversmith. His most famous engraving was the Boston Massacre. His most famous ride was to tell the people that the Redcoats were coming and another name for the Redcoats was Lobsterbacks because they wore the red coats. [Pick another one.] There was Francis Morton. His nickname was Swamp Fox and he was raised in North Carolina and in North Carolina there's a lot of swamps and stuff, so he was raised at the swamps so he knew the area and all this stuff and he led the Redcoats into the swamp and they got lost and sank in the quicksand. He got out of the woods but the Redcoats never got out because they didn't know how to get out.

10. Who were some of the women who participated in the Revolutionary War? Prior to the unit, only Jason could name individuals— Betsy Ross and Sadie Thompson, about whom he was to prepare a report. (Jason had been sick. He was interviewed immediately upon his return to school, but this was 3 weeks into the unit.)

Following the unit, all 10 students identified at least one influential woman. Seven provided details about at least two. Molly Pitcher was mentioned nine times, Sybil Ludington five, and Deborah Sampson four. Nine additional women were recalled one time each. Occasional confusions and conflations appeared, such as Brad's characterization of the continental soldiers as "slaves" and Helen's inclusion of Louisa May Alcott.

Mark: Deborah Sampson, Molly Pitcher, Mary Corbett—that's all I can think of. [Tell me about one of them.] Molly Pitcher, her real name was Mary Hayes. They called her Molly Pitcher because she filled the Patriots' canteens with water and they started calling her Molly Pitcher, and when her husband died in the war, she took his place firing the cannons for them. [What about one of the other ones?] Deborah Sampson was a girl that wanted to be in the army so she dressed up like a man and enrolled in the army and fought for awhile and they found out her true identity.

Sue: Sybil Ludington. [What's her story?] She was like Paul Revere. She warned the people that Danbury was burning. [Who else?] Mary Pitcher. [What's the story with her?] She took her husband's spot at the cannons and General Washington or somebody told the people to abandon the cannons but she stayed there and shot the cannons.

Helen: There was Nancy Hart, Molly Pitcher, Phyllis Wheatley, Abigail Adams, Mary Carey, Louisa May Alcott. [Pick your favorite one and tell me about her.] Molly Pitcher was my favorite. [Did you do your project on her?] No, I did my project on Nancy Hart but I know more about Molly Pitcher. She took water to the soldiers and she was like a messenger and she gave water to the soldiers. Nancy Hart was an Amazon. [What does that mean?] I don't know. There was a group called the "Nancy Harts." She was born in 1771 and died in . . . no, that ain't right. [What kinds of things did she do?] She was born in Georgia and she was famous because . . . I don't really know why she was famous. [What else? How was she involved in the Revolution?] I can't remember. [Why did Molly Pitcher stick in your mind more?] Because she was more important. There were people who really didn't do anything but were in love with the Revolution, but didn't do a lot. But Molly Pitcher stays in my mind. She helped more and she was one of the reasons we won.

11. What happened after the Revolutionary War was over? Prior to the unit, three students did not know. Five deduced that "we" became the United States. Tim and Kay suggested that the country began to expand. Sue made reference to colonial governors, Rita spoke of the Congress and the introduction of voting, and Mark argued that people simply went on about their everyday lives. Few of these answers were offered with much confidence.

Tim: They became a country. [Who's they?] The people in the New World. It's the United States. [Was there a peace treaty?] Yeah. [What did the colonists do afterwards?] They kept on exploring and they explored Texas and had a couple of little wars with France and they just kept getting bigger.

Rita: The colonies weren't colonies anymore. The land became the United States and not colonies. They're united. [So they had one leader instead of 13 different leaders?] Probably there was something like the House of Burgesses. [Did they have a singular leader that led the whole United States?] I think so. [Do you know who that might be?] Abe Lincoln. [Who was the first president?] Washington. [Was he in charge of one colony or . . . ?] It says united so he was in charge of the whole United States, then Congress came. [What was Congress?] They helped support the president's rules and they gave him ideas and stuff. [How did they decide to have a Congress?] Voting.

After the unit, Tim and Ned could not respond. Four students mentioned a declaration of freedom, forgetting that the Declaration of Independence had been issued before the war. Two others noted that the war secured freedom from Britain. Mark and Rita also spoke of the formation of a government for the new country and described the election of a president. Brad and Sue guessed that the colonists threw a party and celebrated.

Jason: Everyone was free.

Brad: I think the Redcoats went back home and the colonists kind of threw a huge party that lasted a long time.

Helen: They declared freedom. [Who?] John Hancock, Johnny Tremain . . . [For whom?] The U.S.A.

Rita: Then we declared our independence. [Then what?] We've got presidents now and we made the rules and we voted and it was fair.

Discussion

These fifth graders' knowledge of the events leading up to the Revolutionary War and of the war itself grew considerably. Except for Jason, they possessed very little prior knowledge, which is to be expected for students taught within the traditional expanding communities curricular sequence.

Lake made use of children's fiction during the unit, reflecting common and widely recommended practice. Barton (1992) also noted an emphasis on children's historical fiction in a case study of a similar fifth-grade unit on the American Revolution. He described heavy reliance, by both the teacher and the students, on five overlapping narrative structures in representing knowledge about this historical period in speech and writing: The unit as a whole was treated as a sequence of causally related events that together formed the "story" of the Revolution; each event was itself treated as a story with characters, problem, and resolution; these stories emphasized the feelings and actions of individuals; fictive conversations were created spontaneously in order to convey information; and nations were endowed with human characteristics. Similar tendencies were seen in our data, both in the teacher's narration of stories about the period and in students' responses to our questions (which emphasized the words and actions of individuals and often personified acts of Parliament or diplomatic exchanges between nations as conversations between the king and colonial leaders).

As we have noted, the narrative mode seems well suited both to history as subject matter and to children as learners, and its power can be seen in the tendency of the students to remember the storylines of the children's fiction to which they have been exposed, often reporting them with considerable elaborative detail. However, the narrative mode and children's fiction in particular need to be used judiciously. Reliance on these resources can lead to distorted understandings if students are not clear about the distinctions between historical accounts and fictional recreations or if they are exposed to fictional selections depicting events that are not historically accurate (Levstik, 1989, 1993a; VanSledright & Brophy, 1992). Some such confusion was seen here in students' inclusion of Johnny Tremain as a revolutionary leader and signer of the Declaration of Independence and Louisa May Alcott as a female participant in the Revolution.

The students' understanding was tilted toward appreciation of American heroes and heroines and toward justification of the war as a defense of colonial rights and liberty. This is consistent with the teacher's bias, which assigned the moral high ground to the colonists. In turn, this is consistent with an educational approach that seeks to make children proud of their cultural and historical heritage and to help them develop some reverence for the efforts that the founders of the nation expended in ensuring freedom and liberty for their descendants. In part, this approach sacrifices the teaching of history as an interpretive discipline. These students came away from their study of the revolutionary period with a singular view of the events of the era.

If history is to be taught as an interpretive discipline, and we believe that it should, then these students will need to encounter other points of view on these events as they grow older (in eighth and eleventh grades if the typical U.S. history sequence is followed). They will need to learn about the British perspective on the war and also might benefit from a more in-depth study of the Patriot–Loyalist dispute, perhaps taking time to role play various points of view. Such activities and the pedagogical outcomes they suggest probably lie within the ability range of most of the fifth graders we interviewed. However, we cannot yet say whether the time spent would be worth the effort and bring about the desired appreciations.

Students acquired only the most rudimentary understanding of the formation of the government of the United States. In later grades, they will need more lengthy and extended treatment of the constitutional convention, the battles over how the Constitution should govern, and the Bill of Rights and the ratification process. Perhaps more time could be taken from studying the war itself and diverted to helping students understand the drama that unfolded as leaders attempted to bring order to the new nation (see Brophy & Alleman, 1996, on this point).

UNIT 6: WESTWARD EXPANSION

During the westward expansion unit, the purview shifted from the 13 eastern seaboard states to the continent as a whole. The emphasis was not on chronology but on developing appreciation of the challenges faced by the pioneers. Children's literature selections were used to bring to life the difficulties involved in crossing the mountains, attempts by Native Americans to resist incursions into their lands, and the many ways in which the pioneers had to be self-sufficient. The students also learned about the Louisiana Purchase, the Alamo, the Oregon Trail, the Gold Rush, and the building of the transcontinental railroad.

Space limitations do not allow us to present the data from this unit in detail, so we will summarize briefly the major findings and implications. As the students began the westward movement unit, they had not acquired much information about who was living west of

the Appalachian Mountains and what had been occurring there between 1492 and 1776. Some remembered that another bone of contention between Britain and the colonies was the British policy forbidding westward expansion, and all of them knew that westward
expansion occurred eventually. Most assumed that it involved additional forceful taking of lands away from Native Americans, accomplished little by little along the frontier by individual families or small
groups of pioneers acting on their own initiative. No one mentioned
the Louisiana Purchase, the Lewis and Clark Expedition, or other
government-sponsored activities. Many assumed that continued immigration and high birth rates had created overcrowded conditions in
the east.

During the unit, the students' learning about the Wilderness Trail
and the initial migration over the Appalachians was informed by selections from children's literature that focused on the logistic difficulties
and hardships involved in travel over the mountains in wagons. This
literature embodied some important advantages but also some potential disadvantages. Well-written stories, especially stories of adventure
or heroism that capture the imagination, tend to stick in the children's
minds. Compared with more analytic approaches, the story approach
is more interesting to students and offers them a narrative format that
makes it easier for them to remember connected elements of information. However, it also focuses their attention on particular incidents or
examples instead of on more powerful concepts or generalizations.
Some of these incidents or examples are lacking in historical accuracy
or even are completely fictional.

In this unit, for example, several students did not remember much
more about the Oregon Trail expedition than that it involved people
named Flaming Hair, Long Knife, and Bird Woman (the names for
Clark, Lewis, and Sacajawea used in the book *Bird Woman and Flaming Hair*, by Clare Thorne, published in 1968 by Child Craft, Chicago).
Similarly, much of what several of them remembered about the Alamo
was focused on the story of *Susanna of the Alamo* (by John Jakes, published in 1986 by Harcourt, San Diego). These and similar literature-
based learnings can be viewed either as effective development of interest and initial ideas about U.S. history or as undesirable development
of distorted knowledge, depending on what one views as desirable and
feasible when introducing elementary students to chronologically organized U.S. history.

Our findings suggest that, if historical narratives are to be used
to create memorable images of historical events, they must be used
judiciously. Care must be given to filling in gaps in students' under-

standings to establish a "bigger picture" perspective in which to situate the discrete occurrences depicted in historical fiction. This will enable young students to leave the study of history with more coherent accounts of developments across time.

The students understood certain major aspects of pioneering such as the need to travel by horse and wagon and to build a home upon reaching one's destination, but they were less clear about clothes, tools, farm implements, and other artifacts used in everyday living. Lessons based on lists of the belongings that a typical pioneer family might take with them would be helpful in this regard, as would exercises calling for students to imagine themselves to be pioneer families deciding what to take with them and what must be left behind. Information about and opportunities to see demonstrations of pioneer crafts such as spinning yarn, weaving cloth, or making soap or candles would be useful as well.

As the unit progressed, it focused more and more exclusively on the activities of the pioneers. Native Americans, and later Mexicans, were pictured primarily as faceless impediments to the pioneers' agendas, rather than as fully developed characters with agendas of their own. A desirable addition to this unit would have been an update about the experiences of Native Americans as the United States expanded westward. At a minimum, this would include reminders that the settlers were taking over lands occupied by Native Americans, who were forced to keep retreating ahead of an advancing frontier if they wanted to maintain their traditional ways of living. A more complete version would inform students about how different tribal groups responded to these pressures, about federal policies and the establishment of reservations, and about key events such as the Ghost Dance Movement and the Trail of Tears. It is not clear how much of this information should be included in an introduction to U.S. history in elementary school (versus saved for eighth- or eleventh-grade U.S. history courses), but, at a minimum, it seems important to keep students aware of the fact that Native Americans were resisting invasion of the lands they occupied, not just attacking settlers because they were unpredictable or hostile people.

Similarly, in addition to exposing students to tales of heroism at the Alamo, teachers might keep the students aware that conflict between the United States and Mexico was rooted in disputed land claims, not in some unexplained tendency of Mexicans to attack Americans. Better yet, teachers might explain that emphasis on western movement from an eastern seaboard base reflects U.S. history told primarily from the English point of view, and that the Spanish point of view produces a story emphasizing movement north and east from a southwestern base.

Finally, although it is a somewhat abstract concept, fifth graders probably could be introduced profitably to the notion of the frontier as a symbol of opportunity and a social safety valve in nineteenth-century America. As part of this process, students could develop at least initial ideas about frontier-related themes of historical importance, such as America as the land of opportunity or "Go west, young man!" Such an introduction might establish important groundwork for instruction in later grades that considers the ways in which historians interpret phenomena such as the "settling of the frontier" and the assumptions that they make in doing so.

KNOWLEDGE DEVELOPMENT ACROSS THE SCHOOL YEAR

Previous sections of this chapter have focused on trends across the group of 10 interviewed students in their understandings of ideas addressed during each successive history unit. We now turn to a consideration of the longitudinal patterns of continuity and change that unfolded across the school year.

These patterns are summarized in Table 4.11. The table illustrates that there were correlations among achievement level, possession of relevant prior knowledge, and indicators of response quality, although more so among the boys than the girls. However, there was only a loose (negative) relationship between achievement level and verbalization of childish ideas indicative of cognitive immaturity. Finally, there was no relationship between achievement level and interest in history or tendency toward reflective, empathetic responses.

The table also brings out the fact that the students who generated extended narrative responses were the same ones whose learning was distorted by persistent misconceptions. These three students (Brad, Helen, and Rita) also were average or low in achievement level, prone to verbalize naive ideas, and yet highly interested in history and able to assume the perspective of the people being studied. Given these commonalities, as well as the contrasts among these students on other variables, it is difficult to infer the degree to which their style of responding to our interviews reflected intelligence, cognitive style, or level of cognitive development.

Some of the most interesting and practically important findings concern the kinds of implicit assumptions and misconceptions that did or did not persist across time and instruction. Misconceptions were

Table 4.11. The 10 Students' Individual Characteristics as Interview Respondents

Name	Gender	Achievement Level	Interest in History	Typical Response Length	Includes Lengthy Narratives	Focuses on Main Ideas	Reflective, Empathetic Responses
Jason	M	High	Medium	Terse	None	Yes	No
Tim	M	High	High	Extended	None	Yes	Yes
Mark	M	Average	Medium	Extended	None	Yes	No
Brad	M	Average	High	Extended	A Few	Yes	Yes
Ned	M	Low	Medium	Terse	None	No	No
Teri	F	High	Low	Terse	None	Yes	No
Sue	F	High	High	Extended	None	Yes	Yes
Helen	F	Average	High	Extended	Many	No	Yes
Kay	F	Average	Medium	Extended	None	Yes	No
Rita	F	Low	High	Extended	Some	No	Yes

Table 4.11 (continued)

Amount of Prior Knowledge	Accuracy of Prior Knowledge	Mentioned Sources of Prior Knowledge					Presence of Naive Ideas	Persistent Misconceptions/ Distorted Learning	Growth Across the Year
		School	Family	TV, Movies	Trade Books	Computer Games			
High	High	Yes	Yes	Yes	Yes	No	Low	No	Medium
High	High	Yes	No	No	Yes	Yes	Low	No	High
High	High	Yes	Yes	No	Yes	Yes	Low	No	Medium
Low	Mixed	Yes	Yes	Yes	Yes	No	Medium	Yes	High
Low	High	Yes	No	Yes	No	No	Low	No	Low
Low	High	Yes	Yes	Yes	Yes	No	Low	No	Medium
Low	High	Yes	Yes	Yes	No	No	High	No	High
High	Low	Yes	Yes	Yes	No	No	Medium	Yes	High
Low	High	Yes	No	Yes	No	No	Low	No	High
High	High	Yes	Yes	Yes	Yes	Yes	High	Yes	High

much more prevalent in the preunit interviews, where many of the students' responses were guesses developed from limited (and sometimes partially incorrect) knowledge. Most erroneous guesses, especially about factual specifics, were replaced in the postunit interviews with accurate information learned during the units. So were most of the inaccurate preunit statements that conflated elements of state history learned in fourth grade with elements of U.S. history learned in fifth grade. These developments are heartening because they suggest that misconceptions embedded in prior knowledge are less likely to persist and distort subsequent learning of fifth-grade U.S. history than they appeared to be at first.

However, certain confusions and misconceptions did persist and distort learning. Examples commonly observed even in postunit interviews included: the belief that historians work like archeologists by reconstructing artifacts dug up or found above the ground (common in students who did not know or appreciate that written records go back several thousand years); the belief that the Plains tribes moved around frequently to find better weather or farmland (common in students who did not yet appreciate what they had been taught about, or could not yet conceive of, the notion of a nomadic hunting and gathering society that moved with the buffalo); the notion that the early European ship captains not only discovered new lands but then went back and recruited settlers and brought them to America to establish colonies (common in students who failed to appreciate that more than 100 years elapsed between 1492 and 1607); and the notion that had it not been for the Louisiana Purchase, most of the Midwest would remain undeveloped wilderness today.

Other misconceptions persisted in one or more individuals: the idea that Europeans wanted to come to America because Europe was overcrowded or because they were slaves seeking to escape their masters; the idea that people stopped coming to America (or even started going back to England) because it started to become too crowded; the notion that slaves were not paid by their masters but could make pocket money by doing odd jobs for someone else; and many more. Some of these misconceptions involved confusion between actual historical people or events and those depicted in children's literature (naming Johnny Tremain as a signer of the Declaration of Independence or Louisa May Alcott as a female leader in the Revolution). These examples were part of a larger set of findings indicating that there are limitations as well as advantages to using children's literature as content sources for history teaching.

Other aspects of these findings will be discussed in Chapter 7, following our presentation of case study material from two other class-rooms. These two teachers differed from each other and from Mary Lake in the ways that they approached teaching history to fifth graders, and the students they taught came from generally higher socioeco-nomic status backgrounds than Lake's students.

CHAPTER 5

Scientific History: The Case of Ramona Palmer

At the beginning of the year, we talked about tools and what tools you use for social studies. We talked about indirect sources and how that would be a tool in reviewing [history]. We always go back to some kind of review, how things fit together, cause and effect: What were the reasons that led up to the Revolutionary War? What led up to this? A professor from my undergraduate college was the one who made history come alive for me. Cause and effect was his way of doing it. That's why I do it now.

—Ramona Palmer

Palmer taught at Matewan Elementary School, a comprehensive K–5 school with a largely middle- to upper-middle-class population of 400 students. The school was located in a suburb of a medium-sized city in the northern Midwest. The student body was approximately 90% white, with about 6% African-Americans and 4% Asian-Americans. There were 28 students in Palmer's class, including three African-Americans and three Asian-Americans. She shared a large room with another fifth-grade teacher. The room was designed to accommodate four classes, but as enrollments declined at Matewan, partitions were erected in one corner to make room for an after-school daycare program. The classroom corner diagonally opposite the daycare room served as a "staging area" for large pedagogical activities and for resource storage. Palmer and her colleague taught opposite one another in the remaining two corners. However, no walls or partitions separated them. The two teachers also shared a sizable office connected to the staging area. This office was cluttered with a rich variety of accumulated teaching and curriculum support materials.

PHILOSOPHY OF TEACHING

Learning about subject matter as a general preparation for future life emerged as a key theme in what Palmer said about her educational philosophy and teaching goals. In different ways, what have been termed the basic subject matters—mathematics, social studies, science, reading—surfaced as important to her teaching efforts. She viewed science and social studies as integrators of the other subjects.

> I think you have to give them the basic structure for mathematics, reading, sociability. The science and the social studies are going to weave in and out, kind of like concentric circles. I think that's our basic responsibility. I think in the process of doing that, you build community, you build a social awareness of the world that they leave to the smaller community that they enter here at school. They learn acceptable behaviors in this society, on a smaller scale—crime and punishment so to speak, the justice system. Also, just what everyday life is. I think also it's to give kids structure for 6 hours in a day in which they can feel safe in an atmosphere in which learning is essential, and that learning is internally exciting.

Palmer explained what she meant about "internally exciting" by saying, "What is internally exciting to me is the awe and wonder. As a teacher I would like to be able to see that at least once a year in every kid."

Palmer's philosophy also entailed high expectations for students— in academics and especially in terms of personal classroom responsibility. She said:

> I basically have very high expectations of [my students]. They know what those expectations are and they know they have to live up to them or there are consequences, personal consequences, and they know I'm high on personal responsibility. My approach to them as a whole group in teaching is that everybody's involved. There's no time to be out in la-la land. I won't say to them that their opinion is wrong. I will say, "I disagree with you. I have a different opinion than you do. I don't expect you to change your opinion," especially when talking in terms of values.

GOAL FRAMEWORKS

Initially, Palmer defined her social studies goals within the context of specific school subjects. She listed them as reading, math, language arts, history, geography, and science. She then elaborated on her main goals for teaching social studies and history by adding:

> Besides knowing about the environmental, political, and socioeconomic aspects of their life and historical parts of their lives, they need to have cultural awareness. It's about acceptance. Acceptance starts at the grass-roots level with acceptance of each other. Environmental awareness, not only of geography and land forms, but environmentally safe practices. . . . You bring in again this relevancy of what's going on today.

In addition to the importance of subject matter, cultural and environmental awareness, making history relevant to students' lives, and developing tolerance for differences, she later added cultivating global political awareness, acquiring social studies skills (map reading, graph analysis, etc.), and fostering patriotism, which was linked to her fundamental belief in American democracy as defined by the Bill of Rights. She also discussed the importance of critical reading skills. In the first weeks of the new year, she indicated that she spent time instructing her students on how to read the history textbook and other textual sources that they would encounter in social studies during the year. These other textual sources frequently were taken from historical fiction tradebooks, a number of which she used during the American Revolution unit. Palmer was interested in integrating historical study with language arts. The use of historical fiction provided an opportunity to accomplish this integration.

Palmer's philosophy and general social studies goals, such as developing personal responsibility for learning, cultural awareness and tolerance for diversity, and a degree of patriotism, were implicitly folded into the rubric of teaching and learning history. Her undergraduate liberal arts exposure to disciplinary history of the "scientific" school (Evans, 1989, 1994), along with social science courses and an early teaching experience with the anthropology-based MACOS (Man: A Course of Study) course, had led her to embed her more general goals within the context of historical study. For her purposes in fifth grade, social studies was history, and history was defined by its practitioners (scientific historians, textbook authors, and, to a degree, historical fiction authors). She came of age pedagogically during the New Social Studies era of the 1960s and 1970s (see Jenness, 1990), so disciplinary purviews toward subject matter of that time period had played heavily on her early experiences. She recalled with fondness the influence of some of her history professors who had focused her attention on the nature and source of evidence and how it was employed to draw scientifically based historical conclusions and compile cause–effect generalizations. Her comment that opens this chapter exemplifies much of this background and influence.

In teaching the American Revolution unit, Palmer employed a variety of pedagogical strategies (games, audiovisual experiences, a simulation, projects and presentations, writing, and several discussions) designed to move her fifth graders systematically toward the goals she had set: (1) making history "come alive" by using this variety of teaching strategies and activities, (2) making it "internally exciting" by attempting to connect it to children's lives, (3) fostering historical inquiry, empathy, and imagination through a variety of historical texts, (4) assisting her students in making causal connections among events that culminated in the revolutionary war, and (5) creating a context for learning and building initial ideas about and an appreciation for the history of the American Revolution period.

CLASSROOM ORGANIZATION

Palmer described her classroom organizational style as "autocratic." By this she meant that she held fairly tight rein over the substance and direction in which history was represented. She made it clear that she was in charge of classroom events and controlled the student-to-teacher and student-to-student discourse. She noted that

> I don't get into a whole lot of kids arguing about what could be right and what could be wrong because of time constraints. In the past, what I used to do was line them up and one would take one side and one would take the other side of the issue. . . . I don't do that anymore. There isn't a whole lot of discourse back and forth between the kids and me. . . . There's not usually a whole lot of, "Let's sit down and discuss." It's usually, "I've got something to tell you. You work with this and come back and show me what you've come up with." I very rarely play devil's advocate. I think expediency-wise, because of the amount of work and academics, for me, expediency dictates. I guess in a lot of ways this is an autocratic society in my room.

Palmer believed that, because her students were studying chronological U.S. history for the first time and had little prior knowledge, direct instruction in the "historical record" was the best approach to enable learning. Classroom observations across the unit bore evidence of this autocratic approach. However, Palmer did promote a degree of "scientific inquiry" into varying interpretations of the period by requiring her students to read from a variety of accounts and to pay attention to the ways in which evidence was used to support assertions. Also, a stimulating 2-day discussion of the Bill of Rights at the conclusion of the unit involved a significant degree of student discourse and focus on multiple interpretations. In it, she promoted the more open-ended, inquiry approach that is valued by those who view history from a scientific perspective (Evans, 1989, 1994).

TEACHING METHODS

Throughout the year, Palmer said that she used a variety of methods to keep her students interested and engaged in the historical content, including such things as game playing, injecting a sense of humor, constructing newspapers, and giving performances.

> We have played Jeopardy . . . for the vocabulary words on the colonies and establishment of the colonies. . . . The idea is to get them not to look at it as drudgery. . . . Then we got to talking about a separatist and what a separatist was, and I said, "Gee, it really seems kind of stupid if you didn't think a separatist was somebody who's separated from the Church of England. Don't call me a separatist because I'm never separated from anybody." And they're all laughing. . . . I think another thing that would be great to do is do a newspaper about the American Revolution. Our fifth-grade performance [usually a play] is always centered around social studies, dates and times from the very beginning of the trek across the Bering Strait right up to the present day.

As her teaching of the American Revolution will indicate, when she could, Palmer also taught by analogy as a method for developing empathy for historical actors and their circumstances. Occasionally, as means for developing empathy and historical imagination, she would ask students to write letters to imaginary characters from the past, and, where possible, she brought in artifacts for students to examine.

She also used films, videotapes, and filmstrips as pedagogical strategies.

CONTENT SELECTION

Palmer explained that the curriculum plate at Matewan was exceptionally full in all subject matter areas. In order to address it, she felt she needed to be efficient. This meant following curriculum guidelines laid down by the school district.

> We have to follow the curriculum. We have to follow those district guidelines and if we go over and above any of those, we have to follow a policy from the Board of Education in which it has to meet certain curricular standards that will indeed fit with the goals of the district. [If] you want to use any materials that haven't been approved by the Board and are not in the curriculum guide, you have to make sure it passes the Board.

Palmer interpreted the curriculum guidelines approved by the school board straightforwardly. For fifth-grade U.S. history, this interpretation meant systematic coverage of the chronological order presented by the textbook. She said that she struggled to "get it all in" during the course of the year. However, she covered some units in more detail than others in order to accommodate her interests in the nature of the history itself. The American Revolution and colonies units received extended attention, while the Industrial Revolution, for example, received shorter shrift. This was one way that she addressed the dilemma of competing demands. It was coupled with a method she had developed (with help from the reading coordinator) for integrating historical content with language arts in a way that enabled her to move through the fifth-grade curriculum more briskly. However, the balance between her interest in spending more time delving deeply into inquiry issues and various interpretations raised by historical study and the requirement to cover the wide-ranging, specified history curriculum was tilted generally in favor of the latter.

ASSESSMENT

Palmer tried to vary her assessment practices as much as her teaching methods. Many of her classroom activities doubled as forms of assess-

ment. For example, students would research the lives of historical figures using multiple sources of information, write a report or biography
about them, and also conduct a dramatization of an important facet of
their experience. Palmer would collect and grade the reports and assess
the quality and historical accuracy of the dramatizations. Occasionally,
she would require that worksheets be turned in and she sometimes
used end-of-chapter tests supplied by the publisher of the textbook
series. Palmer also would ask students to construct timelines and accomplish project assignments that would be collected and assessed.
Furthermore, the class played games such as "historical Jeopardy" to
give Palmer a window into the sort of historical facts and details that
her students had learned. Most of these forms of assessment were in
evidence in the American Revolution unit.

TEACHING THE UNIT

As in Mary Lake's case, we present a summarized account of the unit
as it was taught day by day. It is important to note several key factors
that speak to Palmer's "scientific" approach: (1) her attention to and
interest in cause–effect relationships, (2) her use of multiple texts as
sources of history, (3) her insistence that students back their assertions
with evidence (e.g., when making oral presentations to the class), and
(4) the way in which she attempted to remain neutral or objective
when students raised questions about point of view (especially her re-
luctance to take a position when students pressed her on the morality
of capital punishment near the end of the unit).

Introducing the Unit

Interested in contextualizing the historical period, Palmer began the
unit with a timeline exercise. After a brief explanation of what she
wanted, students set out to create an "overview" of the American Revolution period on a timeline. Using their textbooks (*The United States
Yesterday and Today* by Helmus et al., published in 1988 by Silver
Burdett and Ginn, Morrsitown, NJ), students were to write down key
events and their dates on small squares of green and pink construction
paper and paste them in order on a larger sheet of paper that included
the dates from 1750 to 1800. Students talked quietly among themselves at their desk clusters. This activity consumed the class period.
Palmer ended class by telling students to file their timelines in their
social studies folders. Then she passed out 3 × 5 cards. On these, she

told them to place seven unfamiliar vocabulary words from the textbook chapter on the American Revolution. Students then were dismissed to science period, which followed social studies. Through a semidepartmentalized arrangement, science was taught by the other fifth-grade teacher who shared the large classroom.

Background Context: The French and Indian War

On the second day of the unit, students began by examining a map that depicted the areas of North America controlled by the English, French, and Spanish prior to the French and Indian War. Palmer explained how war broke out over control of North America between the French and the English in 1756. Trying to provide a sense of life in the English colonies at the beginning of this war, Palmer described characteristics of an English colonial village (e.g., houses, weather, clothing, meeting places). The class concluded with a 12-minute filmstrip on life in colonial Williamsburg, followed by an oral review of selected frames from the filmstrip.

Worried by the third lesson that students were confused about who the combatants were in the French and Indian War and that the title exacerbated this confusion, Palmer decided to give her students a 22-item true–false quiz on the assigned section of the textbook that covered this war. She was interested in assessing how well students understood this precursor to the American Revolution. Students reviewed the textbook section for 5 minutes, then took approximately 15 minutes for the quiz. Following the quiz, Palmer took them on a reading-recitation expedition of the textbook section along with a similar section in a second, older textbook, stopping to clarify paragraphs and bold-faced terms. Students, who still had their quizzes in front of them, changed their answers periodically in response to the readings. The period ended before they finished the review. Palmer provided an assignment that asked students to list three reasons why (or why not) the colonists should have been required to pay for the French and Indian War. They were to bring their reasons to class the following day.

In lesson four, Palmer picked up where she had left off, reviewing—item by item—students' responses to the true–false quiz as they followed along on their papers. This proceeded rapidly until they reached an item that read, "The colonists liked belonging to Parliament." An exchange ensued in which Palmer engaged several students in sorting out the relationship of the colonists to the English Parliament. This raised questions about changes in tax policy implemented by Parliament following the French and Indian War and colonial resistance to these policies. Palmer then asked various students to read from their "three reasons" assignments. In the end, four students opposed paying for the French and Indian War in any way, 15 believed partial payment was required, and nine thought that the colonists should foot the bill. Palmer noted that their disagreements paralleled the colonists' disagreements about this issue. Still worried that some students failed to understand the taxation issue, she instructed students to read the textbook section on the matter again for the next day.

Palmer went home at noon on the fifth day of the unit to attend to her sick middle school son. For the lesson, a substitute spent the period reading about colonial developments from two tradebooks that discussed the colonies just prior to the American Revolution and events from the French and Indian War.

Palmer also missed the following Monday. A substitute again took the helm for the sixth lesson and showed a filmstrip to the class. As students watched attentively, the filmstrip chronicled events (e.g., meeting of the Continental Congress, the signing of the Declaration of Independence) that led to the outbreak of war between the colonists and England. After the filmstrip, students were asked to read from their textbooks and answer the "checkup" questions at the end of each text section.

A Simulation of History

As a prelude to a simulation exercise that Palmer had constructed for lesson eight, students spent lesson seven playing historical Jeopardy. Students were grouped by "family teams." As Palmer recited factual questions about the French and Indian War, taxation policies, Parliament, the Continental Congress, and the like, student families excitedly took turns answering the questions as though they were on television. For every "correct" answer, students were awarded a certain number of points (to be referred to as money in lesson eight) depending on the category of the question. Before dismissing the students to science class, Palmer selected two of them to be "the King's helpers" for the following day. Here, she foreshadowed the simulation exercise.

Concerned about making history "come alive" and having her students make causal connections, Palmer devised the following simulation for lesson eight. This vignette helps to illustrate Palmer's interest in what she called making history "internally exciting."

She began the lesson by breaking students into groups of four. She told them that, as on the preceding day, their groups constituted families and, as such, they needed to elect a father and a mother. The remaining students were to play the role of the children. While they quickly set upon this task, Palmer gave each group play money. She instructed them to take only as much money as they had earned the previous day in the "Jeopardy" game. Students drew the money and returned the extra to Palmer.

Palmer then announced that the student groups represented colonial families and she was King George. Students responded with groans, anticipating what they imagined to be poor treatment. The two "helpers" she had selected would be her tax collectors. As she made this announcement, these two boys smiled, while the families groaned. As she continued to introduce the exercise, one family talked among themselves. Palmer stopped in mid-sentence and fined the family two dollars for "talking while the King was talking." This brought immediate silence. She then began to read from the list of taxes she had prepared. As she proclaimed each tax—on tea the families drank, on the paper products they used, and so forth—the tax collectors would go to each family and collect the tax.

As the lesson proceeded, the groans gave way to plots in some families to avoid paying taxes. The plots varied from outright refusals to give the tax collectors money to claims that "we already paid that tax. Get outta here!" When the King spotted these moves, she fined the family double and told them to "fork over the money." After each family's cash had been significantly depleted, Palmer stopped the exercise and debriefed the class. She explained how the anger and the frustration they had experienced were designed to simulate the growing displeasure colonists felt with the tax policies of King George. She told them that she hoped this exercise helped them understand the cause-and-effect relationship between colonial attitudes and British policy that eventually culminated in the Revolutionary War. Students listened attentively. Some nodded in agreement with her, while others complained about how unfair she had been and wondered out loud if the King was actually so ruthless. She indicated that she exaggerated the ruthlessness to get them to empathize, in this lesson at least, with the outrage experienced by some colonists.

She concluded the lesson by asking students what the colonists did to register their disapproval. One student called out, "The Boston Tea Party!" Another said, "Boycotting!" A third announced that some colonists moved west to get away from King George's tax collectors. Palmer smiled and said, "Yes!" approvingly to each answer. Palmer then noted that, in several days, students would assume the roles of angry colonists and write letters to a friend in Great Britain detailing their taxing experience—"pun intended," she added. Students smiled and groaned simultaneously while preparing for the science lesson.

Angry Letters to English Relatives

Students watched a filmstrip on the early years of the Revolutionary War in lesson nine. The filmstrip covered the battles from Lexington to Valley Forge in chronological sequence. The tone of the narrator was decidedly pro-colonist. Following the filmstrip, students worked together to develop responses to a series of vocabulary words (e.g., militia, minutemen, Declaration of Independence) on an assignment sheet associated with the audiovisual materials. Then Palmer reviewed a few selected vocabulary terms, mentioned how Jefferson used the views of French philosophers as he wrote the Declaration, and offered a brief narrative on the reasons for Benedict Arnold's "treason." She then announced, "For Monday, you are to write a letter to a relative in England. Remember, you are colonists. You decide who the relative is and what you want to say."

In the first two lessons of the following week, students took turns reading their letters to relatives in England. In general the letters favored the colonial perspective and spoke of unfair taxes (by name) and rude treatment (by act) from King George particularly. Occasionally humorous, the letters brought snickers and sometimes outright laughter from students.

Grounding accounts with appropriate evidence is important within the scientific approach to history. At a few points following a reading, Palmer would query the writer about historical facts that she believed had been misrepresented or used without sufficient justification. She sometimes asked for clarifications and pressed students for reassessments. Typically she would request that they go back to their books and notes and check on "their information."

Reading Historical Fiction

The next day began a four-lesson (12–15) excursion into the realm of historical fiction and report presentations by students. To augment the perspective of the textbook and convey additional sources of information, Palmer assigned reading from supplemental tradebooks to groups of students (e.g., *And What Happened Paul Revere?* by Jean Fritz, published in 1973 by Coward, McCann, and Geoghegan, New York; *If You Grew Up With George Washington* by Ronald Gross, published in 1982 by Scholastic, New York; *If You Lived in Colonial Times* by Ann McGovern, published in 1964 by Scholastic, New York). Students were to read their assigned books, write a report about what they had read, and design a stimulating presentation for the class. Presentations took several different forms. One group designed a large mural depicting events of the war. Another presented a news report wherein the three female students played newscasters (Jessica Savitch, Leslie Stahl, Connie Chung) who discussed the life of Paul Revere. Presentations lasted 2 days, but not all were completed during that period. Palmer returned to those unfinished presentations near the end of the unit.

Studying the War Itself

Ill, Palmer went home at lunch break on the day of the sixteenth lesson. In her place, a substitute teacher showed two filmstrips. The first dealt primarily with the colonial war victory and the early days of the formation of the Constitution. The second augmented the first by providing more detail on the Constitutional Convention. Students watched both filmstrips attentively, without much deference to the substitute's request that they take notes.

In lesson 17, students continued their study of the war period. Palmer handed out two assignment sheets linked to the filmstrips they had watched on the preceding day. The first exercise involved checking whether 12 different factors were an advantage to the English or to the colonists during the war period. Factors included such examples as, "We had the best navy in the world," "We were fighting for a cause we believed in," and "We had the support of France." The second exercise requested that students write an important event beneath ones that already appeared on the page. Each event was to fall within the same year as the event listed. Students worked on both exercises for approximately 15 minutes.

Palmer then reviewed the answers to the items on the first assignment. Students checked their responses against her explanations. Things moved fairly quickly until they reached the item, "We were fighting for a cause we believed in." Palmer noted that it was an advantage for the colonists. Several boys near the back of the room protested that both sides were fighting for what they believed in. Another boy argued that the colonists were more dedicated. Palmer took their answers in stride, indicating that both responses were justifiable, but that she still believed the colonists were more determined to win and more convinced of the rightness of their cause. Quickly looking at the clock, Palmer ended the exchange and took her students rapidly through the remaining five items. Review of the other exercise waited for another day.

Due to a Safety Patrol meeting on the day of lesson 18, Palmer was short on time. She decided to play the "Red Light–Green Light" game as an exercise in review. She would read a statement, usually factual in nature, that was either "true" or "false." Students would hold up a strip of green construction paper if they believed that the answer was true and a red strip if they believed that it was false. They were awarded points for "correct" responses. Extra points were given to students who could explain why a statement was considered false. Students were required to keep track of their own points on scrap paper. When Palmer mentioned that the class would play the game, the students cheered uproariously.

The game covered items from the textbook reading assignment (the section was entitled "How did the Americans win the Revolution?"). Palmer gave the students several minutes to review the pages they had read as their overnight assignment. They decided to work in groups of 4 or 5 to provide answers, so they skimmed the textbook pages and quietly discussed the reading together. After several minutes, she said, "OK, ready? Here we go." The game proceeded through a series of rapid-fire questions. Students, many on the edge of their seats, waved their hands wildly to attract Palmer's attention in case the group that had the floor missed the item. Then they might be called on to take a turn.

By the end of the 30-minute period, two groups were tied with 38 points. Other groups protested that they had cheated; Palmer, they contended, had not asked enough questions to give any group 38 points. Palmer interrupted, "OK! I have good news and bad news." Several students exclaimed, "Give us the bad news first." Smiling, Palmer complied, "Today is Friday and you won't have school until Monday." "Ooooh! So let's hear the good news," students retorted. "You don't have any homework," Palmer replied.

Student Presentations Continued

The students who had lagged behind the others in completing their report presentations gave their renditions during lesson 19. Palmer also gave an airing to several students who had yet to read their "letter to a relative in England." Following are several samples from this process.

Lorrie, Hadley, and Jessie moved to the front of the room. They announced that they would be "doing a narrative." The story dealt with two brothers, Phillip and Jordan, who had elected to fight on opposite sides in the Revolutionary War. The girls played out the brothers' arguments concerning loyalty to the crown and colonial patriotism. Students listened quietly; some took notes. At the conclusion, Palmer asked Hadley, who had acted as the story's narrator, where the loyalists went when they felt they could no longer remain in the colonies. Hadley noted that many traveled to Canada. In the interest of time, Palmer later noted, she limited the number of questions she asked following each report. Here, the press of the teaching schedule would derail efforts at asking students to provide evidence for their conclusions and discuss their sources.

Palmer thanked them for their presentation. Students applauded. Next, Davey read his "letter to a relative in England" rather phlegmatically. Palmer asked him to put more spunk into his oratory. He discussed the unfairness of the taxes the colonists had to pay, described the work of the Daughters of Liberty and the Boston Tea Party, and condemned the Intolerable Acts. As he returned to his seat, students again applauded. He was followed by Frederic and Barry, who teamed up on a report about Patrick Henry. Barry wrote the report and Frederic delivered it with panache. Palmer complimented him as he sat down. Marvyn got up and read his letter. He likewise was complimented as he finished.

Noting that the time for social studies had elapsed, Palmer announced the assignment for the next day. "I want you to make believe that you are George Washington, Thomas Jefferson, or whoever. Now you realize that you've won the war and you have to have a new government for your country. I want you to name 10 things that your government will be sure to do for its people. Let's try naming some of them right now." Six or seven hands went up.

Kyle: Equal rights.
Barry: Lower taxes.
Cameron: Provide jobs.
Davey: Fair and equal laws.
Palmer: I don't want to give you too many. You can't use the ones we just named. Unless there are questions, I'm assuming you understand the assignment. [no questions are raised] OK, you're dismissed to science.

Exploring Interpretations and the Relevance of the Bill of Rights

Picking up from the day before, Palmer took her students through an elaboration of the list they had begun generating. She continued to record their responses on the overhead. The growing list included such things as housing for everyone, more transportation, free travel, land for everyone, peace, no slavery, freedom of speech, and freedom of assembly. Once students exhausted their ideas, Palmer set them to work in groups of four or five to identify what they believed were the most important five items government should provide its citizens. After several minutes, Palmer made a new list of these "essential guarantees." For example, housing received one vote, freedom of speech four, education one, clean environment one, freedom of religion two, and equal rights one.

Palmer then explained, with sparing detail, the Preamble to the Constitution and the provisions for three branches of government. She followed this by assigning students to write the first 10 amendments to the Constitution in their own words and be prepared to teach them to someone else using examples. Lesson 21 and part of lesson 22 were used to complete the remaining student reports, letters, and presentations. Reports of various types were given on Benedict Arnold, Ben Franklin, a fictional girl named Phoebe who acted as a spy for the colonists, and John and Abigail Adams.

After two final reports at the beginning of lesson 22, Palmer returned to the exploration of the Bill of Rights. She called six students to the chalkboard. They wrote down responses from the class as Palmer went through the first 10 amendments, asking students to explain them in their own words.

Palmer: The First Amendment in your own words. [calls on several students]
Jarron: Choose your own religion.
Jessie: Freedom of opinion.
Junior: Freedom to say what you want.
Drew: Freedom of the press.
Lydia: Freedom of assembly.
Palmer: OK, good! Number two?
Marvyn: Military.
Palmer: What does that mean?
Marvyn: That we have to have the citizens help . . . with the army.
Frederic: Weapons.
Palmer: Do you mean the right to have an army? [Frederic nods.] OK, number three.
Junior: Citizens don't have to house and feed the army during peacetime.
Palmer: Good! Number four?
Jarron: You must have a warrant to search someone's house.

In this fashion, Palmer and her students worked through the first 10 amendments. After they had completed the first six, four more students were called to the chalkboard and asked to keep track of the responses for amendments seven through 10. By the Fourth Amendment, many students had their textbooks open and were quoting directly from the amendments.

When they reached the Eighth Amendment (forbidding cruel and unusual punishment), Palmer asked for a show of hands on student opinions concerning the death penalty. Four students committed themselves as proponents while the same number indicated opposition. The majority remained undecided. The Ninth and Tenth Amendments brought difficulty. Palmer asked the class how many understood these two amendments. Five cautious and tentative hands rose, and Palmer went on to say:

> These two are very complicated. Later in middle school and high school you'll learn about these in much more detail. I think they're probably too difficult for 10- and 11-year-olds. Here's your assignment. Let's just take the first eight. I want you to choose one of the first eight to give up. Let's say that they passed a law saying that one of these amendments had to go. Which would you choose? I want you to write down your reasons after you choose one! OK, get ready for science.

As students switched books, Barry asked Ainsley which one he would give up. He said he was not sure. Excited, several other students asked each other as well. Few seemed ready to pick an amendment.

The examination of the Bill of Rights continued in lesson 23. Palmer was interested in accomplishing several things: (1) breathing life into what students perceived as an old document and thereby making it interesting to them, (2) focusing on the importance of differing interpretations, and (3) attempting to model for her students the value of careful, evidence-based grounding for their assertions about and interpretations of the Bill of Rights.

To begin this part of the lesson, Palmer asked students to take several minutes to write down an amendment they were willing to forego and the reasons for their choice. While students wrote, Palmer pulled down the large screen and lit it up with the overhead projector. She stood and waited, watching the class. After 5 minutes, she said, "If you're willing to give up the First Amendment, then stand up." Cameron, a small wiry boy, stood—alone. Palmer smiled and said, "That's all right, Cameron. There are no right or wrong answers with this; it's what you believe." Palmer repeated process for each of the next seven amendments. For the Second Amendment, two stood. For the Third, four; the Fourth, zero; the Fifth, one; the Sixth, zero; the Seventh, two; and the Eighth, seven. Ten students remain seated throughout the exercise, apparently unable or unwilling to decide.

A discussion of Cameron's eagerness to give up the First Amendment ensued. Palmer asked him to read the amendment from the book. He did and as soon as he finished, he shrugged his shoulders, smiled, and claimed he had changed his mind; he no longer would give this one up.

Palmer: But why were you willing to give it up in the first place? I'm really curious. This amendment protects the rights of free speech, the press, and personal opinion.

Cameron [bashfully]: Well, I just liked the other ones better.

Palmer: If you gave it up, how would this affect you?

Davey [interjecting]: You wouldn't be able to give your opinion!

Palmer: How many of you think that if we gave up this right it would infringe on some very basic American principles? [almost everyone's hand goes up immediately] What would it be like if we didn't know about this, couldn't read about it in the newspapers. I'm going to take Cameron's position for a minute. What about those papers like the Star or the Enquirer?

Several students: Yeah, they exaggerate!

Palmer: Yes. Should there be rules for supplying evidence in these papers?

Cameron: No!

Addie: I think there should be guidelines for what they can print.

Palmer: What about 2 Live Crew [a rap group]?

Marvyn: They're OK! If it bothers some people, they don't have to buy it. They put those labels on there that say there's obscene words and stuff on the record. I guess that's OK.

Sam: I think that the swearing and the words that they use are OK. Everyone does it.

The class erupted into a polyphony of voices. Students competed to be heard above the rapidly rising volume. Palmer told them to stop. She asked them to raise their hands and speak one at a time. They complied. Dancing hands now sliced the air recklessly. Palmer called on Davey.

Davey: I agree with Sam.

Jarron: You could bleep out the bad stuff.

Palmer: But then some records would be all bleep.

Davey: Well, it's OK because people are doing it. It's not really hurting anybody.

Palmer: But it's not really OK to say so just because everyone is doing it. What if everyone was murdering? Is that OK?

Students: No!! That's not OK.

Abigail: I think it's unfair to people who like their music.

Palmer: Davey, you said it doesn't hurt anybody. I disagree with you. The lyrics in some songs—I'm just arguing with you—make me out to be a bimbo. I'm offended.

Davey: But you don't need to listen to it.

Palmer: But what if people start to believe this stuff. I'm just giving you an example.

Adam: But in PG movies, they all swear. What's the difference?

Frederic: I've never heard a song about women's right to vote.

Palmer: I'm just saying, what do you do if it insults women? What about blacks? Marvyn?

Marvyn [a black student]: Well . . . well, if you want to listen to it, it's OK.

Palmer: Marvyn, are you hedging? Should we allow it if it insults blacks? Yes or no, Marvyn?

Marvyn: Well, if . . . yes.

Adam [a white student]: There's a movie out right now called "White Men Can't Jump." And some black people call each other niggers.

Palmer: Should that be allowed?

Addie: You should be allowed to do it in the privacy of your own home.

Palmer: Should we allow a parade . . . if someone was a member of the KKK and wanted to have a parade down the streets of our city, is that allowable? [five hands go up]

Barry: That's freedom of speech!

Palmer: I want you to talk this over with your parents tonight. We have to go on to number two, the right to bear arms. Lots of you are ready to give this one up, why? Brent?

The class shifted to a discussion of the Second Amendment. This amendment created as much disagreement as the first. Throughout the give and take of the discussion, many students sat up on their knees in their desks. Again, their hands beat the air in a frenzied effort to attract Palmer's notice. Aware of their eagerness, Palmer moved around the room calling on students. As soon as one student would finish a statement, she would call on another. At one point she asked students to address each other, not her. Here is an excerpt from this discussion.

Brent: We should be allowed to have guns. We need to be able to defend our town against attack.

Drew: But if no one has guns, we don't have to worry about that.

Frederic: What if Germany wants to start a war and we don't have any guns?

Barry: Yeah, what if a burglar broke into your house and you didn't have a gun?

Abigail: I heard somewhere that there's a lot of accidental shootings of children in homes where there are guns.

Palmer: Put your hands down a minute. How many of you know where your parents' guns are? [three hands go up]

Hadley: This law was made in 1791. Things have changed since then. Now our nation is guarded much better. We don't have the same threats.

Sam: I disagree. What about terrorists blowing things up?

Merry: If you have guns in the house and you have a fight with your wife, she gets shot. [several males snicker]

Palmer: Yes. Some studies show this.

Merry: Yeah, people shoot each other.

Palmer: Yes. The studies say this. By the way, don't make fun of others' opinions. They are entitled to them by the First Amendment!

Lucy: How will guns get into this country if it's illegal to have guns?

Sam: Have you ever heard of the black market?

Davey: I agree with Sam!

Palmer: Davey, what is your dad [a lawyer] lobbying for right now? Gun control?

Davey: Yes.

Palmer: Would it be OK for Davey to disagree with his dad?

Students: Yes!

Palmer: Yes, because the First Amendment is protected here in America.

Frederic and Barry continued to defend their right to bear arms. They challenged Hadley's anti-weapons position. She held fast, suggesting that if in fact no one had guns, there would be no problem.

Palmer sent a courier to check with her colleague about how much more time she needed before the classes would switch subjects. The courier reported that she needed 3 more minutes. Palmer reminded the students that she wanted to cover the additional amendments the following day. She asked them to re-examine their positions and come to class prepared to make statements. With 2 minutes remaining,

Palmer pushed on to a brief consideration of the Fourth and Fifth Amendments, for the moment skipping over the Third.

Palmer: Should the police be able to search your house without a warrant? Kyle?

Kyle: If you were looking for secret chambers, then maybe.

Frederic: Drug dealers—if they see them going into a house, they should be able to follow them in.

Palmer: What if you suspect drug dealing in a house, but you still don't actually see it? Would you need a warrant?

Addie: But in that amount of time [to obtain the warrant], they'd get away.

Palmer: What about the rule "innocent until proven guilty?" How many of you when you watch TV and see a trial, assume the guy is guilty? [four hands go up] What does the Constitution say? Are you to prove guilt or innocence?

Jarron: Innocence.

Palmer: No.

Several students: You have to prove guilt.

Jarron wrinkled his brow and shook his head as though he was confused or disagreed with what had been said. Noticing that her time was gone, Palmer declared dismissal.

Palmer began Lesson 24 by announcing that the class would finish the unit on the American Revolution with a test on the coming Friday. She would discuss it in more detail later. For now, she wanted to return to the discussion of the amendments. She asked Adam to read the Third Amendment from his book. Four students had elected to drop this amendment the day prior. Palmer noted it and asked why. Several students, who opposed dropping the amendment, objected to the fact that, if it was given up, soldiers could enter and live in people's homes. Drew argued that the soldiers could be controlled. Sam raised the possibility of personal harm affecting civilians if the country's enemies knew soldiers were quartered in their homes. Palmer acknowledged Sam's point, then pushed on to the Fourth Amendment (search and seizure limitations), considering it a second time.

Adam, who had discussed this amendment with his parents at Palmer's request, said, "My mom thinks that the police should have to get a warrant every time to protect people." Pushing Adam to examine possible exceptions and their implications, Palmer asked him, "What if some drug dealers had kidnapped you and were holding you in a known drug house? What then?" Frederic jumped in.

Frederic: When human life is involved, I don't think a search warrant is that important.

Junior: My dad said that you don't always need a warrant. If a bank robber ran into a house, and you saw him rob the bank, then you could go in after him without a warrant.

Drew: You don't need a search warrant when a lot of people's lives are involved. [hands wave wildly]

Abigail: I know that if you find evidence in a house and you don't have a warrant, then you can't use it against the person.

Ainsley agreed with Frederic that a warrant should not be necessary when human lives are involved. Palmer thanked Ainsley for his comment and asked Merry to read the Fifth Amendment (due process provisions) from the textbook.

A discussion ensued concerning the double jeopardy clause. Palmer asked several students to explain their understanding of this clause. Students appeared confused. They failed to grasp how the amendment put the pressure on the prosecution for proving guilt, and how the double jeopardy clause protects the accused from being tried repeatedly for the same offense. After several analogies and direct explanations extolling the protective features of the amendment, Palmer seemed convinced that students understood its rudimentary qualities. Students, many again up on their knees in their desks, protested as Palmer asked Cameron to read the Sixth (additional due process provisions), Seventh (right to jury trial), and Eighth (prohibitions against cruel and unusual punishments) Amendments from the textbook. Eyeballing the clock, Palmer firmly insisted that they would have to push on if they were to consider all the amendments.

As Cameron finished the Eighth Amendment, several students sang out, "Cruel and unusual punishment!"

Palmer: We could discuss this one [Eighth] for a long time. Some people would object that capital punishment is cruel and unusual.

Several students: So what's your opinion? Tell us!

Palmer: The [school] district says if I tell you then I run the risk of letting my values influence you. I can't. . . .

Students [objecting]: Oh, we won't tell . . . tell us anyway. . . . Just get on with it!

Another student: My mom will understand!

Palmer: OK. [students fall completely silent, watching Palmer] But this is just my opinion. I have a lot of trouble with this. It's not a black and white issue for me. I really struggle . . . it seems very

cruel to me on the one hand, but if it was my child . . . I think then
I'd want to have capital punishment.

After Palmer paused, Adam interjected his opinion, arguing an eye-
for-an-eye approach. Palmer turned to an analogy. One of her female
friends had been murdered in an altercation with someone being pursued by the police. Her friend's brother frequently objected to paying
taxes that kept the murderer alive in prison.

Sam: Is he in prison for life?
Palmer: Yes. And he had a record for killing others. The reason I'm
   telling you this is to explain how opinions about capital punish-
   ment vary a lot.
Frederic: What if it was your job to pull the lever?
Palmer: It wouldn't be! I could never do that! I'm too afraid of the pos-
   sibility of executing the wrong person. That's a strong argument
   against capital punishment.
Adam: What if someone killed your kids? Could you do it then?
Palmer: I don't know! My emotions might have the better of me.
   That's so hard for me to say.

As she finished her sentence, Palmer began passing out several review
sheets. Students near the front received the papers, groaned, and said,
"Oooh, worksheets! This is capital punishment!" Palmer smiled. She
then assigned the sheets as review for the upcoming test.

Objectivity and neutrality are hallmark characteristics of the scientific history approach. As this vignette demonstrates, Palmer, using
school district policy as a rationale, attempted to beg off answering the
question posed by her students. Even after she conceded, she was careful to note that interpretations and opinions of capital punishment fall
across a range. Indirectly, she was modeling for her fifth graders the
detached or neutral, yet inquisitive, position scientific historians
value.

Reviewing for and Taking the Test

Lessons 25 and 26 were spent reviewing for the test and working
through a set of assignment sheets handed out in lesson 24. Students
typically worked quietly in small groups, consulting the textbook and
writing on the photocopied sheets. On the second day of the review,
about halfway through the period, Palmer began an oral review. The
class managed to work through almost two of the four sheets they were

assigned. Palmer told the students to study the sheets in preparation for the test the following day. The publisher-supplied test consisted of 35 multiple-choice items; their phrasing was derived almost verbatim from the textbook. There were five essay questions that asked for essentially factual recall, again from the textbook. Most of the students took the entire class period (40 minutes) to complete the test.

ASSESSING PALMER'S CASE

Although varied in her selection of teaching practices, Palmer demonstrated a number of the characteristics of the scientific historian. First, her own educational background turned on influences by historians of the scientific school as well as by other social scientists of a positivist orientation. Her undergraduate teacher preparation was forged in the crucible of the discipline-based New Social Studies era. Second, she showed interest in historical cause–effect relationships and the generalizations that could be derived from them. Third, she attempted to build in her students an appreciation for the importance of facts, details, and research in making historical claims. Fourth, she showed interest in inquiry into competing interpretations of history, particularly with regard to the Bill of Rights. Finally, as the discussion of the Bill of Rights revealed, she displayed signs of the objective or neutral stance that scientific historians attempt to take when faced with multiple accounts of the same historical event.

It also should be noted, however, that Palmer's interests in inquiry, multiple interpretations of history, and maintaining an objective stance were most manifest at the end of the unit rather than obvious throughout. As we will see in more elaborate detail in Atkinson's case to follow, approaches that differ significantly from perfunctory content coverage tend to be time-consuming and problematic in practice. Most school districts mandate coverage of considerable ground in these fifth-grade survey courses, so teachers such as Palmer run some risk of failing these mandates if they seriously pursue the inquiry approaches characteristic of scientific historians (and reformers), precisely because they consume so much time. Palmer attempted to deal with this dilemma by adopting a somewhat autocratic organizational style in which she held fairly tight control of and maintained the direction of the class. During several points in the unit, but most notably at the end, she appeared to relax the reins. It was at these moments when she appeared to be at her pedagogical finest (and closest to the scientific historian typology). Palmer seemed comfortable with the sort of temporary truce she created between the autocratic style and the scientific historian approach. However, the kernels of conflict were always there, just beneath the surface.

Despite the limitations produced by this truce, Palmer might earn compliments from those who recommend teaching subject matter in depth and for understanding (cf. Brophy, 1990b; Newmann, 1988, 1990). Her employment of historical fiction, adding a narrative, story-like dimension to an otherwise flat and straightforward textbook chronology, would engender praise from advocates who propose augmenting historical study with good literature (cf. Egan, 1986; Levstik, 1989). Those who point to the value of cultivating empathy and historical imagination, a respect for historical detail, and an appreciation of causal relationships in history (Dickinson & Lee, 1978, 1984; Hertzberg, 1985; Reed, 1989) also would appreciate some of Palmer's efforts. In many ways, Palmer tried to expose her students, to the extent that they seemed developmentally ready, to the view of the community of academic history that she was exposed to as an undergraduate.

Given that she already taught a form of scientific history, her approach might have been even more powerful if it included more of an emphasis on disciplinary inquiry that reflected current scholarship in the field of history (Seixas, 1994; Wineburg & Wilson, 1988), on the interpretive nature of history (i.e., recognizing the differences between fact and conjecture, evidence and assertion; see Reed, 1989), and on the value of sociocultural diversity and change in historical evolution. However, focusing on these dimensions might have pushed past the limits of all but the most able of Palmer's fifth graders, because her class was their initial encounter with history taught in anything resembling a sustained chronological or narrative account. Therefore, Palmer might have been right to assume that their background knowledge and comprehension of the disciplinary discourse of history needed further development before more complex features of historical work could be introduced in detail. There clearly was room for her to extend her introduction to scientific history and the social history that evolved from it, but she would have had to do so cautiously to retain the historical background contexts and the interest and understanding of all her students.

Palmer's approach can be criticized on other grounds as well. Social studies theorists who emphasize inquiry, problem solving, and decision making (e.g., Banks, 1991; Engle & Ochoa, 1988) might argue that, although she demonstrated aspects of scientific history, she could just as easily be described as a conventional knowledge transmitter. Such transmitters, they would argue, often promulgate the teaching of facts and details for their own sake and without regard for the importance of the problem-solving and decision-making contexts in which they could be used (i.e., as a participating citizen of a democracy). Furthermore, they might insist that her classroom generally reflected a passive learning environment, one that lacked inquiry into current human problems and failed to use history as a vehicle to that end. Finally, they might note that Palmer fostered a narrow, indoctrinating view of her citizenship mission, one devoid of social participation and a spirit of democratic involvement. They would cite her organizational style as evidence for such a conclusion. Theorists who take a critical stance would argue many of the same things but would add that Palmer lacked a method for critiquing the very subject matter conclusions she advanced. They might say that her approach was unnecessarily Eurocentric and showed little evidence of attempts to develop an appreciation of difference and tolerance for diversity. In this way, they would insist, her practices unfortunately reproduced unjust and inequitable power relations found in society at large.

These criticisms may have merit. However, to levy them in this fashion is to ignore the pressures and dilemmas Palmer had to manage, ones that help us understand why she chose to operate her class as she did (VanSledright, 1992a, VanSledright & Grant, 1994). Both the community in which she worked and the school in which she taught promoted a philosophy that appeared generally consonant with her own, yet in some ways created discomfort for her. The parents and the principal at Matewan expected strong subject matter teaching and learning; Palmer characterized this as a "no-nonsense approach" in interviews. The curriculum guidelines called for a survey of U.S. history from the explorers to Vietnam (among other things). The curricular plate at Matewan was indeed full; Palmer knew it and responded accordingly. Although she spoke of more far-reaching goals, she accepted the role of primarily a knowledge transmitter within a framework that still allowed her to build in what she perceived to be the inquiry-oriented, cause–effect perspective of scientific history.

Palmer could have mediated the social studies curriculum differently. For example, she could have chosen to orient her teaching even more intensively around disciplinary inquiry and debate or public policy issues made relevant by the study of U.S. history (as she did in the lessons on the Bill of Rights). However, she faced a number of perceived school and community pressures to tend the curriculum gate in the fashion that she did (Thornton, 1991). She responded to these pressures by taking a path that she believed would allow her to do what she could do best. That path is more congruent with knowledge transmission and socialization goals (to middle school particularly) for fifth graders at Matewan School than it is to a full-fledged, inquiry-based, scientific approach. To choose such a path seems reasonable, but it quite clearly comes with a set of trade-offs, some for the better, some perhaps for the worse. These trade-offs go to the core of hotly debated curriculum questions such as: What should students learn in history courses? Why? To what end?

CHAPTER 6

History as a Tool for Reform: The Case of Sara Atkinson

I think you need to tell children [that] . . .if you're talking about coloniza-
tion, and you're talking before that, history was interpreted by white
land-owning, what we call upper-middle-class, men. So then you pose
that question to them, "How do you know we got the straight story?"
The kids say, "You probably didn't." I say, "You're probably right because
history's not dead." All of a sudden you find a diary someplace. You have
people who, through diaries et cetera, invalidate parts of history that
we've always accepted, and you realize that there were some issues or
views that never got stated, because nobody had a place to act as a
sounding board, because no one was asking them questions. So I think
we're rewriting history all the time.

I think my teaching style is what allows kids to think that thinking criti-
cally is a good thing to do. [Students will say,] "I don't agree with your
opinion, Mrs. Atkinson, and the reason I don't is I think that you were
making this oversimplified." I'd say, "Wait a minute; let's talk about some
of these people who came over—for example, the indentured servant
types. Were they really going to have a better life over here?" Again, you
play the devil's advocate to bring out some more.

—Sara Atkinson

Atkinson was a sprightly, effervescent, and talkative veteran of 25 years
of elementary school teaching. She taught fifth grade at Greenwood
Elementary, which is a predominantly white, middle- to upper-middle-
class school of 250 students in the same medium-sized district and
metropolitan area in which Palmer taught. Born and raised on the east
coast, she pursued postsecondary education in the Midwest, receiving
Bachelor of Arts and Master of Arts degrees from a Michigan university. As an undergraduate, she completed a language arts major and
science and social science dual minors. She had taught sixth grade
until the advent of middle schools at which point she transferred to
fifth grade.

PHILOSOPHY OF TEACHING

Atkinson's own childhood had a significant impact on her attitudes
toward the subject matter of U.S. history. This is quite common with
reformers (Evans, 1989, 1994). Her "New England-style" oral tradition
imbued in her a sense of the past that she tried to communicate to her
students. Her sense of this oral tradition was coupled with the belief
that, at its center, the concept of democracy—citizen rights and responsibilities—flourished. For her, this oral tradition was democracy:
the right to argue, negotiate, participate, and decide. Atkinson saw this
process as a vehicle for serving her reformist approach. Her perception
of this democratic tradition had become the historical, curricular
thread with which she tried to weave her classroom. She put it this
way:

> Hopefully, I'm giving examples from day one what a democratic
> classroom is like by giving them some responsibilities for the way
> this class runs. And also, as we're going along, they understand
> that there are times when they have prime responsibility for
> something, and times when I have prime responsibility for some-
> thing, so it's not always a perfect democracy. The first rule in this
> room is respect. Respect is the only rule I've got, and everything
> . . . generates from that. If I'm respecting your point of view, I'm
> going to give you time to generate that with me. We're . . . going
> to give people time to have their say and they are welcome to
> their point of view. It may not be my point of view, but you are
> welcome to yours. Please listen to my point of view to determine
> how you feel about it. We make a lot of decisions in here to-
> gether.

GOAL FRAMEWORKS

Atkinson's goals were tied to constructing a classroom in the spirit of
a participatory, democratic ethos. For her, that ethos was characterized
by a context in which individual rights and personal responsibilities
were often at issue, discussion of issues proliferated, knowledge claims
were understood as tools that gave substance to the process of change,
and informed decision making and action were desired dispositions.

Like Palmer's, Atkinson's goals seemed expansive. She spoke of
them repeatedly and in many different forms, but they were characterized by a relatively consistent thread that emerged from her philoso-

phy. Her specific goals for the study of history can be summarized as (1) stimulating students' interest in history by tying it to their personal lives, (2) fostering inquiry into the sources of knowledge claims and why these claims exist as they do, (3) providing humanistic and affective insight into the human condition, and (4) developing questioning, decision-making, and problem-solving dispositions and applying them to solutions (the heart of the reformist approach).

Atkinson augmented her general social studies goals with several that were specific to the unit on the American Revolution. These unit goals included: (1) developing a basic knowledge of the standard interpretations of the revolutionary period, including specifically the "mistakes" of the past; (2) appreciating the historical significance of the revolutionary era; (3) understanding the importance of the birth of democracy in the United States; and (4) connecting the rights supplied by the Constitution with their accompanying citizenship implications.

TEACHING METHODS

Teaching devices and methods for the unit included use of the textbook, a number of filmstrips and accompanying assignment sheets, discussion of the issues involved and points of view represented, a possible role-playing exercise (a debate), and a concluding videotape describing the struggle over ratifying the Constitution.

Atkinson anticipated considerable teacher–student and student–student discourse during the unit. This discourse was to revolve around open-ended questions that dealt with the issues raised by this turbulent period in U.S. history. One issue that troubled her involved the way in which point of view typically was represented by the textbook. This concern gave way to a generalized criticism of Eurocentric presentations of U.S. history and a reassertion of the importance of understanding opposing positions. She described it this way:

> History is presented pretty much from the colonial point of view. During the time of Columbus—we've done the American Indians such a disservice—we could say when Columbus came, it was the beginning of the end. It was a disaster. If you were a Native American, you saw that as nothing you would like to study. You find it demeaning of you. You became a nonentity and you were driven from your land, and knowing your religious reaction to land, this was above and beyond anything that people of European descent could even relate to. So now when you're here, you have

to say there were two sides. You have to look at the colonists, decision-wise, what they did that was right and what they did that was wrong. You also always have to look at the British side. I always learned we were right; they were wrong. But there are two sides to every story. That was a goal.

CONTENT SELECTION

Atkinson intended to begin the unit by reproaching the singular viewpoint frequently evident in the textbook and filmstrips, not always directly, but often through the process of asking her students to question the sources of their understanding. Reasoning, challenging assumptions, and analyzing claims were to undergird learning. The purpose involved learning the "lessons of the past," avoiding the "mistakes," and using the knowledge to make life better for the present and future. She said:

> I think we do pose oral questions a lot in here. They'll pose them if I don't. I think the decision making comes by the kinds of questions that I ask them. Let's go back to the pros and the cons of the Articles of Confederation. They were looking at both sides of it and instead of saying, "Well, that was around for 6 years and it didn't work," they'll say, "I've got to remember, first came the Articles of Confederation, then the Constitution." I'd like to think that I've laid groundwork so that the next year and the year after that, they're not going to look at things as just black and white. . . . We learned from the good but we also learned from the bad what we needed. The critical thinking and decision making are going to make it meaningful and you've got a chance that they're going to remember [it then].

However, this approach would not be without its difficulties. Atkinson would strive to overshadow coverage with in-depth analysis and argumentation. She complained about the coverage issue: teaching explorers through the Carter years, she lamented, proved to be completely impossible. Her response: "What you can do is to zip through it and feel completely incomplete about what you've done, but if you admit to them that you're zipping through a lot of parts and find some spots that you'd love them to concentrate on. . . . Some parts of social studies, I teach well. Some parts I don't teach well and I zip. That's not fun." She probed the colonial period, the American Revolution, and the Civil War in depth, and "zipped through" the rest (or failed to reach it, as in the case of latter twentieth-century U.S. history). In her classroom, the tension between "digging deeply" and "zipping" manifested itself in a visible race against the clock. This tension reflected one of the trade-offs inherent in teaching from a reformist angle: inquiring, questioning, arguing, and "searching for a path to a better solution" can use up enormous amounts of time. Using history as a tool to improve on the future calls for study of it in depth. Coverage demands, especially those imposed by school districts and reinforced by testing practices, make the reformer's teaching life very problematic. Atkinson's was no exception.

This problem often was compounded by the fact that she knew that her students lacked significant knowledge of U.S. history; after all, most of them had not yet studied it in any systematic way. She found herself needing to lay out and often review a series of historical knowledge claims before her students understood the issues well enough to question or discuss them intelligently (on this issue, see Hallden, 1994). Interpretive analysis and discussion typically were preceded by presentation and sometimes effectively shortened by it.

The tension was compounded further by an illness that caused her to miss several school days during the middle of the unit. When she returned, the race against the clock became much more noticeable, with the lessons marked more by presentation than discussion. Nonetheless, in the descriptions and vignettes that follow, there is evidence that Atkinson, the reformer (1) emphasized the relationship of the past "mistakes" to present-day problems, (2) frequently used past–present comparisons and analogies—the stuff of history (Evans, 1989, 1994)—to drive home her points, and (3) tried to focus her students around inquiry-oriented approaches to the historical record.

ASSESSMENT

Like Lake and Palmer, Atkinson favored a variety of assessment methods. She was especially fond of her own brief teacher-constructed quizzes that asked students to respond in paragraph form to two or three questions reviewing what they had studied over a period of several days. She occasionally required students to complete review sheets supplied by the textbook publisher or conducted review exercises such as historical Jeopardy. Perhaps twice a year, Atkinson would use a publisher-supplied, multiple-choice test as a method for preparing her students for testing practices that they might encounter in middle

school. She also used the oral discussions and debates that she promoted in class as an informal means to assess student learning. Referring to these in-class practices, she said:

> I'm watching as well as listening to them. I'm looking to see how
> many people I have responding in any way, shape, or form and I
> need to go through and sometimes spice up something, I need to
> ask one of those questions that we've referred to earlier so that
> I've got everybody able to come up with an answer. The easiest
> answers are the answers that you can read and find. But if I'm not
> having people taking risks, then I've got to go back and build a lit-
> tle confidence and then go beyond. Assessing by a variety of types
> of questions is important to me. Throw out something; see who's
> responding, how they're responding, and then I'm assessing as to
> whether or not there's a need out there.

TEACHING THE UNIT

Looking for Misrepresentations

An afternoon on a Monday in late November marked the beginning of
study about the American Revolution. Atkinson began the lesson by
telling students to get out their social studies textbooks, but not to
open them. She said that she had wondered over the weekend why she
enjoyed the topic of the American Revolution so much. She concluded
that her enjoyment was connected to the whole idea of "misrepresen-
tation." She immediately asked her 26 students rhetorically what they
thought of when she said "Boston Tea Party," or perhaps "the French
and Indian War." She queried, "Who was fighting? . . . " Several students responded in unison, "The French and the Indians!" Her eyes
sparkled and the corner of her mouth turned up wryly as she feigned
success in conveying how the title of the war curiously misrepresented
the combatants.

She shifted quickly to the word "massacre." "What does this
mean," she asked, "What comes to your mind when I say massacre?"
A girl called out, "Like a riot or something. . . . " A boy followed with,
"Oh, lots of killing, blood . . . !" Atkinson, with a tinge of irony in her
voice, claimed that she was having trouble imagining why anyone
would call it a Boston Tea Party or a French and Indian War or a Boston Massacre.

Before proceeding, Atkinson circled back to review how early colonial life, while both rugged and dangerous, could be characterized by relative peacefulness between British control from afar and colonial self-rule. Only recently in their study of the colonies had they noticed how tensions stirred and open debate and challenge arose. Having foreshadowed the textbook account of the Boston Tea Party with "trouble brewing," Atkinson asked Lisa to read from the textbook. The account began with the crowd gathered at the Old South Meeting House in Boston. Atkinson stopped Lisa after she read the first paragraph. She then commented about how the words "tea party" seemed quite misleading. She wanted to know why misleading terms were necessary, who intended to misrepresent events, and for what purpose. Clearly, something was amiss. "Our goal today," she declared, "is to figure what went wrong and why."

Atkinson proceeded to explain the nature of colonial "propaganda." She discussed with her students how point of view and interpretation of events bear heavily as critical features of reading and understanding this period of history. In short, she prepared her students for "at least two sides of the issue," which in turn would complement her goal of getting her students to listen and carefully read arguments before they "voted" (she meant this both figuratively and literally) to accept or reject them.

She then introduced an upcoming re-enactment of a debate between people on different sides of the issue. Students exuded excitement and asked her when the debate would be held. They began announcing the "side" they wanted to be on. Most if not all of the students declared that they wanted to be Americans. Atkinson cautioned: Students would not know which side they would represent until the day of the debate. As a consequence, they would need to study "both sides." A muffled groan ensued. Atkinson responded by stating that she thought she could be on either side, because to believe that one side was completely right probably suggested a mistake in judgment. She indicated that mistakes in judgment resulted when people were upset and believed irrationally that their way was the only way. She insisted that they, her students, not fall victim to these errors. Thus, students should be able to debate on either side of the issue.

Returning to her goal of discovering "where and why things went wrong," Atkinson reintroduced the French and Indian War. She suggested that wars, including the one they were about to study, solved some problems but always created a host of others. She told her charges, "We call this a generalization." She then asked rhetorically, "What are the problems this war may have corrected and then gone on to create?" She instructed students to read to themselves the section on the French and Indian War. She said, "Look up at me when you're done, so I'll know when you're finished. I want to ask you a bunch of questions about what you've read." Students read silently for 3 minutes. The lesson continued with short readings and brief examinations of what was read. The class explored who was fighting whom in the French and Indian War and how the outcome of that war brought some relative peacefulness to North America.

Near the end of a textbook section, the word "fairness" appeared. Atkinson stopped the oral reading and began a brief monologue about what she called the "fairness ethic." The concept or image of fairness, as it played out in the polemics about who should pay for the war and how, prompted an analogy. How would students react if someone suddenly made the lunchroom rules much more strict without consulting them? Atkinson suggested that the students would balk. This, she claimed, was precisely the problem following the French and Indian War: The colonists suddenly were asked to pay taxes to finance British war debt, taxes that they believed were exorbitant and unfair. She asked Latrice to continue reading orally. She read about how some angry colonists tarred and feathered British tax collectors.

Sensing a need for more analogies, Atkinson wondered out loud what would happen if the rules for her room were changed suddenly so that discussions and collective decisions about classroom activities and rules ceased. A number of students cried foul. They wished to retain voting rights with respect to classroom affairs. The room buzzed with student comments.

Atkinson [voice raised]: But wait, wait, what are these colonists being asked to do?
Zeb: Make decisions. . . .
Gary: Pay taxes to the government.
Atkinson: But why did the government need money?

She told them to quickly "skim and scan" the next two textbook pages for a likely answer. Within seconds, several students replied almost simultaneously that the British needed to pay the French and Indian war debt. Atkinson nodded, then turning to James, asked him, if he were English, how he probably would feel about war payments and the colonists' role. James thought that he would want the colonists to help foot the bill because they benefited from the English victory the most. Atkinson congratulated him for his "logical" response. But why did the colonists remain so angry? Again, she told students to skim and scan.

Seconds later, 10 hands sliced the air. Atkinson called on Alisha, who stated that the colonists had no vote or opportunity to discuss the tax issue in Parliament before laws were changed. Atkinson said that if she were English, she would have wanted to give the colonial resistance a hearing, like she does in class when students raise concerns. "Did they . . . ? That's the big question," she concluded. This prompted two more analogies, one that came in question form, the other in expression of frustration: first, should parents pay attention to their children's opinions and wishes; second, how utterly frustrated she had been at school committee meetings when she was deprived of opportunities to raise questions and discuss options.

She glanced at the clock. With 15 minutes to the end of class, she called attention back to the textbook. After students read three paragraphs dealing with the Boston Massacre and the Daughters of Liberty, she asked, "We've been predicting trouble, but was the Boston Massacre really a 'massacre'?" Students read quietly for about 2 minutes before Atkinson broke the silence by noting how unpopular British troops had become. She said she had a different account of the Massacre from another book that recreated the scene more vividly. She explained how the colonists' snowballs were a form of mockery, how she could feel for the soldiers, in a way not unlike her own experience of having things thrown at her face in a carnival in which she once participated. She said to the class:

> Stop and put yourself in the position of these soldiers! How were they to protect themselves against the iceballs and hardballs being thrown? How angry do you feel when someone hits you on the playground with an iceball? Think about it! These soldiers were taunted and teased. How did the soldiers interpret what was happening to them? Was it a misinterpretation? What happens when misinterpretations are present? Shots were fired in the air, but people continued to pelt the soldiers, and mob-style pushing and shoving began. Is the word massacre a misrepresentation? Headlines in the paper read MASSACRE, but only five died [cautioning that any number of deaths would have been bad]. This is sensationalism—we talked about this in our newspaper unit, and you know we considered this practice invalid. Sensationalism in the press occurred back then too. It contributed to all the trouble.

Time had run out. Atkinson reviewed homework assignments for the next day while the "safeties" departed for their crossing posts.

This reading exercise is an example of what Wineburg (1991) has referred to as reading for subtext, the process that demarcates historian-readers from nonhistorian-readers. Atkinson was no self-proclaimed historian and probably would have eschewed the title. Nonetheless, she seemed intent on teaching her students ways to interpret history (and newspapers, a topic she covered extensively in language arts) in order to develop a critical sense on which to base decisions. Teaching them how to ask questions, to read like historians, served her broader goal of teaching them how to make informed decisions in order to improve society.

Atkinson began the second lesson by shutting off the lights. Students needed a pencil only. A filmstrip projector and tape player stood ready at the center of the room. This day's lesson entailed an excursion into life on the eve of the revolution. Atkinson told her students that the purpose of the lesson involved two matters: (1) encountering more background information for understanding points of view regarding the imminent conflict, and (2) an exercise in the skill of note taking. She circled the room handing out a question guide that accompanied the audiovisual material.

Before turning on the machine, she asked rhetorical questions connected to the preceding lesson: What do you think life was like in the colonies before the Revolutionary War? How do you think the colonists felt about Parliament? To the first question, Atkinson related her memories of the Liberty Bell in Philadelphia and how it evoked images of colonial life: the clothing, the attitudes, and the talk of people grumbling about the latest tax policies. To the second question, she added a third: "What about these 'Parliament types'—any women members?" "No," she immediately retorted.

Atkinson threw the switch on the projector and lit up the screen. The narrator of the filmstrip story emerged as an animated character, a colonist with ties to the Sons of Liberty. He complained that the English Parliament recently had passed tax laws that colonists found objectionable because they were enacted without colonial consent and participation in the law-making process. He traced the roots of the new policies to the French and Indian War and subsequent British debt, and the unfairness of the British desire to finance the war on colonial prosperity. He took up the remaining minutes of the filmstrip by using "unfair" British policy (e.g., the Intolerable Acts) to justify the existence and activity of the Sons of Liberty. The remaining class time was used to discuss the filmstrip and several of the guide questions. Much of the discussion focused on the point of view of the narrator.

To begin lesson three, Atkinson told her students to get out their social studies textbooks, but to keep them closed. She also asked them to take out their "note-taking sheet" from the day before. She briefly discussed the purpose of note taking. The class began with number three (they had finished number two the day prior). Atkinson read the question, "From what nation did England win a huge amount of land west of the colonies?" Students burst into laughter because of her excess emphasis on the word huge. She replaced it with "a big hunk, then." Students continued to laugh. Atkinson, smiling, announced that the answer to the question was France.

The class moved from question to question until they reached number seven. This was as far as they would get for this lesson. Atkinson, and several students, added analogous and anecdotal responses to the questions, often connecting the past to the present. Here is an example. Atkinson commented, "The English soldiers wore something they were very proud of." Adrienne quickly shouted out, "red coats!" Atkinson asked her how these red coats advantaged the colonists. James chimed in, observing that they were bright red. Atkinson noted that they stood out almost anywhere. Allen said, "Those coats were funny looking. The colonists laughed at the soldiers." Robert added, "The coats and the style of combat used by the British made the redcoats easy targets." Atkinson asked if uniforms were related to where one was fighting. Kent immediately noted that camouflaging was popular at the moment. Atkinson added a brief anecdote about the pictures she and probably the students had seen of the Persian Gulf soldiers dressed in their desert gear.

Atkinson was home the next day, having contracted walking pneumonia. A substitute taught using lesson plans sent in by Atkinson. The substitute, in a review-recitation manner, completed questions eight through 12 on the assignment sheet from the day before. She then passed out another assignment sheet on which students were to place an "S" in front of statements that referred to customs common in England, and a "D" in front of statements that suggested customs practiced in the colonies that differed from English customs. While students, in groups of three, selected "S" or "D," the substitute loaded a filmstrip into the projector. Once the filmstrip was loaded, she announced that students had 3 more minutes in which to finish their assignment.

After about 5 minutes, the substitute announced that time was up. Beginning with the first statement on the second assignment sheet, the class moved quickly and without much difficulty through the remaining items. With 5 minutes remaining, the substitute announced that she had time to show a few frames of the filmstrip on colonial expansion westward from the coast. After approximately five frames, she dismissed the class.

For the fifth lesson, Atkinson returned. She claimed that she had too much to do to be home in bed. Yet, it seemed from the sound of her voice and how she labored slightly when she breathed that she had not recovered entirely.

Trouble was brewing as Atkinson's fifth graders came inside from afternoon recess. A girl was crying in the bathroom. Atkinson went to investigate, then returned and launched into a rather stern speech centering on student attitudes and behavior toward one another. "Some days people don't do so well; don't get down on them!" she said. She proceeded to tell them that all people make mistakes (an allusion to the student who was crying as well as to all class members). "I want people to feel comfortable in here! I want them to feel like there's plenty of room to make mistakes!" she stated forcefully. She then added, "Remember, when you go to middle school, friendship from people in this room will be really important—remember that!" Students sat very quietly and listened, some with their heads down.

Atkinson paused for a moment, scanning her children's faces. The air felt heavy. After a long several seconds, she introduced the social studies lesson. "Do you remember," she queried, "that we talked about how diverse life was in the colonies? We read about their differences and similarities. I want us to pull together some ideas from that material and the textbook assignment you are now reading, plus I want to bridge these assignments with the filmstrip and a textbook I used to use." She announced that they would be talking more about the Boston Massacre and the Tea Party—"and they didn't serve tea or sugar either," she interjected, adding levity to a somber group of students who snickered at her remark. She discussed briefly the similarities among and differences between colonies, noting that colonial disagreements with the British fostered a sense of solidarity along the Atlantic seaboard. She then asked her fifth graders to turn to pages 142–143 in their textbooks:

> We talked before about the problem of taxes; let's move on to the Boston Massacre and the battles that began the war. You [students] said to me earlier that you were interested in the battles. I want you to build your background information. Read pages 144–153. You will notice the questions in the gray area on page 146, for example. These are questions that check your comprehension. You don't have to write them out, but ask yourselves these questions once you get there. Then go on and finish the reading up to the section on the Declaration of Independence.

After approximately 5 minutes, Atkinson interrupted them. What they had not yet finished became their homework assignment for the next day. Atkinson then turned to the assignment sheets associated with the filmstrips shown in the preceding several lessons. These, she told them, were to be used as background knowledge and for study purposes. She then began a review of what they had learned from watching the filmstrip earlier that day. (Using a portion of language arts time, Atkinson had completed the filmstrip begun by the substitute on the previous day.)

As review, Atkinson questioned students about why the colonists had risked so much to come to America on a very dangerous voyage. Robert indicated that they had come in search of gold. Gary added land acquisition. Brianne offered the idea that the Indians had controlled the land but had no ownership concept. Atkinson acknowledged Brianne's comment, noting that the Indians used the land but that the explorers, and later the colonists, claimed it as their own. She then assigned note-taking responsibilities for another filmstrip on the maturing colonies. Its narrator took the viewers from colonist–Native American clashes on the frontier, through life in William Penn's Pennsylvania, Scottish immigrant activity in Philadelphia, and Moravian custom in Salem, North Carolina, to an extended discussion of life and times in colonial Williamsburg.

Attempting to deepen students' background knowledge of events leading up to the Revolutionary War, Atkinson next focused attention on economic factors. In a quick exchange with several students, she defined several terms (e.g., boycott) and then discussed how England monopolized colonial markets and limited their trade, and how some colonists responded with boycotts and smuggling.

Narrating rapidly, Atkinson continued, "The English thought that a change in tax policies would solve the economic problem. But the boycotts continued." "Who's acting mature here?" queried Atkinson, referring directly to the British willingness to practice give and take, and obliquely to colonial child-like stubbornness. Several students muttered that the colonists seemed to be acting immature. "As you will see, this kind of behavior will produce open rebellion against the British," Atkinson retorted.

With only several minutes remaining, Atkinson directed student attention to the fact that she had put *My Brother Sam Is Dead* on the board as the next novel on the independent reading list. She used this note as an entree into a brief discussion of the loyalist–patriot issue, in which she shifted back and forth between positions using the pronoun "we" from both perspectives. She noted how neighbors were pitted against neighbors over the loyalist–patriot issue. She wanted her students to remember how crucial point of view was in situations such as these. "Was there a right side? A wrong side? Were the British right or wrong? How about the colonial patriots? Which? We will need to develop some proof before we draw conclusions." With this, she sent the safeties on their way. After this day walking pneumonia and doctor's orders forced Atkinson into bed for a week.

Lessons six through nine were taught by the substitute from lesson plans sent by Atkinson. The lessons focused on a cursory examination of the textbook and several filmstrips (which traced events just prior to the outbreak of war and the war itself) and a series of assignment sheets that accompanied them. On the day before Atkinson's return, the substitute used one of the assignment review sheets as a quiz. It is important to point out that continuity in lessons and learning opportunities was broken temporarily by Atkinson's absence. The substitute, despite good intentions, lacked the enthusiasm and understanding of the subject matter to sustain the level of teaching initiated by Atkinson.

It is difficult to ascertain the degree to which Atkinson's extended absence affected the overall quality of the unit. One important pedagogical casualty was the patriot–loyalist debate she had planned to conduct. From Atkinson's point of view, the unit was failing to go entirely as planned and many of her goals inadvertently were being circumvented. Upon her return she would labor to reinvigorate the reform and participatory spirit she had tried to build. However, feeling "behind," she also would struggle to reteach what she believed her students had failed to learn in the previous four lessons. The tension between building a level of background knowledge and cultivating the time-consuming participatory, reform ethos she favored would be manifest in the remaining lessons.

Atkinson presided over lesson 10 against her doctor's orders, planning to teach only half of this day in order to conserve energy. As a result, she moved social studies to a morning session. Lesson 10's activity, she indicated, would involve a bit of review and an effort to get reacquainted with each other, to have a "little fun." She asked her students to read a magazine called *READ*. The article they were to work through discussed a story of two adolescent boys who terrorized a Jewish rabbi with prejudicial taunts and racial epithets. The story described how the rabbi refused to engage in revenge against the boys and how he worked diligently to challenge their beliefs.

Atkinson used the story to open a discussion of the events and consequences of bigotry. She noted how the days of slavery and the events involving Japanese relocation camps following the Pearl Harbor bombing were embarrassing to our collective history. Adding a customary anecdote, she remarked how she grew up as a "minority person" (she was a Methodist) in a community heavily populated by Jewish immigrants. She knew from their stories about Nazi atrocities how deeply they suffered as a result of unrelenting bigotry. She said that she winced every time she thought about it.

Following a discussion of the story, Atkinson announced that she would postpone the upcoming test because she had heard that students simply were not ready. Turning on the overhead projector, she placed a paragraph about Abigail Adams on the screen. She asked for a volunteer who could read it with great dramatic flair. Aimee agreed. She also indicated that she had a part for a John Adams. Gary agreed to fill this role. The class then broke for lunch.

Violating her plans to go home after a half day, Atkinson returned to finish the history lesson she had begun. Lightheartedly, students teased her about still being there after lunch. She called Aimee and Gary to the front of the room. Atkinson read an introduction from a teacher's guide to the play, explaining Abigail and John Adams's role and relationship to each other. Aimee read Abigail's lines wherein she told her husband John that women could play significant roles in building public support for independence from Britain. But Abigail also worried about who would take care of the children—John went on colonial political business so frequently, she hardly dared follow her instincts in helping the cause locally. John, as Gary read him, responded with what could be construed as condescending placation. He wanted Abigail not to worry, to busy herself with the children, and only after she had done this, to take up the cause.

Atkinson thanked both students as they returned to their seats. She said she wanted students to "get a sense of the innuendoes that passed between Abigail and John."

Atkinson [continuing]: I've probably prejudiced you to Abigail's side because I like her. I think she was a most interesting person. [pausing] Why were we uptight about British control?

Darron: The colonists lacked a say in the rules—no representation, none at all!

Atkinson: How is this like Abigail talking to John? Abigail is torn. She's worried about the war, her involvement in it, John's absence, the children. Do you think John thought she was very bright?

Several students exclaim: No, not at all. . . .

Atkinson: Yeah, John was sort of sarcastic with her—he didn't really understand her very well. . . .

Adrienne [calling out]: It was really sexist. . . .

Atkinson: Yes, an interesting interaction between husband and wife, but Abigail never stopped trying to get better roles for women. She was well read and had guts enough to stand up for what she believed.

Atkinson later indicated that this lesson involved her effort to put a filmstrip about women during the revolution into personal perspective. She wanted her students to empathize with the role of women during this era, to see the woman's point of view in the context of the times. She also was interested in portraying the struggle women experienced exercising their rights in a male-dominated culture.

Lesson 11 began by Atkinson asking, "Were there examples of the king and the colonists making snap judgments with much distance from the problem?" Eduard said, "I think it was about 70% of the time for the King and about 30% of the time for the colonists!" Atkinson then asked students to return for a moment, by way of example, to the French and Indian War. She wanted to run through the "pros and cons" of the war for the British and the colonists.

Atkinson: Pro first. Darron?
Darron: Britain now had all the land [North America] to themselves.
Atkinson: OK, a con statement.
Gary: The British were left in serious debt by the war and the colonists had to pay!
Atkinson: Another pro?
James: They [colonists] didn't really have to worry anymore about Indian attacks.
Atkinson [glancing at the clock]: OK, one more con to even it out.

Emma noted that the British policy makers wanted the colonists to pay for and house the soldiers during and especially following the war. Atkinson reiterated Emma's point, then asked, "So where are these soldiers going to live? In barracks?" Several students in unison called out, "Not! In the colonists' homes [instead]!" Atkinson acknowledged their remarks with a wry smile. She asked them to imagine about the "privacy issue." Atkinson queried, "How do you suppose the houses were chosen?" Carlos speculated that the colonists probably had no choice in the matter and were required to "let the soldiers just come right in their homes." Brianne added, "The soldiers probably felt well treated because the power was on their side—they could get what they wanted."

This comment sparked another Atkinson analogy (Atkinson referred to these as "Atkinsoni's"). She asked the students rhetorically about who had the power that morning while she was recuperating at home (Atkinson was still coming in only half days). She said she was assuming that, perhaps because the substitute was considered an "outsider" to the classroom, she could be thought of in the same vein as the British soldiers in the colonists' homes. She wanted to know how students felt when the substitute asked them to do things. Pushing the analogy home, Atkinson inquired, "Did you treat her well, or did you treat her suspiciously because she was not the 'regular teacher'?" Part analogy to the Quartering Act, but also part challenge to student attitudes about the substitute, Atkinson drove hard to point out the potential consequences of failing to reconcile differences through negotiation on all fronts: colonial and British, student and substitute.

The class ended with a brief discussion of the Intolerable Acts, the Stamp Act, and the Quartering Acts. Atkinson put final closure to the lesson by reminding the students of the depth of the tensions that had grown on both sides. She also pointed out how the British and the colonists both held responsibility for escalating tensions. She then announced that the chapter test would occur the following week. Students appeared relieved.

Test Review

Atkinson began lesson 12 by asking students if they are aware that on this day they should be celebrating a belated birthday party. After a quick review of what belated meant in this context, Zeb announced that it was the birthday of the Bill of Rights the day before. Atkinson smiled approvingly.

She then reminded her students that the book test would occur in 3 days. For the next 10 minutes, Atkinson explained the test in detail. She indicated that it would include 35 multiple-choice items and five essays (the same test Palmer used). The multiple-choice items she generally disliked, but students would encounter more of these items the following year in middle school. She wanted students to have exposure to them. She noted how these questions would be taken directly from the book and assess recall about facts and events surrounding the American Revolution. Before moving on to the essay questions, Atkinson pointed out that each multiple-choice question would have the page number after it, referring to the place in the textbook from which the question was drawn. After she graded and returned the tests, students could consult these page references for the items they had missed. They could challenge the textbook account or the wording of the test question. If their challenge seemed articulate and well argued, she would reverse her decision and give them credit. This approach was consistent with a reformist style of pedagogy.

Atkinson wished to spend the remaining class time in review of what had been studied so far. Aimee suggested that they make a game out of the review process. After a brief debate and vote on rules and changes (a common practice in Atkinson's class), the game proceeded.

Atkinson explained that the questions she would ask could be interesting because she would develop them as she went. "I was not prepared to do the review this way," she said, "but I like the idea, so we'll see how it goes. OK, table 1: I need all three parties involved in the French and Indian War. I need who fought against whom in the right relationship."

Alisha: The French and Indians fighting the British. [Atkinson gave full points to table 1 and marked these down on the overhead]

Atkinson: Table 2: I want to know what good resulted for the colonists as a result of the French and Indian War. [Table 2 confers. Emma responds]

Emma: Because the French and Indians were defeated, the colonists could stop worrying about Indian attacks and competition from the French. [Points for table 2]

Atkinson: Table 3: Name one thing that made the colonists upset at the British.

Robert: The new tax policies, like the Stamp Act and the tea tax— they helped pay for the French and Indian War, but they still bothered the colonists. [Points for table 3]

Atkinson: Table 4: "Taxation without representation," what does this mean?

After a brief conference, Gary responded, "It means that colonists didn't get to vote on these taxes. Only Parliament voted and that made the colonists mad." [Points for table 4] This practice continued in rapid succession from table to table for the remaining 20 minutes of class time. The class resolved by a unanimous show of hands to continue the game the next day in the same fashion.

Review for the test resumed in lesson 13. For 50 minutes, a rapid-fire, question–answer session ensued, similar in format to the preceding lesson. As each new question went to the floor, students hunched up over their tables to confer among themselves. At the conclusion of the lesson, Atkinson reminded students to study again that night. She also told them that she needed to do some lecture-reviewing on the following day. She wanted to make sure they understood the chain of events, their implications, and how winning the war left the colonists to face the interesting dilemma of managing a new country without a clear sense of governmental direction, an irony she found fascinating.

Atkinson began lesson 14 by describing how she had gone back through the chapter and underlined in green ink certain sections she thought were important. She wanted to stress these areas. She turned on the overhead projector and wrote on the screen as she talked. She reviewed four key issues about the time period: (1) how England and the colonies grew apart, (2) the road to revolution or how the colonists consistently failed to find a way to live under British rule, (3) the Revolutionary War itself, and (4) the struggle to create a new nation following the victory. She then discussed the first three in more detail, asserting that she thought of them in a descending order of importance (1) through (3). "I want to pull this all together for you today," she stated.

Atkinson spent the hour telling her version of the Revolutionary War, its beginnings, battles, and aftermath. She punctuated the story with a number of analogies, in order, she said, to draw history closer to students' lives. Students listened attentively and occasionally asked questions. At the conclusion of her story, Atkinson again reminded her students to study for the test.

During lesson 15 students took the test. Several questions were raised about the essays the students began writing. After about 15 minutes of virtual silence, several hands popped up, indicating that these students had finished. Atkinson assigned them to work on a mathematics exercise after they had finished. After 40 minutes, almost everyone had completed the test. Clusters of students whispered quietly as they wrestled with the mathematics exercise. At 3:15, the time for safeties to be dismissed, the last student to complete the test raised her hand to indicate completion.

The Articles of Confederation: Mistakes from the Past

Lesson 16 marked the return from a 2-week winter recess. Atkinson commenced the lesson by describing a Bill of Rights writing contest that had been reported in the local newspaper over the break. One of her recent fifth-grade graduates had written an award-winning essay about children's rights. She read the essay from the newspaper. The student argued that children represent a "minority." He objected to what he perceived as the failure of the Bill of Rights to recognize this

minority and suggested that children needed a "Kids' Bill of Rights."
He concluded by arguing for changes that acknowledge the plight of
children. His argument fronted the age-discrimination issue. Atkinson
challenged her fifth graders to raise similar issues, to recognize the
power of arguments such as this one. She wanted them to consider
engaging in such contests, both formally in newspapers and informally
in class and at home. She stated that she was impressed by the active
involvement in social issues that her previous student's essay represented.

Shifting the activity, Atkinson provided Aimee and Carlos with a
script for a short dialogue she wanted them to enact in several minutes. She requested that they study their roles. While they did, she
asked the class, "What was happening when we left off for vacation;
what were we talking about?" One student mentioned the Intolerable
Acts. Another noted the war and the Continental army. This prompted
a story-setting analogy from Atkinson:

> Sometimes when you win, you have a feeling of elation. These
> colonists had a definite will to win when they fought. Let's make
> a couple of guesses. We [Americans] often don't learn very well
> the first time we do something. We're going to talk about some
> birthdays [that] we don't often talk about because they're about
> mistakes! We don't talk about our mistakes very much in history.
> We don't like to dwell on that. But it has to do with what happens
> when we finally get independence. What do we do? Who would
> get control now? [Several students say, "Me!" jokingly] We are go-
> ing to hear from a conversation [referring to the script] in May
> 1787. At the time, states are worried about too strong a central
> leadership—they wanted to all do their own thing!

She then introduced the dialogue that Carlos and Aimee would
read. They took turns reading their lines. Atkinson played the role of
narrator.

Carlos enacted the role of a lawyer, Aimee, a farmer. They discussed the weaknesses of the Articles of Confederation, the problems
of money and exchange, and Shays's Rebellion. They both hoped that
the forthcoming Constitutional Convention would help resolve rather
severe postwar difficulties. Atkinson followed their reading, saying:

> That's a preview. It's like euphoria when they first won the war,
> but some real practical problems arise. Some things appeared to
> work, but others didn't. So what are you going to do? How are

you going to change? We're going to talk about how we got the Constitution, which has lasted this long! I cringe at the thought that we could write rules for fifth graders that could still be in force 200 years from now. The way they worked out the Constitution would be like us deciding the rules for this school. Which ones would we keep and which would we change to make this a different school. We would have to work together, combine age perspectives, decide on enforceability. We would have to include the principal. Who knows, maybe we should really do this. We could make this school different for your children.

Open your books to Chapter 8. We are not celebrating the anniversary of the Articles of Confederation. They just didn't last that long, and besides, they were like a mistake we're not proud of. None of us are very fond of paying taxes. Your parents will be complaining about that shortly. But, when there's a fire, boy, do we want the fire department there right away! And we want financial protection for when we get older and retire. Are we willing to pay for this? I am! But yet there's a fear angle in all this that I want you to listen for! I think the Articles of Confederation helped produce this fear. James, please read the first section.

Following James's reading, a discussion of "mistakes of the past" ensued.

Atkinson: States wanted the power. Friends and neighbors in each state wanted local control. The southerners didn't think the New Englanders were interested in their problems. . . .

Adrienne: But people would remember what it was like so they wouldn't pass more Intolerable Acts.

Robert: But they [the states] would want all the power themselves and that wouldn't work!

Atkinson: Will someone always abuse power? Once I watched safeties on their posts. I got real insight into how some safeties take advantage of their control over the younger kids. Those problems need to be corrected. People were worried about that kind of abuse from too strong a central government! Let's talk about the pros and cons of the Articles of Confederation. Robert, read the next section on the Northwest Territory.

Atkinson then explained briefly how the Articles of Confederation had rules that helped to organize the Northwest Territory. Organizational plans like that and others helped hold the country together during the war, she noted. With 15 minutes remaining, she told students that they had about 3 minutes to read the section on the "Problems of the Articles." If they read quickly, they were to go on to read about Shays's Rebellion. The room fell silent.

Looking at the clock, Atkinson announced that they had 5 short minutes left to discuss Shays's Rebellion. She quickly presented a short chronology of the events preceding the rebellion. She explained what Shays thought he could accomplish and why. The problem arose when Massachusetts pled with the central government for assistance to put down the rebellion and received no response. Some worried, she noted, that further rebellions would follow and the new country would be forced into civil war or be taken over by a large European power.

Lesson 17 began with Atkinson asking her students to get out their textbooks and leave them closed on their desks. She told the students that in several days she would show them a videotape that does a splendid job explaining Shays's Rebellion. The tape also would deal extensively with the period leading up to the ratification of the Constitution. But before they saw the tape, everyone, including herself, needed more background on the period.

Atkinson next asked several students to identify three things that worked well with the Articles of Confederation. Students mentioned how it prevented the power from concentrating too heavily with government and that it held the country together initially. Atkinson added that it assisted in organizing the Northwest Territory.

Atkinson and her students continued reading excerpts from the textbook. They paused to discuss the problems associated with Shay's Rebellion, the taxation issue, the balance of power between states' rights and the central government, and the sharing of power among states. Atkinson took some time to emphasize the difficulties involved in working out a compromise to satisfy all the states. Using an analogy at one point, she asked students to remember back to when there had been problems in their classroom. She wanted them to imagine what might happen if her class were allowed to make decisions to solve problems for all fifth graders in the district. "And what if we were a small class, the smallest in the district, say 15 or so students. Who would get more say proportionately in the decisions?"

Gary: I could go both ways here over who gets more say. It's not the small class's fault they only have 15! But the larger groups probably should still have more influence.

Atkinson: Yes, this is a problem. Take the states of Pennsylvania and Rhode Island—one very large state and the smallest one. If you give them each two votes, they are equal in power. So how do you solve this? I am really impressed with how the conventioneers struggled with this, how they could see both sides of the issue [balancing power within and between the states]. They didn't give up. They kept working on this difficult issue 'til they came up with two houses of Congress.

Realizing she had run out of time, she assigned seven pages in the textbook for the next class. Students were to read about the Constitution and study its various sections. "Tomorrow, I am going to ask you to explain to me how these sections were organized and why. I also will ask you to give your interpretations of what certain sections mean. I've signed things in lawyers' offices and I wanted to be able to interpret and understand what I was signing. I want you to do the same with the Constitution. I know you can make sense out of it!" she concluded.

The Bill of Rights, the Constitution, and Citizen Action

Lesson 18 began with an examination of the Bill of Rights. Students opened their textbooks. Here, each of the 26 amendments to the Constitution appeared chronologically with brief descriptions. Atkinson led students through the amendments, noting how most of them expanded civil rights and social justice. She paused for several minutes to discuss this process and stress its importance, noting how many of the amendments "corrected flaws" in the original Constitution and limits in the Bill of Rights.

Atkinson had begun the lesson with the rhetorical question, "Why would you refuse to sign the Constitution?" After the brief look at the amendments, she returned to this question as a preface to a filmstrip. Before running the filmstrip, she told students to focus on the balance of power provisions, the need for the Bill of Rights to support ratification, and the struggle between the Federalists, personified by Hamilton, and the Anti-Federalists, represented by Jefferson. After the filmstrip concluded, the following dialogue ensued:

Atkinson: We said that between 1775 and 1971, we saw amendments being made and only in 1913 did we see two in one year. . . . [Several students call out that they had 10 in one year in 1791 and also two in 1933; Atkinson smiles and thanks them politely] But how did this Constitution get passed, that's the question. [Gary's hand goes up] If your hand isn't up, I'm really nervous!
Kent: Can you say the question again?

Atkinson: After 1791, we only had 2 years when there was more than one amendment to the Constitution, and then only two in each of those years. Why did we get 10 in 1791?

Robert: They had many amendments, but they decided to pass them all in one year.

Elena: They needed nine of the 13 states to ratify the Constitution, so they needed the first 10 amendments to get enough votes!

Atkinson: Yes. They needed to compromise to settle the debate between the Federalists and the Anti-Federalists. But, as I said earlier, some of these basic rights were open to interpretation. For example, why was the right to bear arms allowed?

Brett: For military reasons. In case there was a war or a surprise attack.

The conversation continued, surrounding the nature of terms elected officials could serve initially and how limits were placed on these terms later.

Beginning lesson 19, Atkinson stated, "The other day we were talking about how people were nervous about giving too much power to the central government. We talked about compromise. I have a diagram [holds it up] I want you to do. Do it quickly. I'm going to ask which box you put each of the three branches of government in." Diagrams were passed out and students began filling in the boxes.

After several minutes, Atkinson announced that students had 45 seconds left. After a minute, she instructed them to stop. The class then worked through which government branches belonged in which box and what their functions and powers included. Atkinson told students that people who worked in each of the branches did very different things. Stressing the importance of this understanding, she asked the class why three branches of government were necessary, why one would not do as a central decision-making body. The discussion that followed continued to demonstrate Atkinson's reformist approach. At one point, she implored her students to take active roles in local and national politics by holding herself to the same standard.

Jeb [responding]: If you had only one, then that group would make all the decisions.

Allen: Yeah, one group shouldn't be allowed to do it all.

Atkinson: What if I made all the decisions as the teacher? What's wrong with that?

Adrienne: You'd have all the power—we couldn't make any of the decisions.

Atkinson: So how do we have input now?

Latrice: We can vote and write letters. . . . [pauses]

Atkinson: We can write to our representatives. Why would this work?

Gary: We have power through our votes!

Dan: And we [the people] have lots of votes!

Atkinson: Yes!! Congressmen might not get re-elected if they don't pay attention to the voters. But we have a problem: A lot of people don't vote. Apparently, it's too much trouble. But you know what? I can't just sit around and complain. I have to do something! I have to exercise my rights by making a contribution.

The class finished the assignment. Atkinson collected the papers while asking students to take out their textbooks.

She noted that their study had taken them close to the end of the chapter. They had completed a survey but would study this period in U.S. history in much more detail in eighth grade and again in high school. Then Atkinson turned to the importance of being an active reader.

Atkinson: Why do you think adult types want you to study this so much and in so many grades? Why three times?

Darron: It has a lot to do with everyday life.

Atkinson: Yes and people know this! But some adults know less about this than you do. I'm proud of all of you! The average reading level of adult types is about fifth grade.

Darron: That's disgusting!

Atkinson: Newspaper people are worried that people will stop reading. I teach you "Newspaper" [the unit] to get you to read instead of just watching the news. Why do you think they always take negative viewpoints on the news?

Zeb: To catch your attention.

Atkinson: Too much sensationalism, but it sells! I want you to learn to get different points of view, to read for different positions. We're almost out of time. I want to give you an assignment. [students groan] I need you to know about President Washington. Look on page 179. What's a debt?

James: It's borrowing money that you have to pay back.

Atkinson: Yes. We're going to talk about banks. We're going to hear an argument that forms two political parties—watch [for] this closely.

With that, she asked students to read to the end of the chapter for the next lesson.

A number of Atkinson's lessons included references to civic action.

For her, making history come alive meant connecting it to the decision-making process, taking rights and responsibilities seriously. She tried to give substance to this purpose by constructing a classroom environment in which students were allowed room to negotiate and decide about matters important to them, up to and sometimes including what they were to learn and how. She appeared less interested in U.S. history as a disciplinary frame of reference (in contrast to Lake and Palmer) and more interested in what it could do for her and her students as they confronted decisions and tried to solve present problems. Again, use of history in this way is consistent with the reformist approach and underpins the teaching and curriculum recommendations of some social studies theorists (e.g., Banks, 1991; Parker & Jarolimek, 1984; Shaver, 1987).

Lessons 20 and 21 were spent watching a videotape entitled "The Empire of Reason." The program traced the developments at the Constitutional Convention. Following the many debates about the relative strengths and potential dangers of central government under the Constitution, the program used contemporary actors and actresses, TV personalities, and newscasters to re-enact this period in U.S. history. The setting was late-twentieth-century America, but the subject matter was late eighteenth century. The actors and personalities were contemporary household names (e.g., Connie Chung, Walter Cronkite, Mario Cuomo, Phil Donahue) but the roles some of them played (e.g., Hamilton, Madison, Representative Lansing) effectively took students back in time. Newscasters (e.g., Cronkite) presented information on a network-type broadcast that followed the events of the convention. The program ran for one hour and was filled with suspense and intrigue.

Atkinson showed two 30-minute segments, one each day. Students watched attentively and occasionally wrote on question-and-answer sheets that she had prepared as a guide for watching the program. Following the viewing of the entire videotape, Atkinson conducted a rushed review, mindful that she already had exceeded her own time limit for the unit by more than a week. She noted the arguments for and against constitutional ratification, the struggle and debate between disagreeing parties, and how Hamilton's influence combined with the Bill of Rights may have been the decisive factors in final ratification.

Lesson 22 concluded her treatment of the American Revolution. It ended with a brief quiz. Students were asked to identify the branches of government under the Constitution and write out their responsibilities and powers. The last item asked students to write an essay in which they described something they found interesting and worthwhile in their study of the Constitution and Bill of Rights.

ASSESSING ATKINSON'S CASE

Atkinson appeared to use as many opportunities as she could locate to turn history to her reform orientation. For example, she used reading for subtext as a method for teaching her students to be critical readers, to hunt down word usages designed to persuade and propagandize. The issue of women's roles in the past was used to address the need to change women's roles in the present. Constitutional amendments were noted as reformist examples, redressing historical social and economic grievances. The Articles of Confederation illustrated "mistakes of history" in need of correction. Atkinson used numerous analogies and anecdotes to drive home these points. These are many of the characteristics of reformist-oriented practice.

However, unchecked reformist approaches sometimes degenerate into zealotry; virtually everything suffers from the need for change. Atkinson walked this edge. Her unit consumed more classroom time than those of the other two teachers (and this probably would have been true even if she had she remained healthy). She knew that time was precious and that she had to balance her reformist desires with the need to provide sufficient background knowledge of the period for her students. Consequently, we observed a rush to finish the unit, coupled with myriad, often quickly delivered references and analogies to and anecdotes about "mistakes needing correction." They were plugged into the story at opportune moments but seldom pushed to the depth that Palmer's study of the Bill of Rights entailed. Time constraints tugged more heavily on Atkinson.

Consistent with Banks's (1991) recommendations, Atkinson tended to use history as a tool pressed into the service of understanding and acting on present problems and social issues. Her "social studies" approach to the study of history was designed to produce critical readers, inquirers, and active citizens more than storytellers or young historians. Lake's and Palmer's approaches were generally more efficient; they covered considerable ground and in some depth. Atkinson hoped to do the same. However, when history presents many opportunities to invoke stories of reform, reformers attempt to take advantage. Herein lies the trade-off. Taking advantage means stopping to make connections, past to present. This provides important learning opportunities for students, but leaves little time for in-depth treatment of unique "mysteries" of history (the disappearance of the first Virginia colony) or the struggle to understand history's causal relationships (the French and Indian War to the American Revolution).

Atkinson cognizantly walked a fine line between a set of opposing expectations concerning what it meant to teach history-social studies to fifth graders at Greenwood. On the one hand, she tried to model her particular definition of democracy, which valued wrestling with ideas (sometimes absent fixed properties) and often demanded some type of action for the benefit of the community (in her case, the classroom and school). This definition questions the nature of authority, renders decision making problematic, and is often time-consuming and onerous in practice. Atkinson once told her students, "I want to teach you how to argue with your parents and win. And that goes for the principal here at school too." To teach her students to argue in this way required using the subject matter of history (whether U.S. history or the more immediate history of the classroom) in a different manner, one that involved treating it as a tool in service of the argument itself. To argue and negotiate this way requires a significant time commitment. In classroom sessions devoted to the discussion of issues raised by the study of history, large portions of the hour often were spent considering only one key point (e.g., the status of women during the war period). Students would engage deeply, but content coverage would suffer.

Atkinson's reformist approach contrasted with the more traditionally defined nature of role responsibility and organizational authority found at Greenwood and the larger community it served. Teachers were considered knowledge sources. Knowledge, presented in textbooks and in the authoritative stories of teachers, was to be transmitted to students. Coverage, in the case of history, was crucial; district curriculum guidelines for fifth-grade social studies said as much and, to a degree, middle school teachers expected to receive students from elementary school who had knowledge of "the facts." The principal at Greenwood encouraged (sometimes pressed) teachers to follow the guidelines and exercise their roles as knowledge purveyors in getting their students ready for the rigors of life beyond elementary school.

Atkinson spent considerable energy traversing the shaky bridge connecting these opposing expectations. As she put it, she had democratic and nondemocratic days. Her approach to teaching and curriculum gatekeeping (Thornton, 1991) reflected this vacillation. In some social studies lessons, issues would be discussed. In other lessons, they would not. Time was seldom on her side and her extended absence exacerbated the press she experienced in the unit. On occasion, she would begin a discussion, find her students interested in exploring the issue, notice the clock, and somewhat abruptly shift gears to the next topic (VanSledright, 1992b). She was interested in the students' contributions to each lesson, but she also was aware that she needed to retain the authority to the class through the material. Yet, most of the time she seemed willing to push at the boundaries of Greenwood's traditional ethos, which called for a more linear and structured approach to subject matter.

Atkinson could be criticized for vacillating, for failing to be consistent to her reformist orientation, for slipping into occasional knowledge transmission approaches. As result of her "inconsistencies," some would argue that she may have given students mixed and confusing messages about the nature of historical knowledge and what it means to understand history. Others might criticize her for not taking her reformist approach far enough and teaching students to be more ardent critics of the unjust practices found in history and the present. These criticisms become possible primarily as a result of the inevitable trade-off decisions teachers must make when they teach history. Often, these gatekeeping trade-offs have implications that reach beyond the students and the classroom walls, as these cases make plain. Teachers' trade-off decisions, in turn, are influenced by a number of factors not entirely under their control. This puts teachers in the middle of managing myriad dilemmas (Lampert, 1985; VanSledright & Grant, 1994), a process that appears to require vacillation and flexible judgment in any number of instances.

STUDENT DATA FROM THE PALMER AND ATKINSON CASE STUDIES

The pre- and postunit data obtained from students in Palmer's and Atkinson's classes suggested several trends, ones consistent with their different emphases. Generally speaking, Palmer's students demonstrated a slightly better grasp of the details, persons, and events of the American Revolution period, mirroring her stress on being able to make evidence-supported claims about the past. Reflecting the importance she placed on using history as a tool for reform, Atkinson's students were quicker to recount those historical episodes discussed in class that involved actions that were perceived as historical "mistakes" that were "corrected" by later decisions (e.g., replacing the Articles of Confederation with the Constitution). Atkinson's students also were more apt to stress the importance of democratic principles in history and in the classroom, a consequence of the democratic ethos that she tried to create. For more details concerning these trends and a complete report of the results, see VanSledright (1995b).

CHAPTER 7

Implications for Curriculum and Instruction

We have reviewed the scholarly literature on teaching history to elementary school students, presented case studies of three fifth-grade teachers who took contrasting approaches to teaching U.S. history, and traced 10 fifth graders' progress across the school year as they studied chronologically organized U.S. history for the first time. In this final chapter we consider the implications of our findings concerning issues related to the learning and teaching of history in elementary school.

Before doing so, we wish to remind readers that the data from our studies came from students who attended primarily middle- and upper-middle-income suburban schools that were located in the Midwest and served predominantly Anglo-American populations. Also, only 6–10 students were interviewed in depth in each study. Therefore, caution should be observed in generalizing from the findings.

On the other hand, it is also worth noting that Lake's students came from a community with socioeconomic status indicators at or only slightly above national averages, and that all of the case studies were done in schools that followed the "de facto national curriculum" in social studies, which featured the expanding communities content sequence that introduces students to chronological historical study in fifth grade. Thus, the students we studied were representative of a great many fifth graders in contemporary U.S. schools. Also, McKeown and Beck's studies of students in the Pittsburgh area, Levstik's studies of students in Kentucky, Barton's studies of students in the Cincinnati area, and VanSledright's studies of students in southern Maryland all have yielded findings that are similar on comparable dimensions to the findings from our studies of students in Michigan.

These findings suggest that fifth graders in schools that use the expanding communities social studies sequence are more similar than different in their prior knowledge of and readiness to study U.S. history. The differences lie primarily in the specifics of the historical content included in their state studies in fourth grade. The students we interviewed had studied Michigan history and thus had learned about Native American tribes that lived in Michigan, the coming of Europeans as represented by French explorers and fur traders traveling on Michigan rivers, and later French and Indian War conflicts that took place in or near Michigan. Students located in other states learn quite different historical content as part of their fourth-grade state studies.

Otherwise, however, it appears that entering fifth graders exposed to a typical K–4 social studies program share a lack of familiarity with history as a discipline or school subject. They have general knowledge about "life in the olden days," and they usually have been exposed to some historical information through lessons on holiday themes or units on Native Americans or the pioneers. However, they have not yet learned much if anything about the history of the nation as a nation. Nor do they know much yet about the nature and extent of historical source material, about the data collection and reasoning processes involved in constructing historical accounts, or about the need to empathize with and appreciate the points of view of historical figures. Thus, most American fifth graders are novice history learners who are unfamiliar with history as a knowledge domain and do not yet possess a coherently organized network of historical knowledge.

FIFTH GRADERS' READINESS FOR HISTORICAL STUDY

Although they are relatively sophisticated learners in many respects, fifth graders' readiness for historical study is limited not only by their prior knowledge but also by their cognitive development. The students' questions and comments in class, their written KWL responses and work on assignments, and especially their oral responses to our interview questions consistently reminded us that they were still primarily concrete thinkers, not yet very skilled at abstract thought.

As children, they lack an experiential knowledge base (beyond their own personal histories) to provide them with raw material to use in constructing historical understandings. Their opportunities to develop knowledge about history through their own personal exploratory learning are limited. Consequently, they are more dependent on cultural transmission when developing ideas about history than they are when developing ideas about mathematics or science. They can learn about the physical world, about plants and animals, and about numbers and quantitative relationships through direct, experiential contact with manipulable aspects of their environments. Most of what they learn about history, however, is communicated to them by parents, teachers, books, audiovisual media, or other socialization sources. Thus, their historical knowledge is composed primarily of ideas that they have heard or imagined rather than ideas that they have developed through direct personal experience (Coltham, 1971; Little, 1989).

Much of the historical information they learn as fifth graders is new to them, and where prior knowledge does exist, it tends to be vague, spotty, and sometimes distorted by naive conceptions or imaginative and inaccurate assumptions. When conceptual change must occur, it is less a matter of changing experience-based misconceptions than a matter of reconstructing historical understandings that have been pieced together from unsystematically acquired bits of information or extrapolated imaginatively from limited direct experience.

In recounting these limitations, we do not mean to suggest that children cannot learn history meaningfully or that the subject should not be taught in elementary school. On the contrary, we believe that our findings justify a position of tempered optimism with regard to fifth graders' readiness to engage in chronological study of history. They support the body of work that has developed in recent years indicating that elementary students are interested in history and capable of constructing meaningful historical understandings even though many of them are not yet very skillful at abstract thought. Elementary students are not adult thinkers, let alone disciplinary specialists, so it is not reasonable to expect them to develop the kinds of historical knowledge and reasoning abilities that the discipline expects of academic historians. However, as Levstik (1986) noted, it is reasonable to expect elementary students to develop historical knowledge of limited validity—knowledge that is incomplete in content and limited in purview but valid as far as it goes (that is, consistent with current disciplinary views). Gardner and Boix-Mansilla (1994) expressed similar views in discussing commonsense knowledge and proto-disciplinary knowledge that precede development of disciplinary knowledge.

Our findings also support arguments that issues related to children's historical thinking are addressed usefully with reference to work on novice versus expert differences in domain-specific knowledge and to the ideas of Bruner, Egan, and others who have contrasted narrative forms of understanding (Levstik & Pappas, 1992). In the students we studied, most historical knowledge was represented in the form of story-like narratives that featured a setting, a plot focused on the motives and goals of one or more focal individuals or groups, and a resolution that carried implications for the futures of these people and others included in the story. The stories featured themes such as monarchs competing for power and glory through land claims and territorial wars, colonists uniting to proclaim and fight for their freedom from British rule, and pioneers struggling against adversity to establish new communities.

Less sophisticated versions often were vague or inaccurate about the temporal and geographical specifics of the settings, and many of them featured overtly narrative renderings of stories personalized around hero figures. More sophisticated versions were more specific and accurate about time and place, were formulated more as cause-and-effect explanations than as conventional stories, and described larger historical trends involving sizable populations or geographical areas rather than only recounting what happened to a particular individual or small group during the course of a particular event. However, even the most sophisticated versions still tended to be primarily narrative descriptions (with explanations) of historical events and trends, delivered primarily as factual information. There were few comments on the nature and quality of the evidence, characterizations of the points of view of various stakeholder groups, references to alternative interpretations, or other indications of the kinds of historical reasoning brought to bear by disciplinary specialists.

The fifth graders we studied were able to overcome tendencies toward presentism and other biases in order to identify and empathize with some of the people they studied, especially if these people were portrayed as heroic figures or as victims of oppression (see Levstik, 1986, on children's interest in reading stories about human suffering). This was especially the case with slaves and with Native Americans, although in the latter case, the focus of identification shifted to the (white) pioneers as the school year progressed. To the extent that the students were encouraged and helped to do so, they also showed an ability to see both sides of an issue, such as the contrast between King George's views and the American rebels' views of the events that led to the American Revolution. However, these fifth graders did not display advanced forms of historical empathy reflecting deep and contextualized knowledge of the people they studied. They did not, for example, evaluate historical figures' goals or strategies by taking into account the information available to those individuals at the time in question, or point to the individuals' prior philosophies or experiences that might have predisposed them toward particular views or courses of action.

Given the limited experience elementary students have with these forms of advanced historical reasoning (and in some cases, lack of developmental readiness), and especially given their lack of a rich base of prior knowledge to inform their efforts at such reasoning, we view it as unrealistic to argue that the elementary history curriculum should be developed primarily as socialization of students into history as an academic discipline. Elementary students can and should acquire basic understandings about history as an interpretive discipline, about the kinds of historical evidence that are available and the processes that historians use to construct accounts based on this evidence, and about how contrasting agendas lead historians (and other stakeholders in historical accounts) to emphasize different aspects of history and adopt different points of view about the aspects they address in common. However, we believe that these and other aspects of history as a discipline should be developed within an overall emphasis on introducing history primarily as citizen education rather than primarily as disciplinary socialization.

Limitations in most elementary students' levels of cognitive development and prior historical knowledge also lead us to question the feasibility of using issues analysis as the primary basis for organizing the elementary history curriculum. The kinds of critical thinking and decision making emphasized in issues-analysis approaches are vital to citizen education in general and social studies in particular. However, issues analysis is most useful when it is informed by richly detailed and well-connected networks of prior knowledge. With respect to history, elementary students are just beginning to develop such knowledge networks. In these circumstances, a chronological survey of major trends and events makes more sense than a list of issues as the basis for organizing the historical content taught in elementary school. However, each unit should include an issues-analysis dimension, in which students are engaged in critical thinking and decision making about issues related to the historical content they are studying. With the support of age-appropriate teaching of key understandings and elucidation of issues, elementary students can appreciate and debate many of the ethical and civic policy issues raised by major historical events.

HELPING STUDENTS WITH THE TIMELINE

Elementary students can understand general chronological sequences (e.g., that land transportation developed from walking to horse-drawn carriages to engine-powered vehicles), even though they may have difficulty mapping these advances onto timelines or keeping track of particular dates. The latter problems need not be significant impediments to good historical teaching and learning, because the most powerful historical knowledge is focused around chronological sequences rather than precise dates, and especially around the cause-and-effect relationships that explain the trends that developed (Levstik & Barton, 1996). Even so, we see some value in helping students to locate historical events in time and space and to keep track of advances on timelines and maps as their historical studies progress.

In one sense, we mean this literally. At the beginnings or ends of units, and in some cases at key points within units, teachers might lead their students through reviews of when and where the events being studied took place and where they fit within important macro-level trends that were in progress at the time. For this purpose, it helps to develop collections of timelines and maps that vary in scope (e.g., a macro-level timeline showing key events in the eighteenth century as well as a micro-level timeline showing key developments between 1750 and 1776). In the case of maps, the collection should vary not only in scope (e.g., world, North America, Atlantic seaboard) but also in levels of detail that reflect historical developments (e.g., maps of the United States at various dates, showing which states had become part of the nation at the time). Periodic reference to such timelines and maps helps students to keep track of the big picture and develop a larger historical context as they study more specific historical events (Patriarca & Alleman, 1987; Willig, 1990).

Even more important than helping students to be able to place what they are studying on timelines and maps is helping them to keep track of advances in technological developments and the general "state of the world." Many of the most persistently inaccurate assumptions or misconceptions expressed by the students we interviewed concerned the temporal and spatial relationships among the people and events being studied. The students clearly needed help in seeing how the historical content they were studying fit within the broader sweep of human history.

We do not mean to suggest that historical study must start with the beginnings of recorded history and proceed forward in strict chronological order. However, we do believe that the study of U.S. history (which typically begins in the fifteenth century except for brief reference to Native Americans crossing the land bridge thousands of years earlier and Vikings visiting the continent somewhere around 1,000 A.D.) needs to be contextualized with reference to timelines, landmark events and inventions, and social and political developments. An adequate context for supporting the traditional (primarily Eurocentric) introduction to U.S. history would include introduction to

1. several broad themes in sociopolitical developments through time (progression from nomadic hunting and gathering societies, to stable but small farming communities, to the rise of towns as centers of commerce and culture, to city-states and federations, to larger nations, and progression in European perceptions from a world centered around the Mediterranean, to a world centered around the Middle East, to a world centered around the Atlantic Ocean);
2. life in Europe during the fifteenth and sixteenth centuries (modern in many respects but without engine-powered transportation, electronic communications, etc.); and
3. the leading European nations' economic agendas and rivalries (shipbuilding and navigation advances that increased the scope and importance of trade with other nations, search for better routes to the Far East, and the establishment of colonies).

An adequate context for supporting a less traditional (multicultural) introduction also would include information about pre- and post-Columbian life among Native American tribes who experienced early encounters with European explorers and colonists, as well as life in Africa and in America among people who became enslaved. At least in some areas, the context also might include description of native life in Mexico and the southwest, before and after colonization by the Spanish. To encourage their students to invest themselves in historical studies, teachers will need to tailor their curricula so that the students understand themselves to be studying "our" history, not "their" history (Alton-Lee, Nuthall, & Patrick, 1993; Holt, 1990; Seixas, 1993a).

Establishing a context would provide students with a much better sense of who the different people were that they were studying, what agendas they were pursuing, and what resources they had available to them. A few lessons devoted to this purpose would go a long way toward helping students to remain aware of relevant timelines (and what they represent about conditions of everyday life and about world political and economic developments) as they study U.S. history. They also would lay a foundation for later studies of "Encounter" phenomena at the state and local levels.

WHEN TO STUDY STATE HISTORY

Like McKeown and Beck (1990), we found that timeline confusion and other difficulties experienced by many students as they began to study U.S. history in fifth grade were exacerbated by conflations with information remembered from their studies of state history in fourth grade. These findings raise questions about the wisdom of teaching state history prior to U.S. history. It appears that students would experience less confusion if they studied U.S. history first (contextualized along the lines described above). This would seem to be likely even for students living in the eastern seaboard states, clearly true for those living in states in the middle of the country that were established later, and especially true for those living in the southwestern states whose early histories featured Spanish rather than English colonization.

If U.S. history were taught first, what would happen to state history? Some might argue for its elimination, noting that state history appears to be less important than it once was as citizen preparation, for three reasons. First, the influence of the federal government increasingly has overshadowed that of the states, to the point that, in most states at least, national affairs receive much more media coverage and policy debate than state affairs. Second, even though it is much larger, the nation is a more comprehensible entity to children than states are, and students usually show earlier and more accurate knowledge of the nation than of the state or region. Third, the marked residential mobility of the American population means that many students will move from one state to another, often several times. This again raises questions about the value of systematically teaching state history to elementary students.

As a practical matter, we do not advocate elimination of state history (many state legislatures insist on it). However, we suggest that it might better be taught in fifth grade than in fourth grade. Depending on the state, this could be accomplished either by incorporating state history content within the more general U.S. history content as it unfolded (for the original 13 states) or by teaching a separate state history unit following the U.S. history content (for the other states). These changes would require adjusting the traditional expanding communities framework, although only in minor ways. Although it is not essential, this framework makes reasonable sense for organizing the sociological, cultural, economic, and geographic strands of elementary social studies. However, the historical strand may be taught more effectively by beginning with larger entities to provide a context and only then moving to state and local aspects.

This approach would still leave room for a great deal of emphasis on the state in teaching regional geography (and related social and cultural content) in fourth grade. Brief references to historical developments might be included (e.g., noting that fur trading was important in Michigan's early economic history, and that logging, farming and orchards, and the auto industry became important later). However, systematic chronological treatment of state history would be saved for fifth grade. This would minimize development of the conflations of national and state history that were observed so frequently in our interviewees.

A second alternative would be to teach chronological American history in both grades 4 and 5, roughly dividing the timeline between the two grades. State history and geography could be embedded within this chronological treatment and taught in an integrated fashion. Some history units would be taught in the historical survey when it made chronological sense to include them (e.g., during the colonial period for eastern seaboard states, the antebellum period for many midwestern states, etc.).

More generally, we suggest that units dealing with people or events from the past that are taught prior to fifth grade might be taught with emphasis on their anthropological or citizen education aspects, without much emphasis on historical chronology. That is, units on Native American tribes or on pioneers can emphasize their daily lives and activities, units on holidays can emphasize our reasons for celebrating, and units on famous Americans can emphasize their accomplishments and values as role models, but without attempting to place these topics within a chronology of history. Again, this would minimize students' conflations and misconceptions as they began systematic study of history in fifth grade.

CLEAR GOALS AS THE BASIS FOR DEVELOPING POWERFUL CURRICULUM AND INSTRUCTION

We have argued that a chronologically organized survey of major trends and events, taught primarily as citizen education but with secondary emphasis on disciplinary socialization and issues analysis, appears most suitable as a way to introduce elementary students to systematic historical study. We hasten to add, however, that we do not mean this as an endorsement of the objectivist tradition in selecting and representing content or the emphasis on breadth over depth that produces parades of ill-organized and soon-forgotten facts. Instead, we would emphasize the principles involved in teaching school subjects for understanding, appreciation, and application to life outside of school, especially the notion of structuring the content around key ideas developed in depth (Brophy, 1990b; Good & Brophy, 1995, 1997; Newmann, 1988; VanSledright, 1995b).

The process of developing powerful curriculum and instruction begins with identification of clear purposes and goals for the history component of the social studies program. In turn, the process of identifying what key ideas to develop proceeds most smoothly when the historical content (and indeed the curriculum as a whole) is viewed as a means to be used to accomplish the ends represented by the purposes and goals of instruction. We would emphasize the goals of socializing children into American democratic traditions and preparing them to be citizens. There are many ways to do this, however, including the approaches described in Chapters 3, 5, and 6.

As a rule, goal-oriented approaches that structure content around key ideas selected for development in depth because they foster progress toward major instructional goals will be superior to parade-of-facts treatments developed primarily in response to content coverage lists. This assumes, however, that the goals are feasible given the characteristics of the students and the time available for instruction in the subject. Unfortunately, the Bradley Commission and the groups involved in writing the national curriculum standards for history, besides being focused somewhat narrowly on disciplinary history rather than more broadly on citizen education, were overly optimistic in their assumptions about what elementary students will be interested in and able to learn meaningfully, as well as about how much curricular "air time" would be available for history teaching. Furthermore, the same has been true of the groups that developed standards in civics, economics, and geography.

The curriculum standards developed by the National Council for the Social Studies (1994) call for interdisciplinary citizen education and are more realistic for elementary school, although still formidable in their implied expectations for student learning. Wholesale adoption of these national curriculum standards and guidelines appears difficult at the least, so curriculum developers and teachers will need to engage in thoughtful adaptation of these guidelines in planning history instruction for elementary students.

Teachers frequently identify multiple purposes and goals for teaching history. Teachers interviewed by Patrick (1990), for example, expressed the following views: Students should enjoy studying history; the subject is valuable as the study of humanity, to teach about people's lives and motivation, and to develop the ability to empathize with others; such learning should make students more tolerant and understanding of fellow human beings from different cultural backgrounds; history should act as an introduction or background to world affairs or current political events; more generally, the past acts as a context for understanding the present and thus helps to increase students' awareness, self-confidence, understanding, and vicarious experience; and history can be used to teach critical thinking and decision-making skills. However, further probing revealed that many teachers did not translate these general aims and purposes into specific objectives for their individual lessons and activities. Consequently, their day-to-day teaching usually amounted only to content coverage for its own sake, without evident planning or movement toward goals supportive of larger purposes.

In comparison to one another, thoughtfully developed goal-oriented approaches typically offer trade-offs rather than clear-cut superior or inferior choices. Consequently, rather than argue for one particular set of goal priorities for elementary history, we would encourage curriculum developers and teachers to engage in the very kinds of value-based critical thinking and decision making that should be emphasized throughout the social studies curriculum. That is, we suggest that they inform themselves by studying the standards documents and curriculum guidelines issued by national organizations, states, and school districts; inspecting available curriculum materials (not just textbook series but also specialized educational materials and tradebooks, videos, CD-ROMs, and other potential sources); consider their own values and philosophies concerning the purposes and goals of education; and then establish goal priorities to guide their selection of historical content and learning activities. As Rogers (1987) noted, decisions about what history to study are not fundamentally questions about history at all; they are questions about what *things* are important, and therefore about which "histories" are most important to study.

For example, Brophy and Alleman (1993, 1996) described an American Revolution unit intended to develop fifth graders' understanding and appreciation of the origins of U.S. political values and contrasted it with a unit on this same period that might be taught in a military history course in one of the service academies. Given its goals, the fifth-grade treatment would emphasize the historical events and political philosophies that shaped the thinking of the writers of the Declaration of Independence and the Constitution. Content coverage, questions, and activities would focus on the issues that developed between England and the colonies and on the ideals, principles, and compromises that went into the construction of the Constitution (especially the Bill of Rights). Thus, students would learn about "no taxation without representation," but also about the colonists' experiences that led them to want to limit governmental powers, protect against unwarranted search and seizure, guarantee free speech, and separate church and state.

Assignments calling for research, critical thinking, or decision making would focus on topics such as the various forms of oppression that different colonial groups experienced (and how this influenced their thinking about government), as well as the ideas of Jefferson and other key framers of the Constitution. Thus, there might be critical discussion or research on the methods that the framers developed to limit governmental powers and protect minority rights, the grievances that King George and the American rebels had against each other, the merits of the Boston Tea Party as a revolutionary act, or how things might have developed differently if the Revolution had never occurred or had been suppressed by the British.

There would be little emphasis on Paul Revere or other revolutionary figures who are not known primarily for their contributions to U.S. political values, and little on the details of each of the individual Intolerable Acts. There would be no emphasis at all on the details of particular battles, and no activities such as time-consuming construction of dioramas depicting those battles. In contrast, a military history course in a service academy would concentrate heavily on the military aspects of the Revolution, analyzing overall strategy and the factors that influenced the outcomes of noteworthy battles.

HISTORY AS MEANINGFUL AND USABLE KNOWLEDGE

Goal-oriented development of history curriculum and instruction will go a long way toward helping students to appreciate the value of history as a subject of study. To further encourage such appreciation, we recommend stressing two advantages to historical study that never occurred to most of the students we interviewed. First, although it also has social science aspects, history is one of the humanities and thus is worthy of study as such: It can enhance one's quality of life. Learning about and reflecting on history can enhance one's sense of identity by helping to "place" oneself within the broad sweep of the human condition. Such experiences can be powerful for individuals of all ages, but especially for children, who still have strong potential for experiencing awe and wonder at aspects of the human condition that they become aware of for the first time. Children also can learn to appreciate the history that is all around them and to enjoy reading about history and visiting historical sites.

Second, we would stress history's value as citizen education. Although the "lessons of history" notion can be overdone, it remains true that a good working knowledge of history includes information about individual and national decision-making situations that repeat themselves periodically because they are part of the human condition. Equipped with knowledge about the possible trade-offs involved in various courses of action (based in part on knowledge about the past outcomes of these courses of action), students will become better prepared to make good personal, social, and civic decisions.

Personalizing the Content

Theory and research on teaching history for understanding suggests several additional principles for helping elementary students learn it as meaningful and usable knowledge. One widely recommended set of principles calls for focusing on the study of particular individuals and groups of people (rather than on impersonal abstractions), studying these people with emphasis on developing understanding of their contexts and empathy for their points of view, and emphasizing general trends in the evolution of social systems rather than particular dates or detailed chronologies (Barton & Levstik, 1996; Knight, 1993; Levstik & Barton, 1996; Low-Beer & Blyth, 1983; Willig, 1990). Children in the primary grades are interested in and can understand accounts of life in the past that are focused on particular individuals or groups (cave dwellers, Native American tribes, the Pilgrims, people living on a plantation or on the frontier in the eighteenth century). Fifth graders are interested in and can understand an introduction to chronological study of U.S. history. However, this content needs to be represented to elementary students in the form of narratives that depict people with whom they can identify, pursuing goals that they can understand.

For example, primary grade children can understand that the "Pilgrims" were persecuted for their religious beliefs and left England because they wanted to be free to practice their religion as they saw fit, but they would struggle to follow an abstract analysis of the theological differences between the "Separatists" and the Church of England. Similarly, fifth graders can understand a discussion of trade routes in colonial times that includes the notion that the colonists sold raw materials to England and purchased finished products manufactured in England, but many of them would have difficulty following an abstract discussion of the rise of mercantilism as an economic theory.

Using Varied Data Sources

There is broad agreement on the value of exposing students to varied data sources and providing them with opportunities to conduct historical inquiry, to synthesize and communicate their findings, and to learn from listening to or reading biography and historical fiction selections as well as conventional textbooks (Downey & Levstik, 1988; Harms & Lettow, 1994; Lamme, 1994; Low-Beer & Blyth, 1983; Sunal & Haas, 1993). It is important, however, for teachers to screen these varied data sources and guide students in their use.

Fictional sources need to be historically accurate and free from bias and stereotyping (unless they are going to be used explicitly as examples of fictionalized or biased portrayals). Elementary students lack a rich base of prior knowledge to inform their efforts at critical thinking and decision making, so they have difficulty knowing what to believe or how to assess conflicting accounts. They will need to learn that textbooks, and even eyewitness accounts and diaries, tend to emphasize aspects of events that support their authors' biases and interests (VanSledright & Kelly, 1995). In studying the American Revolution, for example, one might expose them to information sources that will help them to realize that King George had a quite different view from that of the American rebels concerning how the events leading up to the Revolution should be interpreted, and thus whether the Revolution was justified. Similarly, the students might come to see that the Boston Massacre would be viewed (and described later) quite differently by a British soldier seeking to avoid a confrontation than by an American rebel seeking to provoke one.

History-based fiction helps to "make history come alive" for elementary students. Comparisons of children's historical tradebooks with social studies textbooks indicate that the tradebooks have a great deal to offer as substitute or supplementary sources of curricular content. However, teachers need to exercise care in selecting historically based tradebooks because so many of them offer romanticized rather than realistic portrayals of historical figures and events, feature chauvinistic or otherwise biased interpretations, or reflect other problems in content selection or representation that undermine their value as historical content sources.

Teachers will need to help their students keep fictional sources in perspective, so that they do not confuse the real with the fictional (like the student who named Johnny Tremain as a leader of the American Revolution) or overgeneralize from the specific (like the students who developed the notion that life for all children in all of the colonies was like Sarah Morton's life among the Puritans). These examples illustrate how the motivational and insight benefits that might be derived from using fictional sources must be balanced against their potential for inducing distorted learnings. Some distortions are probably inevitable, and most will be cleared up without great difficulty. Still, teachers should minimize such problems by screening historical fiction sources for authenticity and by helping their students to understand the differences between fictional and historical representations (Levstik, 1989; VanSledright, 1994; VanSledright & Kelly, 1995).

Fostering Historical Empathy

Virtually all sources of advice on teaching history emphasize the importance of fostering empathy or perspective taking with the people being studied, although Knight (1989a) and Little (1989) cautioned that empathy needs to be discussed with emphasis on the understandings and skills that children need to develop, rather than on its affective aspects (lest it be confused with sympathy). Children are especially prone to presentism, often believing that people in the past were not as smart as we are today because they didn't have all of the social and technical inventions that ease our contemporary lives. Teachers can foster their development of empathy by helping them to appreciate such things as bow-and-arrow hunting, horse-drawn carriages, or butter churns as ingenious inventions that represented significant advances for their times, not just as tools from the past that seem primitive when compared with today's technology.

Teachers also can help their students avoid presentism and the often negative judgments it produces by asking them to imagine themselves in the place of historical persons they encounter in studying history. Accomplishing this would require the use of multiple sources of information taken from interesting historical accounts and good historical literature, then putting these accounts within the larger historical context. However, care must be taken, particularly with young students, to avoid over-romanticizing the lives of the people in question. Providing different perspectives placed within the context of the historical era under study can help students understand that, in making judgments about the past, we have the benefit of hindsight and a comparative framework unavailable to our ancestors, who could not foretell the future. One might draw the analogy for students about future generations looking back at us and wondering about our presumably "archaic ways." Presentism needs to be tempered by these realizations, which are within the reach of fifth graders.

POWERFUL CURRICULUM AND INSTRUCTION

We have suggested several guidelines for teaching history effectively to elementary students. Of the many other suggestions that might be offered, most are implied in a position statement issued by the National Council for the Social Studies (1993) concerning powerful teaching and learning. This statement argues that social studies teaching and learning is most powerful when it is meaningful, integrative, value-based, challenging, and active.

• *Meaningful:* The content selected for emphasis is worth learning because it promotes progress toward important social understanding and civic efficacy goals, and it is taught in ways that help students to see how it is related to these goals. As a result, students' learning efforts are motivated by appreciation and interest, not just accountability and grading systems. Instruction emphasizes depth of development of important ideas within appropriate breadth of content coverage.

• *Integrative:* The curriculum cuts across disciplinary boundaries, spans time and space, and integrates knowledge, beliefs, values, and dispositions to action. It also provides opportunities for students to connect to the arts and sciences through inquiry and reflection.

• *Value-based:* Powerful teaching considers the ethical dimensions of topics, so that it provides an arena for reflective development of concern for the common good and application of social values. The teacher includes diverse points of view, demonstrates respect for well-supported positions, and shows sensitivity and commitment to social responsibility and action.

• *Challenging:* Students are encouraged to function as a learning community, using reflective discussion to work collaboratively to deepen understandings of the meanings and implications of content. They also are expected to come to grips with controversial issues, to participate assertively but respectfully in group discussions, and to work productively with peers in cooperative learning activities.

• *Active:* Powerful social studies is rewarding but demanding. It demands thoughtful preparation and instruction by the teacher and sustained effort by the students to make sense of and apply what they are learning. Teachers do not mechanically follow rigid guidelines in planning, implementing, and assessing instruction. Instead, they work with the national standards and with state and local guidelines, adapting and supplementing these guidelines with their own ideas and instructional materials in ways that support their students' social education needs.

Powerful teaching makes use of a variety of instructional materials, employs field trips and visits by resource people, develops current or local examples to relate to students' lives, provides for reflective discussions, and scaffolds students' work in ways that encourage them to gradually take on more responsibility for managing their own learning independently and with their peers. Assessment systems are made compatible with these goals and methods.

Surveys and case studies of good teaching practice in history and social studies reflect the attributes featured in the National Council for the Social Studies (1993) position statement. In elementary history, these suggestions feature content representations that "put students at the scene" of historical developments and learning activities that engage them in active inquiry, critical thinking, and decision making. For example, assigning students to interview family members and develop a family and personal history (illustrated with a timeline and artifacts) appears to be an effective way to introduce both history as a field of study and some of the processes involved in collecting and synthesizing historical data. A bonus to this assignment (and others that involve interviewing family members) is that it enhances familial bonds and involves family members in the school's curriculum in enjoyable and supportive ways.

Role-taking questions or activities are useful for encouraging students to empathize with the people they are studying and to develop their abilities to appreciate multiple points of view. For example, Brophy and Alleman (1996) suggested that some of the following activities might be included in a unit on the American Revolution:

1. Have students role play journalists or pamphleteers writing about the Boston Massacre or the Boston Tea Party. Have some individuals or groups pretend to be Sam Adams or another colonist seeking to foment rebellion, others to be a newspaper reporter seeking to write a neutral or balanced account, and still others to be a Tory dismayed by unjustified defiance of legitimate authority.

2. Have the class simulate a town meeting (or a Continental Congress meeting) called to decide whether, and if so how, the group should support the people of Boston in resisting the Intolerable Acts.

3. Simulate a debate or trial concerning whether or not the American Revolution was justified. Include arguments or testimony by King George and other defenders of the view that British actions prior to the Revolution were not only consistent with established laws and customs but reasonable and respectful of the colonists' concerns, as well

as arguments or testimony by Tom Paine and other defenders of the view that the colonists were justified in breaking away from England to form an independent nation.

4. Have small groups of students simulate family discussions of whether the father or one of the sons should join the Continental Army. Assign different geographical locations and life circumstances to different groups (e.g., the families of a Boston shop owner, a Massachusetts farmer, a farmer in rural Pennsylvania, a plantation owner in Georgia, and a former slave now living in New York City).

5. Have students pretend to be citizens of Boston beginning to get caught up in the events preceding the Revolution, discussing among family members or writing to friends elsewhere about their experiences and how they might respond to them (a family forced to quarter British troops, a family whose son threw a rock at British troops and barely escaped when they gave chase, a Tory family trying to decide what they will do if conflict with England continues to escalate, or formerly close friends who find that disagreement over political issues is ruining their friendship).

An advantage to role-taking activities is that they involve collaborative learning among pairs or small groups of students. Other forms of collaborative learning (such as assigning pairs or groups to research a historical person or event, synthesize their findings, and then make a report to the class) also are desirable because they engage students in active construction of historical understandings.

As opportunities arise, it also is desirable to make connections between past events currently under study and present events that embody parallel features or issues. Developing these connections helps students to appreciate the relevance and potential applicability of historical learning, particularly for developing perspectives on and making predictions or decisions about significant current events. However, in doing so, it is important to avoid encouraging presentism in students' interpretations of the past.

ENCOURAGING AND ASSESSING CONCEPTUAL CHANGE

As illustrated in our case studies, there is potential for applying principles of conceptual change teaching in history as well as in mathematics and science. Teachers who are aware of their students' inaccurate assumptions and naive conceptions can minimize their frequency and persistence, as Mary Lake showed in her treatment of slavery during the second year in which we interviewed her students. Commonly observed naive conceptions can be prevented or cleared up for most students by incorporating reference to them in the process of providing clear and accurate information when introducing the content. Where this has been insufficient, or where students have developed unanticipated misconceptions, these can be addressed during subsequent content development and application activities.

To become aware of these naive conceptions, teachers will need to employ learning activities and assessment devices that encourage students to express their understandings at length and in their own language. Pretests or less formal KWL-like exercises are useful for eliciting students' prior knowledge and thinking whenever new units or topics are introduced. Thereafter, teachers can keep abreast of developments in their students' understandings by emphasizing open-ended questions that call for explanations or other extended statements rather than recitation of brief words or phrases. They also can emphasize activities, assignments, and assessment instruments that call for students to reflect upon, synthesize, and communicate connected understandings of what they are learning.

Attempts to assess changes in students' historical knowledge and thinking will be complicated by the tendencies of some students to engage in fanciful constructions and elaborations. For example, what constitutes accurate assessment of entry-level knowledge? Should one "credit" accurate elements when they are embedded in a larger narrative that includes imaginary elaborations or conflated details? How can one assess what was learned as a consequence of teaching in the current course as distinct from bits and pieces gleaned from instruction in earlier grades or, for that matter, from watching the "Chipmunks" show? Should one even try? These are difficult questions that defy simple answers.

Similarly thorny questions arise with respect to pedagogical practices. Social educators often recommend socratic questioning and inductive concept development strategies. However, these instructional approaches appear to be contraindicated for introducing chronological study of history to children who lack a background context and are prone to generate imaginative narratives. With some students, it may be necessary to emphasize that questions or activities meant to function as knowledge assessment instruments call for summaries of what one has learned as historical information, not for generation of fictional stories or fanciful elaborations.

USING SUPPLEMENTARY RESOURCES

Curriculum developers and teachers interested in following the recommendations outlined here do not need to start from scratch. Along with textbook series, a great many fictional and nonfictional trade-books, activities packets, computer programs and CD-ROMs, and other ancillary materials suitable for use in teaching history to elementary students have been developed, and more are appearing each year. As examples of the opportunities for curriculum enrichment that these materials provide, we offer brief profiles of three of the more useful sets of materials that we have encountered. These include a handbook for developing one's own family history, a series of guidebooks for teachers, and an activities supplement.

A Family History Handbook

A Family History Handbook (Rife, 1985) is a 113-page textbook/workbook that provides students with information about families and family histories and guides them in developing their own family histories. It comes with a teacher's manual and a large family history pedigree chart covering seven generations.

The text begins by describing different types of families and terms used to discuss family relationships, then engages students in recording information about themselves and their families. Next comes a series of lessons, examples, and exercises relating to different sources of information that may be mined by students in developing family histories: Bibles and other family records, church records, diaries and journals, cemeteries, census records, photographs, immigration records, interviewing of relatives, wills, family coats of arms, vital statistics records, newspapers, and military service records. In addition to focusing directly on the nature of these sources of information and ways that students might tap them to develop their own family histories, these sections teach more general concepts and information about each of the topics addressed and seek to develop students' skill in understanding and interpreting the information found in these sources. Thus, questions and exercises call students' attention to some of the details of photographs from earlier times; question them about the information embedded in sections of a diary written in 1870; and invite them to interview relatives, to interpret and write wills, and to take a mini-census in their own neighborhoods using a simplified census form.

The material appears to have been written with junior high students in mind, but most of it would be understandable to and usable by fifth graders. Few teachers would want to invest the time needed to work through the entire program, but teachers interested in having their students develop their own family histories as part of a history course will find useful information and handouts here. The materials include a variety of reproducible documents: a funeral program, a diary, a will, an obituary, military service records, pension records, and sample birth, death, and marriage certificates and census forms.

Guidebooks for Teaching U.S. History

U.S. History: Book One. Beginnings to 1865 (McBee, Tate, & Wagner, 1985) is a 225-page guidebook designed to help teachers teach the "conceptual history" of the United States. It is one of four guidebooks designed for that purpose, intended to be used in conjunction with whatever textbook the teacher is using. Much of the material is too advanced for elementary students, but adaptations of some of the key concepts and themes could help provide a conceptual base to fifth-grade U.S. history courses.

The guidebook is predicated on some interesting assumptions and contains some important goals and objectives. Key assumptions are that our history reveals cooperation, coexistence, and occasional conflict among three visions of America: a nation founded on belief in the rights of the individual; a pluralistic society in which various groups coexist; and a nation that reveals a sense of homeland, patriotism, or being American. Students are to learn about these themes as well as come to understand that we are products of the past, live in the present, and shape the future. History is portrayed as an evolutionary process composed of recurring themes, so the curriculum emphasizes examining why and how changes occur and how these themes have shaped the current world.

Creative Activities for Teaching U.S. History

Creative Activities for Teaching U.S. History (1988) is a series of packets of reproducible blackline masters containing problem-solving and critical thinking activities for use in U.S. history courses. For example, the "westward movement" packet contains 20 puzzles, games, and activities focusing on life and times in the American west during the nineteenth century.

Some of these activities focus on relatively minor details (constructing a covered wagon from a milk carton; guessing the names and functions of personal, household, and horse/wagon items illustrated through drawings; interpreting cattle brands; and guessing the meanings of colorful but obsolete terms used by cowboys and miners in the old west. Other activities, however, allow for more substantive critical thinking or decision making. For example, one activity calls for students to make a series of seven decisions that had to be made by the Donner Party (a snowbound group whose survivors eventually resorted to cannibalism). After students discuss and make each decision, they find out what decision the Donner Party made, and with what results.

Other activities provide students with basic information about key issues or events in the development of the west and call for them to take the roles of the original decision makers (as the state governor, to decide whether to call out the militia to put down vigilantes; as a Mexican miner, to decide how to respond to newly passed laws designed to drive Mexicans out of California; as a citizen of Owens Valley, to choose among strategies for trying to stop construction of the aqueduct that would divert water to Los Angeles). There is also an interesting decision-making exercise involving a railroad developer who must decide whether to go along with potential investors who will invest only if they are promised kickbacks and other forms of special treatment. Finally, there is a simulation exercise calling for a team representing the U.S. government to negotiate with a team representing the Nez Perce tribe concerning land claims and ways of life.

Elementary teachers might use several of these decision-making activities in "westward movement" units, as well as comparable activities from other packets dealing with other historical periods. The activities will be most effective, however, if they are structured and scaffolded optimally by the teacher and followed up by appropriate post-activity debriefing discussions (Brophy & Alleman, 1996). Unfortunately, the materials provide no guidance to teachers about these aspects of implementing the activities in the classroom.

CONCLUSION

In this chapter, we have made a number of recommendations based on our research with three fifth-grade teachers and their students and on the research literature on teaching and learning history in elementary school. We believe that our research syntheses and especially our detailed accounts of teachers and students provide valuable insights into the process of teaching and learning history. We hope that prospective and practicing elementary teachers have found themselves and aspects of their efforts within these portraits and accounts.

However, our primary purpose for writing this book has been to foster reflectiveness about teaching and learning history in the elementary grades. The research suggests repeatedly that unreflective practice produces history instruction that features parades of facts, perfunctory content representation, and bored and disdainful students. If this result becomes established in fifth grade, students are likely to approach subsequent history courses that they take in eighth grade and in high school with a level of disregard that is difficult to change. We advocate that teachers approach the subject of history by asking themselves penetrating questions such as: Can I teach everything from A to Z? If not, then what are the big ideas I want to get across to my students? How can the study of history pique my students' curiosity? How can I encourage them to ask important questions about what happened in the past? What do they already know? What conceptions do they hold that might be inaccurate? How can I help them to understand the past and get inside the experience of others? How can I help them to understand that history is an interpretive construction based on evidence and that they also can construct history, say, by interpreting their own lives from collected evidence? How can I help my students to see that learning history is essential to their growth as democratic citizens? What can I read that will help me address these questions and provoke still others?

We recognize that we offer not only recommendations but questions as well, and that teachers undoubtedly will have many of their own, if they stop to ask such questions. These need to be assessed and reassessed regularly, with attention to the trade-offs that apply when they are addressed in different ways. The trade-offs stem from disagreements about best practice in teaching history (e.g., arguments about national history standards, conflicting ideas about what and how to teach, concerns about what students at various grade levels are capable of learning). These debates are unlikely to be resolved any time soon, but they make teaching history a lively, active, and potentially exciting endeavor. Teachers will have to make their way through the process as reflectively as they can. This is why asking questions, reading research, and thinking about purposes, goals, and strategies are so important. The research described in this book provides one framework for doing that. We hope that readers have found it useful and have been motivated to go on to explore other sources as well.

References

Alton-Lee, A., Nuthall, G., & Patrick, J. (1993). Reframing classroom research: A lesson from the private world of children. *Harvard Educational Review, 63*, 50–84.

Andres, P. N. (1981). Social studies orientations and educational attitudes of secondary classroom teachers in the state of Indiana. *Dissertation Abstracts International, 42*, 5082A.

Armento, B. (1986). Research on teaching social studies. In M. C. Wittrock (Ed.), *Handbook of research on teaching* (3rd ed., pp. 942–951). New York: Macmillan.

Ashby, R., & Lee, P. J. (1987). Discussing the evidence. *Teaching History, 48*, 13–17.

Banks, J. A. (1991). Social science knowledge and citizenship education. In M. Kennedy (Ed.), *Teaching academic subjects to diverse learners* (pp. 117–128). New York: Teachers College Press.

Barr, R., Barth, J., & Shermis, S. (1977). *Defining the social studies.* Washington, DC: National Council for the Social Studies.

Barton, K. (1992, November). *"It seems a lot like a story": Narrative presentation of the American Revolution.* Paper presented to the College and University Faculty Assembly of the National Council for the Social Studies, Detroit.

Barton, K. (1993, November). *History is more than a story: Expanding the boundaries of elementary learning.* Paper presented to the College and University Faculty Assembly of the National Council for the Social Studies, Nashville.

Barton, K. (1994). *Historical understanding in elementary children.* Unpublished doctoral dissertation, University of Kentucky, Lexington.

Barton, K., & Levstik, L. (1996). "Back when God was around and everything": Elementary children's understanding of historical time. *American Educational Research Journal, 33*, 419–454.

Beck, I., & McKeown, M. (1994). Outcomes of history instruction: Paste-up accounts. In M. Carretero & J. Voss (Eds.), *Cognitive and instructional processes in history and the social sciences* (pp. 237–256). Hillsdale, NJ: Erlbaum.

Beck, I., McKeown, M., & Gromoll, E. (1989). Learning from social studies texts. *Cognition and Instruction, 6*, 99–158.

273

Biggs, J. B., & Collis, K. (1982). *Evaluating the quality of learning: The SOLO taxonomy.* New York: Academic Press.

Bloch, M. N. (1986). Social education of young children. In C. Cornbleth (Ed.), *An invitation to research in social education* (Bulletin 77). Washington, DC: National Council for the Social Studies.

Booth, M. (1979). *A longitudinal study of cognitive skills, concepts, and attitudes of adolescents studying a modern world history syllabus and an analysis of their adductive historical thinking.* Unpublished doctoral dissertation, University of Reading.

Booth, M. (1993). Students' historical thinking and the National History Curriculum in England. *Theory and Research in Social Education, 21,* 105–127.

Bragaw, D., & Hartoonian, M. (1988). Social studies: The study of people in society. In R. Brandt (Ed.), *Content of the curriculum* (pp. 9–30). Alexandria, VA: Association for Supervision and Curriculum Development.

Brophy, J. (1990a). *Mary Lake: A case study of a fifth-grade social studies (American history) teacher* (Elementary Subjects Center Series No. 26). East Lansing: Michigan State University, Institute for Research on Teaching, Center for the Learning and Teaching of Elementary Subjects.

Brophy, J. (1990b). Teaching social studies for understanding and higher-order applications. *Elementary School Journal, 90,* 351–417.

Brophy, J. (1992a). The de facto national curriculum in US elementary social studies: Critique of a representative example. *Journal of Curriculum Studies, 24,* 401–447.

Brophy, J. (1992b). Fifth-grade U.S. history: How one teacher arranged to focus on key ideas in depth. *Theory and Research in Social Education, 20,* 141–155.

Brophy, J. (1993). Mary Lake: Introducing fifth graders to U.S. history. In J. Brophy (Ed.), *Advances in research on teaching: Vol. 4. Case studies of teaching and learning in social studies* (pp. 101–156). Greenwich, CT: JAI Press.

Brophy, J., & Alleman, J. (1993). Elementary social studies should be driven by major social education goals. *Social Education, 57,* 27–32.

Brophy, J., & Alleman, J. (1996). *Powerful social studies for elementary students.* Fort Worth, TX: Harcourt Brace.

Brophy, J., & Good, T. (1986). Teacher behavior and student achievement. In M. C. Wittrock (Ed.), *Handbook of research on teaching* (3rd ed., pp. 328–375). New York: Macmillan.

Brophy, J., VanSledright, B., & Bredin, N. (1993). What do entering fifth graders know about U.S. history? *Journal of Social Studies Research, 16 & 17,* 2–22.

Bruner, J. (1960). *The process of education.* Cambridge, MA: Harvard University Press.

Bryant, B. K. (1982). An index of empathy for children and adolescents. *Child Development, 52,* 413–425.

California State Board of Education. (1988). *History-social science framework.* Sacramento: Author.

Chase, W. L. (1961). American history in the middle grades. In W. Cartwright & R. Watson (Eds.), *Interpreting and teaching American history* (pp. 329–343). Washington, DC: National Council for the Social Studies.

Cheney, L. (1987). *American memory: A report on the humanities in the nation's public schools.* Washington, DC: National Endowment for the Humanities.

Coltham, J. (1971). *The development of thinking and the learning of history.* London: The Historical Association.

Cornett, J. (1990). Teacher thinking about curriculum and instruction: The case of a secondary social studies teacher. *Theory and Research in Social Education, 18,* 248–273.

Crabtree, C. (1989). Improving history in the schools. *Educational Leadership, 47,* 25–28.

Creative Activities for Teaching U.S. History. (1988). Stockton, CA: Stevens & Shea.

Cuban, L. (1984). *How teachers taught: Constancy and change in American classrooms: 1890–1980.* New York: Longman.

Cunningham, L., & Gall, M. (1990). The effects of expository and narrative prose on student achievement and attitudes toward textbooks. *The Journal of Experimental Education, 58,* 165–175.

Davis, J., & Hawke, S. (1992). Seeds of change: Cutting edge knowledge and the Columbian Quincentenary. *Social Education, 56,* 320–322.

Dawson, I. (1989). The Schools History Project—A study in curriculum development. *History Teacher, 22,* 221–238.

Dewey, J. (1950). *The child and the curriculum.* Chicago: University of Chicago Press. (Original work published 1902)

Dickinson, A. K., & Lee, P. J. (1978). Understanding and research. In A. K. Dickinson & P. J. Lee (Eds.), *History teaching and historical understanding* (pp. 94–120). London: Heinemann.

Dickinson, A. K., & Lee, P. J. (1984). Making sense of history. In A. Dickinson, P. Lee, & P. Rogers (Eds.), *Learning history* (pp.117–153). London: Heinemann.

Downey, M. T., & Levstik, L. S. (1988). Teaching and learning history: The research base. *Social Education, 52,* 336–342.

Downey, M. T., & Levstik, L. S. (1991). Teaching and learning history. In J. Shaver (Ed.), *Handbook of research on social studies teaching and learning* (pp. 400–410). New York: Macmillan.

Egan, K. (1983). Social studies and the erosion of education. *Curriculum Inquiry, 13,* 195–214.

Egan, K. (1986). *Teaching as storytelling: An alternative approach to teaching and curriculum in the elementary school.* Chicago: University of Chicago Press.

Egan, K. (1988). *Teaching as storytelling: An alternative approach to teaching and the curriculum.* London: Routledge.

Egan, K. (1989). Layers of historical understanding. *Theory and Research in Social Education, 17,* 280–294.

Elbaz, F. (1983). *Teacher thinking: A study of practical knowledge.* New York: Nichols.

Engle, S., & Ochoa, A., (1988). *Education for democratic citizenship: Decision making in the social studies.* New York: Teachers College Press.

Estvan, F., & Estvan, E. (1959). *The child's world: His social perception.* New York: Putnam.

Evans, R. (1989). Teacher conceptions of history. *Theory and Research in Social Education, 17,* 210–240.

Evans, R. (1994). Educational ideologies and the teaching of history. In G. Leinhardt, I. Beck, & C. Stainton (Eds.), *Teaching and learning in history* (pp. 171–208). Hillsdale, NJ: Erlbaum.

Fraenkel, J. (1980). *Helping students think and value: Strategies for teaching the social studies* (2nd ed.). Englewood Cliffs, NJ: Prentice-Hall.

Gagnon, P. (Ed.). (1989a). *Building a history curriculum: Guidelines for teaching history in schools.* Washington, DC: Educational Excellence Network.

Gagnon, P. (Ed.). (1989b). *Historical literacy: The case for history in American education.* New York: Macmillan.

Gardner, H., & Boix-Mansilla, V. (1994). Teaching for understanding—Within and across the disciplines. *Educational Leadership, 51*(5), 14–18.

Good, T., & Brophy, J. (1995). *Contemporary educational psychology* (5th ed.). White Plains, NY: Longman.

Good, T., & Brophy, J. (1997). *Looking in classrooms* (7th ed.). New York: Longman.

Goodlad, J. I. (1984). *A place called school.* New York: McGraw-Hill.

Goodman, J., & Adler, S. (1985). Becoming an elementary social studies teacher: A study of perspectives. *Theory and Research in Social Education, 13,* 1–20.

Green, R. P., & Watson, R. L., Jr. (1993). American history in the schools. In V. Wilson, J. Litle, & G. Wilson (Eds.), *Teaching social studies* (pp. 65–91). Westport, CT: Greenwood.

Greene, S. (1994). The problems of learning to think like a historian: Writing history in the culture of the classroom. *Educational Psychologist, 29,* 89–96.

Gross, R. (1952). What's wrong with American history? *Social Education, 16,* 157–161.

Guzzetta, C. (1969). Children's knowledge of historically important Americans. In W. Herman (Ed.), *Current research in elementary school social studies* (pp. 392–400). New York: Macmillan.

Hahn, C. (1986). Advocating early childhood social studies. In V. Atwood (Ed.), *Elementary school social studies: Research as a guide to practice* (Bulletin 79, pp. 165–174). Washington, DC: National Council for the Social Studies.

Hallam, R. N. (1978). An approach to learning history in the secondary schools. *Teaching History, 21,* 9–14.

Hallam, R. N. (1979). Attempting to improve logical thinking in school history. *Research in Education, 21,* 1–24.

Hallden, O. (1994). On the paradox of understanding history in an educational setting. In G. Leinhardt, I. Beck, & C. Stainton (Eds.), *Teaching and learning in history* (pp. 27–46). Hillsdale, NJ: Erlbaum.

Hanna, P. (1934). Social studies in the new Virginia curriculum. *Progressive Education, 11,* 129–134.

Hanna, P. (1963). Revising the social studies: What is needed? *Social Education, 27,* 190–196.

Harms, J., & Lettow, L. (1994). Criteria for selecting picture books with historical settings. *Social Education, 58,* 152–154.

Hertzberg, H. W. (1985). Students, methods, and materials of instruction. In D. Alder & M. Downey (Eds.), *History in the schools* (Bulletin 74, pp. 25–40). Washington, DC: National Council for the Social Studies.

Hirsch, E. D., Jr. (1987). *Cultural literacy.* New York: Vantage.

Holt, T. (1990). *Thinking historically: Narrative, imagination, and understanding.* New York: College Entrance Examination Board.

Howard, J., & Mendenhall, T. (1982). *Making history come alive: The place of history in schools.* Washington, DC: Council for Basic Education.

Howe, K. (1990). Children's literature and its effects on cognitive and noncognitive behaviors in elementary social studies (Doctoral dissertation, University of Minnesota, 1990). *Dissertation Abstracts International, 51/12A,* 4044.

Jenness, D. (1990). *Making sense of social studies.* New York: Macmillan.

Jurd, M. F. (1973). Adolescent thinking in history-type material. *Australian Journal of Education, 17,* 2–17.

Kinder, D., & Bursuck, W. (1993). History strategy instruction: Problem-solution-effect analysis, timeline, and vocabulary instruction. *Exceptional Children, 59,* 324–335.

Knight, P. T. (1989a). Empathy: Concept, confusion and consequences in a national curriculum. *Oxford Review of Education, 15,* 41–53.

Knight, P. T. (1989b). Research on teaching and learning history: A perspective from afar. *Social Education, 53,* 306–309.

Knight, P. (1993). *Primary geography, primary history.* London: David Fulton.

Kobrin, D. (1992). It's my country, too: A proposal for a student historian's history of the United States. *Teachers College Record, 94,* 329–342.

Kovalcik, A. (1979). The effect of using children's literature to change fifth grade students' attitudes toward social studies as an area of instruction (Doctoral dissertation, University of Northern Colorado, 1979). *Dissertation Abstracts International, 40/5,* 2585A.

Lamme, L. (1994). Stories from our past: Making history come alive for children. *Social Education, 58,* 159–164.

Lampert, M. (1985). How do teachers manage to teach? Perspectives on problems in practice. *Harvard Educational Review, 55,* 178–194.

Larkins, A., Hawkins, M., & Gilmore, A. (1987). Trivial and noninformative content of elementary social studies: A review of primary texts in four series. *Theory and Research in Social Education, 15,* 299–311.

Laville, C., & Rosenzweig, L. W. (1982). Teaching and learning history: Developmental dimensions. In L. W. Rosenzweig (Ed.), *Developmental perspectives on social studies* (Bulletin 66, pp. 54–66). Washington, DC: National Council for the Social Studies.

League of Women Voters. (1975). Children's impressions of American Indians:

A survey of suburban kindergarten and fifth-grade children: Conclusions. In A. Hirschfelder (Ed.), *American Indian stereotypes in the world of children: A reader and bibliography* (pp. 7–14). Metuchen, NJ: Scarecrow.

Levstik, L. (1986). The relationship between historical response and narrative in the classroom. *Theory and Research in Social Education, 14,* 1–15.

Levstik, L. (1989). Historical narrative and the young reader. *Theory Into Practice, 28,* 114–119.

Levstik, L. (1990). The research base for curriculum choice: A response. *Social Education, 54,* 442–443.

Levstik, L. (1993a). Building a sense of history in a first-grade classroom. In J. Brophy (Ed.), *Advances in research on teaching: Vol. 4. Case studies of teaching and learning in social studies* (pp. 1–31). Greenwich, CT: JAI Press.

Levstik, L. (1993b). "I wanted to be there": The impact of narrative on children's historical thinking. In M. Tunnell & R. Ammon (Eds.), *The story of ourselves: Teaching history through children's literature* (pp. 65–77). Portsmouth, NH: Heinemann.

Levstik, L. (1995). Narrative constructions: Cultural frames for history. *Social Studies, 86,* 113–116.

Levstik, L., & Barton, K. (1996). They still use some of their past: Historical salience in elementary children's chronological thinking. *Journal of Curriculum Studies, 28,* 531–576.

Levstik, L., & Pappas, C. (1987). Exploring the development of historical understanding. *Journal of Research and Development in Education, 21,* 1–15.

Levstik, L., & Pappas, C. (1992). New directions for studying historical understanding. *Theory and Research in Social Education, 20,* 369–385.

Little, V. (1989). Imagination and history. In J. Campbell & V. Little (Eds.), *Humanities in the primary school* (pp. 33–53). London: Falmer.

Low-Beer, A., & Blyth, J. (1983). *Teaching history to younger children.* London: The Historical Association.

Marker, G., & Mehlinger, H. (1992). Social studies. In P. Jackson (Ed.), *Handbook of research on curriculum* (pp. 830–851). New York: Macmillan.

McBee, T., Tate, D., & Wagner, L. (1985). *U.S. history: Book One. Beginnings to 1865.* Dubuque, IA: William C. Brown.

McCabe, P. (1993). Considerateness of fifth-grade social studies texts. *Theory and Research in Social Education, 21,* 128–142.

McKeown, M. G., & Beck, I. L. (1990). The assessment and characterization of young learners' knowledge of a topic in history. *American Educational Research Journal, 27,* 688–726.

McKeown, M. G., & Beck, I. L. (1994). Making sense of accounts of history: Why young students don't and how they might. In G. Leinhardt, I. Beck, & C. Stainton (Eds.), *Teaching and learning in history* (pp. 1–26). Hillsdale, NJ: Erlbaum.

McKinney, C. W., & Jones, A. J. (1993). Effects of a children's book and a traditional textbook on fifth-grade students' achievement and attitudes toward social studies. *Journal of Research and Development in Education, 27,* 56–62.

McNeil, L. (1986). *Contradictions of control: School structure and school knowledge.* New York: Routledge & Kegan Paul.

Myers, J. (1990). The trouble with history. *History and Social Science Teacher, 25,* 68–70.

National Board for Professional Teaching Standards. (1994). *Social studies-history: Draft standards for National Board certification.* Detroit: Author.

National Center for History in the Schools. (1994). *National standards for U.S. history: Exploring the American experience.* Los Angeles: University of California.

National Commission on Social Studies in the Schools. (1989). *Charting a course: Social studies for the 21st century.* Washington, DC: National Council for the Social Studies.

National Council for the Social Studies. (1992). The Columbian Quincentenary: An educational opportunity (NCSS Position Statement). *Social Education, 56,* 248–249.

National Council for the Social Studies. (1993). A vision of powerful teaching and learning in the social studies: Building social understanding and civic efficacy. *Social Education, 57,* 213–223.

National Council for the Social Studies. (1994). *Curriculum standards for the social studies* (Bulletin 89). Washington, DC: Author.

Naylor, D., & Diem, R. (1987). *Elementary and middle school social studies.* New York: Random House.

Newmann, F. (1988). Another view of cultural literacy: Go for depth. *Social Education, 52,* 432–436.

Newmann, F. (1990). Higher order thinking in teaching social studies: A rationale for assessment of classroom thoughtfulness. *Journal of Curriculum Studies, 22,* 41–56.

Ogle, D. (1986). K-W-L: A teaching model that develops active reading of expository text. *Reading Teacher, 39,* 564–570.

Parker, W. (1989). Participatory citizenship: Civics in the strong sense. *Social Education, 53,* 353–354.

Parker, W., & Jarolimek, J. (1984). *Citizenship and the critical role of the social studies.* Washington, DC: National Council for the Social Studies.

Patriarca, L., & Alleman, J. (1987). Studying time: A cognitive approach. *Social Education, 51,* 275–277.

Patrick, H. (1990). Investigating the relationship between aims and practice in the teaching of history. *Research Papers in Education, 5,* 97–126.

Ramsey, P., Holbrook, H., Johnson, H., & O'Toole, C. (1992, April). *The effects of a multicultural curriculum on children's perceptions of Native Americans.* Paper presented at the annual meeting of the American Educational Research Association, San Francisco.

Ravitch, D. (1987). Tot sociology, or what happened to history in the grade schools. *American Scholar, 56,* 343–353.

Ravitch, D., & Finn, C. (1987). *What do our 17-year-olds know? A report of the first national assessment of history and literature.* New York: Harper & Row.

Reed, E. (1989). For better elementary teaching: Methods old and new. In

P. Gagnon (Ed.), *Historical literacy: The case for history in American education* (pp. 302–319). New York: Macmillan.

Resnick, L., & Klopfer, L. (Eds.). (1989). *Toward the thinking curriculum: Current cognitive research.* Washington, DC: Association for Supervision and Curriculum Development.

Richgels, D., Tomlinson, C., & Tunnell, M. (1993). Comparison of elementary students' history textbooks and trade books. *Journal of Educational Research, 86,* 161–171.

Rife, D. (1985). *A family history handbook.* Logan, IA: Perfection Form Company.

Rogers, P. (1987). History—The past as a frame of reference. In C. Portal (Ed.), *The history curriculum for teachers* (pp. 3–21). London: Falmer.

Sansom, C. (1987). Concepts, skills and content: A developmental approach to the history syllabus. In C. Portal (Ed.), *The history curriculum for teachers* (pp. 116–141). London: Falmer.

Saxe, D. (1992). An introduction to the seminal social welfare and efficiency prototype: The founders of the 1916 social studies. *Theory and Research in Social Education, 20,* 156–178.

Seefeldt, C. (1993). History for young children. *Theory and Research in Social Education, 21,* 143–155.

Seixas, P. (1993a). Historical understanding among adolescents in a multicultural setting. *Curriculum Inquiry, 23,* 301–327.

Seixas, P. (1993b). Parallel crises: History and the social studies curriculum in the USA. *Journal of Curriculum Studies, 25,* 235–250.

Seixas, P. (1994). Students' understanding of historical significance. *Theory and Research in Social Education, 22,* 281–304.

Shaver, J. (1987). Implications from research: What should be taught in social studies? In V. Richardson-Koehler (Ed.), *Educators' handbook: A research perspective* (pp. 112–138). New York: Longman.

Shaver, J. (Ed.). (1991). *Handbook of research on social studies teaching and learning.* New York: Macmillan.

Shaver, J., Davis, O. L., Jr., & Helburn, S. M. (1979). The status of social studies education: Impressions from three NSF studies. *Social Education, 43,* 150–153.

Shemilt, D. (1980). *History 13–16 evaluation study.* Edinburgh: Holmes McDougall.

Shemilt, D. (1983). The devil's locomotive. *History and Theory, 22,* 1–18.

Shemilt, D. (1984). Beauty and the philosopher: Empathy in history and classroom. In A. Dickinson, P. Lee, & P. Rogers (Eds.), *Learning history* (pp. 39–84). London: Heinemann.

Sinatra, G., Beck, I., & McKeown, M. (1992). A longitudinal characterization of young students' knowledge of their country's government. *American Educational Research Journal, 29,* 633–661.

Sunal, C., & Haas, M. (1993). *Social studies and the elementary/middle school student.* Fort Worth, TX: Harcourt Brace Jovanovich.

Sylvester, D. (1989). Children as historians. In J. Campbell & V. Little (Eds.), *Humanities in the primary school* (pp. 19–31). London: Falmer.

Thornton, S. (1990). Should we be teaching more history? *Theory and Research in Social Education, 18,* 53–60.

Thornton, S. (1991). Teacher as curricular-instructional gatekeeper in social studies. In J. Shaver (Ed.), *Handbook of research on social studies teaching and learning* (pp. 237–248). New York: Macmillan.

Thornton, S. (1993). Toward the desirable in social studies teaching. In J. Brophy (Ed.), *Advances in research on teaching: Vol. 4. Case studies of teaching and learning in social studies* (pp. 157–178). Greenwich, CT: JAI Press.

Thornton, S. (1994). The social studies near century's end: Reconsidering patterns of curriculum and instruction. In L. Darling-Hammond (Ed.), *Review of Research in Education* (Vol. 20, pp. 223–254). Washington, DC: American Educational Research Association.

Torney, J. (1977). Socialization of attitudes toward the legal system. In J. Tapp & F. Levine (Eds.), *Law, justice, and the individual in society* (pp. 134–144). New York: Holt, Rinehart & Winston.

Tyack, D., & Tobin, W. (1994). The "grammar" of schooling: Why has it been so hard to change? *American Educational Research Journal, 31,* 453–479.

VanSledright B. A. (1992a). *Stories of the American Revolution period: Comparisons of two fifth-grade teachers' curriculum mediation practices* (Elementary Subjects Center Series 67). East Lansing: Michigan State University, Institute for Research on Teaching. Center for the Learning and Teaching of Elementary Subjects.

VanSledright B. A. (1992b). *Teaching about the American Revolution: The case of Ramona Palmer* (Elementary Subjects Center Series No. 68). East Lansing: Michigan State University, Institute for Research on Teaching, Center for the Learning and Teaching of Elementary Subjects.

VanSledright, B. A. (1992c). *Teaching about the American Revolution: The case of Sara Atkinson* (Elementary Subjects Center Series No. 69). East Lansing: Michigan State University, Institute for Research on Teaching, Center for the Learning and Teaching of Elementary Subjects.

VanSledright, B. A. (1994, November). *How to read history? The content-form problem in fifth-grade classrooms.* Paper presented at the annual meeting of the National Reading Conference, Coronado, CA.

VanSledright, B. A. (1995a). "I don't remember—the ideas are all jumbled in my head": Eighth graders' reconstructions of colonial American history. *Journal of Curriculum and Supervision, 10,* 317–345.

VanSledright, B. A. (1995b). The teaching–learning interaction in American history: A study of two teachers and their fifth graders. *Journal of Social Studies Research, 19,* 3–23.

VanSledright, B., & Brophy, J. (1992). Storytelling, imagination, and fanciful elaboration in children's historical reconstructions. *American Educational Research Journal, 29,* 837–859.

VanSledright, B. A., & Brophy, J. (1995). "Storytellers," "scientists," and "reformers" in the teaching of U.S. history to fifth graders: Three teachers, three approaches. In J. Brophy (Ed.), *Advances in research on teaching: Vol.*

5. *Learning and teaching elementary subjects.* (pp. 195–243). Greenwich, CT: JAI Press.

VanSledright, B. A., & Grant, S. G. (1994). Citizenship education and the persistent nature of classroom teaching dilemmas. *Theory and Research in Social Education, 22,* 305–339.

VanSledright, B. A., & Kelly, C. (1995, April). *Learning to read American history: How do multiple text sources influence historical literacy in fifth grade?* Paper presented at the annual meeting of the American Educational Research Association, San Francisco.

West, J. (1978). Young children's awareness of the past. *Trends in Education, 1,* 9–14.

West, J. (1981). School children's perceptions of authenticity and time in historical narrative pictures. *Teaching History, 29,* 8–10.

Whelan, M. (1992). History and the social studies: A response to the critics. *Theory and Research in Social Education, 20,* 2–16.

White, C. S. (1982). A validation study of Barth–Shermis Social Studies Preference Scale. *Theory and Research in Social Education, 10,* 1–20.

Willig, C. (1990). *Children's concepts and the primary curriculum.* London: Paul Chapman.

Wilson, S. M. (1991). Parades of facts, stories of the past: What do novice history teachers need to know? In M. Kennedy (Ed.), *Teaching academic subjects to diverse learners* (pp. 99–116). New York: Teachers College Press.

Wilson, S. M., & Sykes, G. (1989). Toward better teacher preparation and certification. In P. Gagnon (Ed.), *Historical literacy: The case for history in American education* (pp. 273–289). New York: Macmillan.

Wilson, S. M., & Wineburg, S. S. (1993). Wrinkles in time and place: Using performance assessments to understand the knowledge of history teachers. *American Educational Research Journal, 30,* 729–769.

Wineburg, S. S. (1991). On the reading of historical texts: Notes on the breach between school and academy. *American Educational Research Journal, 28,* 495–519.

Wineburg, S. S., & Wilson, S. M. (1988). Models of wisdom in the teaching of history. *Phi Delta Kappan, 70,* 50–58.

Wineburg, S. S., & Wilson, S. M. (1991). Subject matter knowledge in the teaching of history. In J. Brophy (Ed.), *Advances in research on teaching, Vol. 3. Planning and managing learning tasks and activities* (pp. 305–347). Greenwich, CT: JAI Press.

Wood, F. H. (1966). *A study of social studies education in the rural, urban, and suburban high schools of Missouri.* Unpublished doctoral dissertation, University of Missouri, Columbia.

Wooster, J. (1992). Choosing materials for teaching about the Columbian Quincentenary. *Social Education, 56,* 244–247.

Index

About the Authors

Jere Brophy is University Distinguished Professor of Teacher Education in the College of Education at Michigan State University. Well known for his work on teacher expectations, teacher effects on student achievement, classroom management, and student motivation, Dr. Brophy has focused in recent years on social studies teaching and learning. He is coauthor (with Janet Alleman) of *Powerful Social Studies for Elementary Schools* (1996), and editor of the *Advances in Research on Teaching* series. (Volume 6 in this series, to be published in 1997, focuses on history teaching and learning.)

Bruce A. VanSledright is Assistant Professor of Education in the Department of Curriculum and Instruction at the University of Maryland, College Park. He was a social studies and American history teacher for 13 years before completing doctoral work at Michigan State University. His research interests have centered on how teachers teach and students learn American history. Research articles he has written have appeared in the *American Educational Research Journal*, *Journal of Curriculum Studies*, and *Theory and Research in Social Education*.

250 /5th Park famely

Renk